Julia Davydova
**Quotation in Indigenised and Learner English**

# Language and Social Life

Editors
David Britain
Crispin Thurlow

**Volume 16**

Julia Davydova

# Quotation in Indigenised and Learner English

A Sociolinguistic Account of Variation

ISBN 978-1-5015-2451-6
e-ISBN (PDF) 978-1-5015-0706-9
e-ISBN (EPUB) 978-1-5015-0700-7
ISSN 2192-2128

**Library of Congress Control Number: 2018961670**

**Bibliographic information published by the Deutsche Nationalbibliothek**
The Deutsche Nationalbibliothek lists this publication in the Deutsche Nationalbibliografie; detailed bibliographic data are available on the Internet at http://dnb.dnb.de.

© 2020 Walter de Gruyter Inc., Boston/Berlin
This volume is text- and page-identical with the hardback published in 2019.
Typesetting: Integra Software Services Pvt. Ltd.
Printing and binding: CPI books GmbH, Leck

www.degruyter.com

For
Alla N. Davydova,
Alexandra J. Gapeeva,
Larisa M. Khokhlova,
and
Valentina P. Leskova,
*the four remarkable women who came before me.*

# Acknowledgements

This book was written as part of my *Habilitation* at the University of Mannheim. First and foremost, I would like to acknowledge the financial support provided by a gender-equality initiative called the WOVEN-Programme at the University of Mannheim, and to thank Prof. Dr. Rosemarie Tracy for hosting my postdoctoral position at the Chair of English Linguistics, *Anglistik I*. I acknowledge with gratitude the funding of the project "Determinants of sociolinguistic variation in ESL/EFL English" (DA 1678/1-1) provided by the *Deutsche Forschungsgemeinschaft* (DFG). Moreover, the work presented here would not have been possible without the financial support of the *Landesexzellenzcluster* (Hamburg, Germany), which sponsored the fieldwork trip to Jawaharlal Nehru University in 2011. I also thank the Collaborative Research Centre on Multilingualism (SFB 538 "Mehrsprachigkeit") and Prof. Dr. Peter Siemund for sponsoring the fieldwork trip to Jawaharlal Nehru University in 2007.

I would like to thank Prof. Dr. Pramod Pandey and Prof. Dr. Tatiana Oranskaia for their invaluable help in organising my two fieldwork trips to Jawaharlal Nehru University. I also thank all the students from Jawaharlal Nehru University and the University of Mannheim for the time they have taken to participate in this project.

Many thanks to my (senior) colleagues and mentors: Prof. Dr. Isabelle Buchstaller, Prof. Dr. Erik Schleef, Prof. Dr. Carola Trips, and Dr. Agniezska Ewa Tytus for their continued support throughout the project.

Finally, I would like to thank my two wonderful singing teachers, Marina Ivanova and Beate Mewes, my friends from the Venice Beach sports studio, and from the CreaDom dancing school, as well as my Facebook-gang for helping me achieve the necessary work-life balance. Most of all, however, I would like to thank my friends and family in Bryansk for their unconditional love. Theirs are the shoulders I am standing on.

# Contents

Acknowledgements —— VII

Abbreviations —— XI

1 Introduction —— 1
1.1 Aims and scope —— 1
1.2 The object of study —— 3
1.3 The structure of the book and terminology —— 5

2 Globalisation of English: Forms and contexts —— 7
2.1 English as a Second Language —— 7
2.2 English as a Foreign Language —— 11
2.3 Variationist sociolinguistics and the study of World Englishes —— 13

3 The worldwide reality of English quotative marking —— 17
3.1 Quotation: Definition and some theoretical preliminaries —— 18
3.2 Quotation: The method of study —— 20
3.3 English quotation in real time: A cross-varietal perspective —— 21
3.4 English quotation: systemic constraints —— 26
3.5 Quotative *be like* and grammaticalisation theory —— 29

4 Tackling non-native speakers' attitudes —— 33
4.1 Attitudinal questionnaire —— 34
4.2 Verbal guise test —— 39
4.3 Sociolinguistic interviews —— 45

5 The nativised ecology of quotation —— 55
5.1 English-dominant speakers —— 65
5.2 Hindi-dominant speakers —— 70
5.3 Mixed bilinguals —— 75
5.4 Exposure to mass media —— 81
5.4.1 High levels of exposure to mass media —— 82
5.4.2 Low levels of exposure to mass media —— 85

6 The Learner ecology of quotation —— 91
6.1 North American exposure dominant learners —— 96
6.2 UK exposure dominant learners —— 100
6.3 Mixed exposure learners —— 103

| 6.4 | Lingua franca exposure learners —— 106 |
| --- | --- |
| 6.5 | Low-level naturalistic exposure learners —— 111 |
| 6.5.1 | High levels of exposure to mass media —— 111 |
| 6.5.2 | Low levels of exposure to mass media —— 114 |
| 7 | **Quotation in non-native English: Bird's eye perspective —— 121** |
| 7.1 | Modelling the variable grammar for *be like* in nativised and Learner English —— 123 |
| 7.2 | Acquiring a variable grammar —— 136 |
| 8 | **Non-native speakers' perceptions and adaptation of global linguistic innovations —— 145** |
| 8.1 | Verbal guise test —— 153 |
| 8.2 | Overt attitudes' task —— 164 |
| 9 | **Putting it all together —— 175** |
| 9.1 | Frequency —— 178 |
| 9.2 | Salience —— 187 |
| 9.2.1 | Cognitive salience —— 189 |
| 9.2.2 | Sociolinguistic salience —— 193 |
| 9.2.3 | Socio-cognitive salience —— 197 |
| 9.2.4 | *Be like* as a socio-cognitively salient feature —— 198 |
| 9.3 | Other factors —— 205 |
| 9.4 | Concluding remarks —— 207 |

**References —— 209**

**Appendix A: Interview Schedule —— 225**

**Appendix B: Background Questionnaire (JNU) —— 228**

**Appendix C: Background Questionnaire (UM) —— 232**

**Appendix D: Goldvarb Analyses —— 235**

**Appendix E: *Be like* survey —— 238**

**Index —— 251**

# Abbreviations

| | |
|---|---|
| ANOVA | analysis of variance |
| AmE | American English |
| AusE | Australian English |
| BrE | British English |
| CanE | Canadian English |
| CHP | Conversational Historical Present |
| DisPrt | Discourse particle |
| EFL | English as a Foreign Language |
| ESL | English as a Second Language |
| EurE | European English |
| GerE | German English |
| HCNVE | The Hamburg Corpus of Non-Native Varieties of English |
| HKE | Hong Kong English |
| HME | high-levels of exposure to the media (but low levels of naturalistic exposure) |
| IndE | Indian English |
| JNU | Jawaharlal Nehru University |
| KenE | Kenyan English |
| L1 | first language |
| L2 | second language |
| LG | lingua franca |
| LME | low-levels exposure to the media (and low levels of naturalistic exposure) |
| MaCGE | The Mannheim Corpus of German English |
| NA | North American |
| NZE | New Zealand English |
| PhE | Philippines English |
| SD | Semantic Differential (scale) |
| SinE | Singapore English |
| UM | University of Mannheim |
| VGT | Verbal Guise Test |

# 1 Introduction

## 1.1 Aims and scope

This book is a variationist account of quotative marking in English-speaking communities that emerged through colonisation and interethnic linguistic practices on the one hand and classroom environment and learners' stay-abroad experiences on the other. Its overarching goal is to tap into and advance our knowledge of the mechanisms guiding language variation and language change in non-native Englishes, thereby revising the well-established dichotomy of English as a Second Language vs. English as a Foreign Language (henceforth, ESL vs. EFL) (see Kachru 1985; McArthur 1998) and its contribution to our understanding of the sociolinguistic processes shaping the evolution of the newly emerging Englishes. The following two general questions inform the book:

> RQ1: How do non-native speakers, i.e. second- and foreign-language learners, appropriate patterns of sociolinguistic variation attested in native-speaker English? Crucially, how and to what extent do they adopt the global linguistic innovations attested in native-speaker varieties?

> RQ2: Which system-internal, socio-psychological (attitudinal), and psycholinguistic mechanisms underpin the evolution of the newly emerging forms of English and shape its linguistic outcomes?

Direct comparisons of indigenised (ESL) and Learner (EFL) English in selected language domains have become an increasingly important avenue for sociolinguistic research of World Englishes over the past decades, as documented in Davydova (2011, 2012), Edwards (2014), Edwards and Laporte (2015), Hundt and Gut (2012), Meriläinen and Paulasto (2014), Mukherjee and Hundt (2011), Nesselhauf (2009), and Williams (1987). All of these studies have focused on developing an integrated view of ESL and EFL, thereby putting this issue on the agenda of English linguistics (Hundt and Mukherjee 2011: 1). The pertinence of this approach is motivated by the fact that, presently, English is employed as a non-native language far more often than as a native idiom. It is estimated that English is spoken as a first language by approximately 329,140,800 people, and as a second language by a further 430,614,500. Moreover, the number of speakers who adopt English as their primary foreign language is growing daily and is thus difficult to estimate. Yet some experts suggest that the entire English-speaking population amounts to some 2,236,730,000 speakers (Jenkins 2015: 2). Indeed, English is second only to Chinese in terms of speaker numbers; more importantly, the English-speaking population is not circumscribed to one geographic locale delimited by national boundaries. It is dispersed virtually all over the globe, yielding a variety of scenarios accompanying the acquisition of the global lingua franca and linguistic practices of its speakers. Given this unprecedented case in human history, linguists of all affiliations (but especially sociolinguists) are then invited, indeed urged, to tap into the socio- and psycholinguistic complexities of the dynamics underlying the emergence of World Englishes. Such an undertaking is a vital assignment because it aims at honing our understanding of the inner workings of our linguistic capacity on the one hand, and the socio-cultural evolution of language on the other.

This book has been envisaged with these principal goals in mind. It goes beyond the existing publications on the topic in the following respects. First and foremost, it explores the variation across distinctive varietal types of non-native English in the sense of Kortmann et al. (2004) and Siemund et al. (2011), while drawing on the methodologies well-established in the field of variationist sociolinguistics (Buchstaller 2014; Labov 2010[1972a]; Tagliamonte 2006, 2012). In so doing, the book aims to advance our understanding of the mechanisms guiding adaptation of new linguistic variants within local varietal ecologies, while assessing the role played by language-internal, extralinguistic and socio-psychological determinants of variation.

Secondly, most studies carrying out contrastive comparisons between ESL and EFL English do so, while exclusively relying on production-based data. Taking spontaneous data as a baseline for analyses and a starting point of the discussion, the book extends its scope to comprise attitudinal data revealing speakers' socio-psychological orientations towards the donor varieties, i.e. North American English and UK English, as well as their perceptions of linguistic variants associated with them. The major motivation for such an expanded agenda derives from a well-received (variationist) wisdom that "one cannot understand the development of a language change apart from the social life of the community in which it occurs" (Labov 2010[1972a]: 293). If we expand this idea further, it becomes clear that "the way language varies and the way it changes can only be understood through the prism of people's attitudes, both covert and overt, towards incoming variants" (Davydova 2016c). With this said, the book assesses the role of language attitudes in the process of adaptation of linguistic innovations.

Furthermore, existing studies on ESL/EFL English rely extensively on the spoken data stemming from the International Corpus of English (ICE) and the International Corpus of Learner English (ICLE) collected back in the 1990s/the early 2000s (but see Edwards 2014) and thereby representing relatively older stages in the development of the new linguistic varieties. This study draws on two corpora of indigenised and Learner data collected at Jawaharlal Nehru University (henceforth, JNU), New Delhi, India and at the University of Mannheim (henceforth, UM), Germany, in the time period from 2007 to 2015, which allows the researcher to explore the latest trends in cross-varietal dynamics. Collected under very similar methodological conditions, the corpora contain data stemming from 177 young adults (aged 18 to 26) – 80 from India and 97 from Germany. The Indian data is part of the Hamburg Corpus of Non-Native Varieties of English (henceforth, HCNVE). The German data stems from the Mannheim Corpus of German English (henceforth, MaCGE). In addition, the study takes into account attitudinal data obtained from both student communities. The data taps into ESL/EFL learners' attitudes towards the two mainstream forms of native English, i.e. British English and American English, and contrasts those with their perceptions of non-native Englishes, including the respective local variety. It furthermore elicits learners' attitudes towards a global linguistic innovation attested in native Englishes worldwide – a linguistic variant called quotative *be like* and demonstrated in (4).

Importantly, the study places an explicit emphasis on exploring ESL/EFL learners' local sociolinguistic ecologies as they are, I argue, the key to understanding intra- and intervarietal variation and, finally, the processes guiding the evolution of the English language. In so doing, it offers new insights into the existing research on ESL/EFL contrasts which has singled out learners' proficiency and norm orientation as major determinants of variation (see, for instance, Edwards and Laporte 2015). Following the research agenda outlined in Davydova (2012), the study explores sociolinguistic profiles of individual speakers within a speech community, while accounting for variation in non-native speaker English. These include: (i) the amount and type of contact with (other speakers of) English; and (ii) exposure to mass media.

## 1.2 The object of study

While elaborating on the contrasts and similarities between ESL and EFL English, I draw on the domain of quotative marking for illustration. Quotative markers are strategies illustrated in (1) through (5) to report speech, thoughts and feelings, in addition to non-lexicalised material throughout narrative structures and dialogues in speech.

(1) And then she raised those soulful eyes at me and **said**, 'How come you didn't know about this?'[1]

---

[1] All examples are mine, unless otherwise documented.

(2) And I **went**, 'Well, I didn't care to ask. I **thought**, 'Maybe this will get sorted out all by itself.'

(3) She glanced at me searchingly one more time and, 'Make sure this doesn't happen again.'

(4) And I **was like**, 'Whatever it takes darling to deserve your forgiveness. I swear (making an expressive gesture).'

(5) One hour later, we **were all** (making a dramatic pause), 'Tears and heaven on earth!'

I explore this feature for five major reasons. First and foremost, quotation is a highly variable domain of L1 English vernacular that has been reported to have been undergoing proliferation and expansion as well as robust and large-scale change (D'Arcy 2012; Tagliamonte 2012; Tagliamonte, D'Arcy, and Rodríguez Louro 2016). It has furthermore been argued to "be a good place to look for, and 'catch', the burgeoning global 'mega trends' of language change" (Tagliamonte and Hudson 1999: 168). More precisely, it is the innovative variant *be like* that has proven to be "a robust heuristic in the ongoing effort to hone an empirical theory of language change" (D'Arcy 2013: 3). More importantly, its rampant spread in English vernaculars all over the world has been described as "one of the most striking and dramatic changes [...] offering sociolinguists an opportunity to study rapid language in progress on a large scale [...]" (William Labov, cited in Tagliamonte and D'Arcy 2004: 494). Given that this feature is being mainly put forward by the younger generation in native-speaker communities, the crucial question is, 'How do young speakers living in different parts of the non-Anglophone world appropriate this feature in their L2 English?'

Secondly, "it is precisely at the blurred margin between the syntactic and the extrasyntactic that the study of syntactic variation is particularly revealing and has the most to contribute" (Sankoff 1988: 156). Thirdly, quotatives are frequent features that can yield generalisations on the basis of medium-sized corpora (Meyer 2002: 12–13). Fourthly, this linguistic variable has been meticulously examined for native-speaker vernaculars and the research has yielded robust generalisations. The variationist analyst working on non-native English is thus supplied with a stable and replicable L1 benchmark for cross-varietal comparisons. Finally, quotative *be like* has been described, by linguists and non-linguists alike, as a highly salient feature of speech. This observation raises two further questions, 'How can salient features be defined in linguistic terms? In other words, which properties do they exhibit? And how do these then contribute to the acquisition of sociolinguistic variation and the propagation of language change in the newly emerging forms of English?'

The argumentative thread of narration is grounded in a mix of approaches and methods that complement each other and, in so doing, pinpoint the forces guiding the evolution of English worldwide in "an extraordinary dynamic domain" of language (Buchstaller 2014: 1). These include acquisitional sociolinguistics and World Englishes, usage-based and cognitively oriented theories of second-language acquisition, as well as approaches tapping into speakers' attitudes employed in social psychology. Such a perspective is majorly motivated by the search for the new synergy effects stemming from the different subfields of sociolinguistics and the science of the human mind more generally.

## 1.3 The structure of the book and terminology

The monograph is organised as follows. I start out with a very brief exposition of the spread of the English language worldwide (Chapter 2). In so doing, I elaborate on the socio-historical forces that shaped the formation of two distinct forms of non-native English and the resulting psycholinguistic realities of their speakers, while taking recourse to Indian English and English spoken in Germany for illustration. Here, I also introduce the variationist method and explain how it can be complemented with other methods to inform the study of World Englishes. Chapter 3 examines the worldwide reality of English quotative marking, while tracing the rise and subsequent spread of innovative *be like* in speech communities across the globe. In so doing, it also introduces the major predictors constraining the variable occurrence of *be like* reported from previous studies. Chapter 4 taps into ESL/EFL learners' evaluations of the two major target varieties of English, i.e. British English and American English, while comparing them with two non-native varieties, Indian English and English spoken in Germany/Europe. This chapter serves as a background specifically designed to enhance our understanding of the nature of structured variation in indigenised and Learner English introduced in Chapters 5 and 6. Relying on the comparative method established in variationist sociolinguistics, Chapter 7 provides contrastive analyses in ESL/EFL data in order to explore commonalities and differences in the patterns of use of innovative quotative *be like* as well as the major linguistic and non-linguistic determinants of its variable realisation. It also assesses the degree to which non-native speakers of English tested in this study have acquired the variable grammar underlying occurrence of the innovative variant. Chapter 8 taps into ESL/EFL learners' attitudes towards quotative *be like*, while pinpointing the extent to which attitudinal data can explain patterns of structured variation. Finally, Chapter 9 provides a synthesis of the major findings and, in so doing, takes recourse to the concepts of frequency and salience as important explicatory tools in the presented analyses of data. The monograph is concluded with a portrayal of directions for future research into L2 English variation.

Before we begin, I would like to make two remarks about the terminology used in the study. While describing the domain of quotative marking throughout this book, I will be referring to non-native speakers of English discussed here as 'ESL/EFL speakers (learners)', while being mindful of the fact that the actual sociolinguistic situation in India is, as we shall see, far more varied and complex than the label suggests. In a similar vein, I will be using the labels 'second-language acquisition' and 'L2 acquisition' interchangeably to describe the settings in which English has evolved both as a second and a foreign language. The term 'L1 (speakers)' is reserved for those contexts where English thrives as a monolingual native idiom.

# 2 Globalisation of English: Forms and contexts

It would not be much of an exaggeration to state that the gradual emergence of English as a linguistic giant on the global arena of modern communication is an unprecedented case in the recorded history of our species. To be sure, an expert well versed in the study of language could also point to Latin with its vibrant literary heritage, Spanish, French (and to some extent, Portuguese) with their colonial histories, Arabic with its dominance in the Middle East, or Chinese with its impressive speaker numbers. And let's not forget about Russian, which still holds a firm (albeit substantially weakened) foothold in the countries of the former Soviet Union.

Yet English is a 'special case' requiring relentless attention from a trained linguist. The main reason why English is so important to study in real time is this: No other language has yielded such a diversity of linguistic variants coming about as a result of different, yet in some cases related, cognitive and sociolinguistic processes. English is spoken as a native language, as a second (additional) language and as a foreign language in various parts of the world. It is spoken in metropolitan cities and in urban centres but also in geographically isolated enclaves and rural areas; it is used as a link language among ethnically diverse population groups; it is spoken by monolinguals and multilinguals alike; it can be heard as a sole language in a friendly banter, but it is also easily mixed with other lects and idioms. The psycholinguistic realities of English, alongside as its sociolinguistic scope, are as broad as they are astounding. With this said, the major concern of this monograph are those forms of English that have been emerging as a result of a psycholinguistic process broadly termed as second-language acquisition. Experts unanimously agree that the latter has yielded two distinctive types of English – ESL English and EFL English (Galloway and Rose 2015; Jenkins 2015; Kachru 1985; Kirkpatrick 2010).

## 2.1 English as a Second Language

As a second language, English is thriving in countries with colonial heritage. It was introduced in the 16th – 18th centuries through the geopolitical expansion of the British Empire. With time, English was adopted on these territories not only as a *de facto* language of administration, education as well as the ruling elite. More importantly, it became a lingua franca spoken on the streets by people not sharing a common language. Against this backdrop, India serves as a textbook example of the ESL ecology, to the discussion of which I now turn.

In India, there are 350,000 native speakers of English and 200,000,000 L2 users of English (Jenkins 2015: 3). Having been introduced on the South Asian subcontinent in 1600 through the Royal Charter granting English merchants from the East India Company the permission to carry out commercial transactions, English continuously gained prominence in various parts of India during the 17th and 18th centuries not only through the British trade and military activities but also, more importantly, through the British missionary schools, which provided educational facilities attracting the indigenous elite. By the early 19th century the British had managed to gain control over almost entire India (Mukherjee 2010: 169) and contacts with English, both formal and informal, increased as a result. During that period, two historical events, the Great Revolt of 1857/1858 and the establishment of absolute monarchy under the British rule in 1877, secured the political supremacy of English in relation to native languages and, by and large, initiated nativisation of English. Also known as indigenisation, nativisation is a process characterising the emergence of a new linguistic variety and resulting from heavy phonological and lexical borrowings from the mother tongues as well as morphosyntactic and phraseological innovations.

In the 20th century, English entered a new stage of its development on the South Asian subcontinent. Contrary to the initial aspirations and expectations following India's independence in 1947, English was not with time replaced with Hindi as the only national language of the multilingual country. The Official Language Act of 1963, also amended in 1967, reaffirmed the status of English as a dominant lingua franca and a language of prestige and socioeconomic prosperity. Since then, English has played a vital role in various spheres of public and domestic life including education and interpersonal communication. The important position occupied by English at all levels of Indian education has promoted the educated variety of Indian English with ensuing attempts at its codification (Nihalani et al. 2004). To some linguists, this is a sign that Indian English has undergone endonormative stabilisation, a phase marking the acceptance of local standards and norms (Schneider 2003, 2007). Chapter 4 of this monograph provides details regarding Indian speakers' attitudes towards their own variety. Significantly, English is used widely as a means of communication in speakers' daily face-to-face interactions. Some population groups use English easily (and often deliberately) combined with other languages such as Hindi (see also Chapter 4). The result of these constant linguistic practices is a mixed code, referred to as Hinglish.

Previous sociolinguistic research shows that as a second language, English is acquired under extremely varied conditions in India (Davydova 2011, 2015b, 2016a). There is what may be termed as the elitist mode of second-language acquisition leading to the acrolectal forms of language (Davydova 2011; Mukherjee 2010). In this scenario, speakers begin to acquire English from very early on, in many cases at the age of two or four. Such kids usually speak English with one of the parents, typically the father or grandfather, but in some cases also the mother. Coming from prosperous upper-class families in New Delhi and other metropolitan cities in India, these young individuals are then sent to English-speaking convents or missionary schools where they hone their command of English to the extent that the latter becomes their dominant means of linguistic expression, native tongues being demoted, in some cases, to the status of a heritage language. What these sociolinguistic observations imply is that these speakers are in the process of language shift towards English, slowly but surely abandoning the native idiom of their parents. In fact, these individuals tend to consider themselves native speakers of English rather than any other language. They are clearly dominant in English and take recourse to Hindi in cases of great necessity (when, for instance, at the market or while communicating with their grandparents). My ethnographic research in the JNU community shows that the described patterns of incipient language shift primarily characterise upper-class communities of New Delhi. The elitist circles in the West (Bengali-speaking families) and in the South (Dravidian-speaking families) seem to have retained their bilingualism so far.

Conversely, large parts of India remain virtually unaffected by the influence of the English language. These are smaller towns and rural areas in many northern Indian states such as Rajasthan, Haryana, Bihar, Uttar Pradesh, Jharkhand, Chhattisgarh and others. Here, English is typically learned as one of the subjects in so-called vernacular schools, institutions of secondary education which provide instruction in the regional language, i.e. Hindi. In so-called public schools, which are private schools, English is the official language of instruction although teaching is effectively carried out in Hindi. These speakers need to work very hard (if they do so at all) to obtain good working knowledge of English by the time they reach late adolescence. They are clearly dominant in Hindi as it is their native tongue and a medium of instruction at schools. English is essentially a foreign language mastered through books and other printed sources since the Internet and other devices of mass communication is still a rarity in these parts of the country.

In between these two extreme societal circumstances, there is a third one representing middle-class families living in the regional capitals or big cities such as, for instance, Ranchi, the capital of Jharkhand; Lucknow, the capital of Uttar Pradesh; Jhansi, a historical city in Uttar Pradesh; Patna, the capital city of Bihar; Purnea, a big city in Bihar; Jaipur, a capital city of Rajasthan, and so on. This population group is perhaps best described as upwardly mobile. In these families, knowledge of English symbolises good education and ensuring social advancement as well as economic prosperity. Therefore, English is introduced typically as an additional language (alongside Hindi and/or another Hindi-related mother tongue) starting at the age of five or six. English is usually spoken with one of the parents, typically father, and is often used among siblings and close friends. Supported by educators, such parents make efforts to advance and maintain their children's proficiency in all the languages involved. Their secondary education is often in English, although many receive mixed (Hindi/English) instruction as well. These children effectively grow up speaking two and in some cases three or more varieties simultaneously, English being an inherent part of their linguistic repertoire.

Crucially, these diverging sociolinguistic contexts underlying acquisition of English in India have significant consequences for speakers' day-to-day psycholinguistic realities. To explain how this is the case, I take recourse to the language mode model proposed by Grosjean (1998, 2001). The model presupposes the existence of two language modes, a monolingual language mode and a bilingual language mode, from which a bilingual speaker can operate in their informal social interactions. A mode is a state of cognitive activation of language processing mechanisms in both languages and as such, is a continuum, as illustrated in Figure 1.

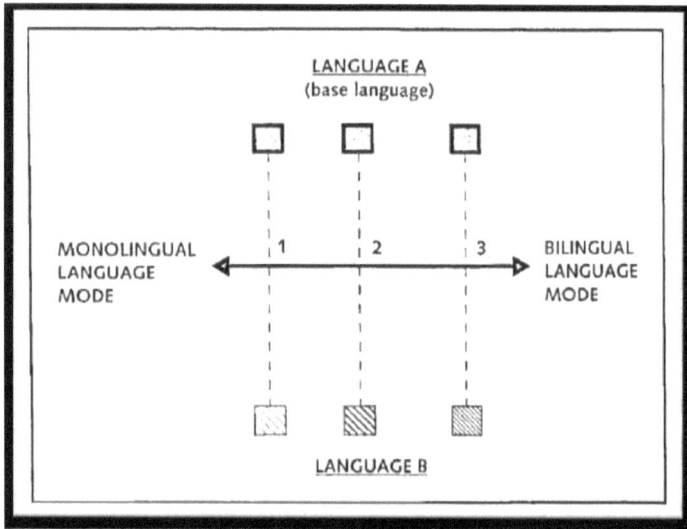

**Figure 1:** Language mode continuum (Grosjean 2004: 41).

Grosjean draws a distinction between Language A, which is the base language, and Language B. Also known as the matrix language, the base language is always activated, as Figure 1 indicates, providing a baseline for speakers throughout the verbal interaction. The degree of activation of a second language allows bilingual speakers to navigate between the monolingual and bilingual states. In the monolingual state (position 1), Language A is active, whereas Language B is largely suppressed. In contrast, both languages are fully operating in the bilingual state (position 3), although, as Grosjean (1998) points out, Language A is slightly more active than Language B as it is currently the language of communication. The model allows for an intermediary mode as well (position 2), which may arise when a bilingual is interacting with another bilingual who is not as proficient in both languages. In those circumstances, Language A will be the most active language, although Language B will also be activated, albeit to a lesser degree.

When considered against the sociolinguistic background characterising modern India, the model informs us that the younger generation of the upper-class elite in Delhi is, probably, operating from the monolingual mode while interacting with their peers in spontaneous interactions, English being their base language. Similarly, young Hindi speakers with rural/smaller towns' background and with limited exposure to English also live in a monolingual (Hindi) state of mind. Crucially, it is the offspring of the upwardly mobile, middle-class families who are trained from very early on to operate in the bilingual language mode as a matter of prestige ('I know more than one language, and I am proud of it') and as a matter of day-to-day necessity ('I need to speak two (or more) languages to be a functional member of my social group'). What this effectively means is that these young speakers have adopted and routinely practise code-switching as a default strategy in their spontaneous, intimate interactions. I return to the discussion of these issues and their relevance for the theory of acquisitional sociolinguistics in Chapters 4, 5 and 9.

## 2.2 English as a Foreign Language

As a foreign language, English is taught as one of the school subjects in the countries of Western Europe, Russia, East Asia, and South America. It is a major means of international communication and a gateway to information in various spheres of life (academia, business, tourism, and global social networks). All over the world, foreign-language learners are faced with the ongoing growth of English in terms of its presence and functions (González 2010: 332), although the exact impact of English may vary from country to country. Many European universities and other institutions of higher education offer degree programmes taught (almost) exclusively in English (Dimova, Hultgren, and Jensen 2016). The Business School in Mannheim is one notable example. Some universities (for instance, the University of Freiburg, Germany) offer degree programmes in intercultural communication requiring prolonged stays abroad. Native-like knowledge of English offers numerous possibilities on the job market and is inextricably linked to well-paid positions. Given their exonormative, target-variety oriented mindset (see also the discussion in Chapter 4), younger EFL speakers find themselves under ever-increasing pressure to attain native-like proficiency in English.

In that regard, the economically advanced countries of Western Europe offer young individuals relatively easy opportunities for travel which increases their contact with English in natural-interaction settings. As one of the most prosperous West European societies, Germany serves as a canonical example. "Whether during a gap year, as an *au-pair* or funded by the German exchange service DAAD or by a range of scholarship providers such as Erasmus or Fulbright, German adolescents and young adults are spending increasing amounts of time in English-speaking countries, with an average of 5–6 months abroad" (Davydova and Buchstaller 2015: 445). Furthermore, it is not unusual for German students to spend a semester at a university in another country (e.g. Norway, Sweden, China, etc.; possibilities are, indeed, numerous), where they get instructed in English and use primarily English for informal interactions with speakers. Here, they encounter English in an international lingua franca context. The intriguing question is then whether the English spoken by learners with a high level of exposure to naturalistic L1 contexts is any different from the English spoken by learners who spent prolonged periods of time in a lingua franca setting.

From a psycholinguistic perspective, foreign-language learners in the Western cultures tend to supress one of their linguistic codes during spontaneous interactions naturally. Let us consider as an example a young adult undertaking a PhD in social science at the University of Mannheim. While visiting a German friend in Kaiserslautern, she is most likely to converse in German. In contrast, she will, probably, use English while presenting and interacting with people at an international conference. Naturally enough, both situations will demand that one of the codes be activated, while the other inhibited. What this effectively means, is that, in contrast to speakers of the indigenised ecology, EFL learners always (or at least most of the time) operate from the monolingual language mode.

To be sure, it is quite possible to encounter scenarios in which EFL learners operate from a bilingual mode. To give one example, being a native speaker of Russian living in Germany and teaching courses in English linguistics at a university, I sometimes code-switch between German and English while interacting with one of my German colleagues who, in all appearance, finds this practice entertaining and fun, indulging himself occasionally in a bilingual mode of communication where both languages work in tandem and at the same time. This is, however, not how he talks to, let's say, his family, students and other colleagues. It is, therefore, possible to occasionally encounter circumstances in the EFL settings licencing the balanced and simultaneous activation of two linguistic codes in a learner's mind although the overall sociolinguistic context arguably does not predict such a situation as a default-case scenario.

Despite obvious differences relating to socio-cultural contexts and psycholinguistic modus operandi, there is one linguistic practice shared by the speakers of both varietal types. This linguistic practice is the result of recent technological advancements allowing learners to encounter (native-speaker) English, most importantly American English, through the media of mass communication. Thus, speakers of indigenised and Learner English are subject to varied exposure to American (and to some extent British) films and television series, both of which reproduce, at least to some degree, L1 vernaculars (Sayers 2014: 187; Tagliamonte and Roberts 2005: 296). Indeed, "[t]elevision is the dominant medium for young people – and adults – around the world" (Gigli 2004: 4). The Intermedia Survey reported in Gigli (2004) informs that the daily use of television by school children ranges between one and a half and four hours. Consequently, young individuals "come to spend more time exposed to non-local varieties than to their local vernacular" (Foulkes and Docherty 1999: 15). Furthermore, "many are exposed to the same programmes, the same characters and the same marketed spin-off products" (Gigli 2004: 3). But perhaps more importantly, "[t]he prominence of television in young people's daily lives makes it one of their major information sources about the world around them" (Gigli 2004: 4).

Given that television and film viewing habits permeate young adults' life all over the world, the implicit assumption underlying much of sociolinguistic research has been that mass media must be one important conduit for the propagation of linguistic innovations (Buchstaller 2008: 37; Buchstaller and D'Arcy 2009: 316–317). The premise is, in a way, a necessity in the context of World Englishes since many ESL/EFL learners do not have the financial resources allowing for sustained face-to-face contact with native speakers. Furthermore, we know that global linguistic innovations have been attested even in sociolinguistic settings where contact with the (alleged) donor group has been severely restricted (Davydova 2015b, 2016a; Sayers 2014). However, the evidence demonstrating a clear causal link between mass media viewing habits and linguistic behaviour has remained so far elusive (see, for instance, Buchstaller 2014: 93–97). I will come back to this issue in Chapter 3, while discussing the global spread of *be like*.

## 2.3 Variationist sociolinguistics and the study of World Englishes

In view of the fact that the newly emerging varieties of English exhibit such high levels of internal sociolinguistic and psycholinguistic heterogeneity, the pertinent question arises, 'How can we ensure reliability in sociolinguistic research of ESL/ EFL Englishes?' Here I propose that variationist sociolinguistics provides a stable framework for the study of English varieties spoken worldwide licencing methodologically rigorous comparisons of empirical data. The major benefit offered by this paradigm is that it is grounded in four theoretically motivated and empirically substantiated postulates: (i) orderly heterogeneity (Weinreich, Labov, and Herzog 1968: 100); (ii) language change; (iii) social identity (Tagliamonte 2006: 6–7), and (iv) sociolinguistic competence or sociolinguistic knowledge (Clark and Schleef 2010: 300; Davydova, Tytus, and Schleef 2017; Meyerhoff and Schleef 2012: 399).[1] The first principle claims that language is inherently variable: Different linguistic items naturally compete with each other in the system for the expression of a specific language function. Speakers, however, do not choose linguistic variants randomly; rather their choice is predicted from a set of intra- and extralinguistic conditions. Patterns of structured variation characterise not only those forms of language that are spoken as a native idiom. Crucially, language of non-native speakers is variable but structurally ordered as well.

The second principle states that language is in constant flux (Tagliamonte 2006: 6). In other words, the mainstream English as we know it today is not what it used to be 400 years ago. The language has undergone significant changes on all the levels of linguistic structure. The variationist analysis "put[s] linguistic features ... in the context of where each one has come from and where it is going – how and why" (Tagliamonte 2006: 7). Relying on the principle of accountability, which requires that we account for all the variants vying for the expression of a specific language function, the variationist analysis is a stringent method allowing us to capture a linguistic change in progress across different forms of language, both native and non-native.

The third principle highlights the fact that as a means of human communication language is not merely used to communicate a series of referential meanings, i.e. reporting on the state of affairs in the external or internal world. Importantly, speakers recruit various pieces of language material, either consciously or subconsciously, to communicate crucial pieces of extralinguistic information revealing not only their age, sex, and social class but also other socio-psychological, oftentimes community-specific characteristics. From a sociolinguistic perspective, the study of the evolution of the English language should account for the heterogeneity of the sociolinguistic environments and resulting speaker identities attested in World Englishes today.

---

**1** These principles might also reflect general ways in which systems involving conscious agents (individuals) are structured.

The fourth principle focuses on the acquisition of variable linguistic systems known as 'vernaculars' by language learners. Vernaculars are initially acquired linguistic codes associated with the most spontaneous and unmonitored speech register devoid of any overcorrections and style-shifting. In other words, this is the kind of language that people use when they are at their most relaxed. This speech style characterises informal situations. The study of this register is given primary importance in variationist sociolinguistics as it is here, so the contention, that many linguistic innovations naturally emerge and develop to contribute to systemic variability which may (or may not) with time result in a language change.

While getting familiar with their native informal varieties of language, children do not simply pick up on certain linguistic features and their frequencies of use; they also acquire quite intricate patterns of language-internal and language-external triggers conditioning the use of a specific variant. They furthermore internalise the social evaluations of linguistic variants. Empirical investigations show that this is a laborious, although by and large subconscious, process that results in the gradual emergence of *sociolinguistic competence* by L1 speakers. Sociolinguistic competence is a highly complex network of speakers' tacit knowledge about the patterns of structured variation within a given language as well as their socio-cultural assessments. It becomes fully fledged and stabilised in the speaker's mind at around the age of 17 (Tagliamonte 2012: 45). (Probably, the major reason for such a 'delay' in acquisition has to do with the fact that the acquisition of social patterns and their evaluations requires interactions in more global social contexts or with a wider community, see also Labov 2013: 249).

Against this backdrop, variationists concerned with the acquisition of sociolinguistic competence by language learners (Clark and Schleef 2010: 299; Meyerhoff and Schleef 2012: 409) have ascertained that the acquisition of native-like competence necessarily entails the acquisition of:
(a) the relevant variants and their relative frequencies;
(b) the language-internal and sociolinguistic predictors of variation;
(c) the ordering of specific constraints;
(d) similar social evaluations of specific variants.

The skill listed in (d) is also referred to as *sociolinguistic awareness* in the relevant literature (Clark and Schleef 2010; Davydova, Tytus, and Schleef 2017). The main goal of this study is to determine how (and to what extent) non-native ESL/EFL learners cope with patterns of sociolinguistic variation within their local sociolinguistic ecologies.

To be sure, no one would expect speakers of indigenised English to strive to replicate native-speaker norms of sociolinguistic variation (see also discussion in Chapter 4). The major point here is that such an approach provides an analyst with a set of clearly defined parameters, listed in (a) through (d) that she may use as a tool in her comparisons of both norm developing and norm dependent English-speaking communities. Carried within a methodologically unified framework, the analyses of data might be able to yield informative generalisations across the board.

Focusing on analyses of structured variation, current research methods allow variationist sociolinguists not only to assess how linguistic variables are used in a speech community (see *inter alia* Tagliamonte 2006, 2012). Collaborations with researchers working in the field of social psychology also allow us to use techniques tapping into speakers' implicit and explicit evaluations of linguistic variants. These complementary methodologies allow for differentiated, yet largely comprehensive descriptions of L2 speakers' sociolinguistic competence.

In conclusion, the analysis of sociolinguistic variation needs to be extended to the exploration of the newest forms of English as these are the real-world laboratories for the exploration of global linguistic innovations and their patterns of use. Crucially, both indigenised and Learner English can sharpen our understanding of L2 variability and its language-internal determinants. It can furthermore pinpoint sociolinguistic and psycholinguistic mechanisms underlying acquisition of the variable grammar in a second language.

# 3 The worldwide reality of English quotative marking

The world we live in today is characterised by the increased levels of interactions, interconnectedness, and interdependence (McGrew 1992: 23). This recent societal development has shaped the agenda of the social science which has become increasingly interested in how "things – ideas and practices – get from here to there" (Katz 1999: 145). In sociolinguistics, this research trend has opened a discussion about the spread of linguistic innovations around the globe and how these are adopted by the local speech communities (Meyerhoff and Niedzielski 2003). One linguistic domain, the one of English quotation, has caught linguists' special attention (Buchstaller 2008; Buchstaller and D'Arcy 2009; D'Arcy 2012; Tagliamonte and Hudson 1999) largely because it is an "extraordinarily dynamic" niche of language (Buchstaller 2014: 1) featuring a number of innovative variants, also called non-canonical quotative innovations, illustrated in (6) through (14). Some of these variants are geographically restricted (see also Cheshire et al. 2011: 155; Buchstaller 2014: 2): *I'm here*, *be all* (California), *I'm sitting there* (Alabama), *this is + speaker* (London, England), *here's + speaker* (Ireland), *be pure* (Scotland) and *be just* (York and Glasgow, Great Britain). Others, such as *go* and most importantly *be like*, illustrated in (13) and (14), have, in contrast, been spreading around the globe at an unprecedented speed presenting a sociolinguist with a remarkable opportunity not only to study the patterns of language variation and change in real time. Crucially, this linguistic variable allows the analyst to explore language-internal and socio-psychological mechanisms underlying the adaptation of the innovative variant in L2 speech, thereby enhancing our understanding of the processes underpinning second-language acquisition.

(6) Here **was I**, 'Then I must be hard of hearing or something you rapped the door and I didn't hear you.' (Milroy and Milroy 1977: 54, cited in Buchstaller 2014: 2)

(7) S/**he's all**, [with hands on hips and falsetto voice], 'Why don't you ever do what you are told?' (Alford 1982–83: 6, cited in Buchstaller 2014: 2)

(8) **I'm sitting there**, 'Wow! Dude! Slap bracelets!' (Stein 1990: 303, cited in Buchstaller 2014: 2)

(9) **This is me**, '(does an action which makes the interviewer laugh)' (Cheshire et al. 2011: 178)

(10)  ... **Here's me**, 'Have youse took leave of your senses?'... (Cheshire et al. 2011: 176)

(11)  She**'s pure**, 'You got it wrong.' (Macaulay 2006: 275, cited in Buchstaller 2014: 2)

(12)  Angela**'s just**, 'Did you do anything last night?' (Tagliamonte and Hudson 1999: 155)

(13)  And I **was like**, 'Whoosh.' (Tagliamonte and Hudson 1999: 163)

(14)  ... So, I **went**, 'Go on then get me.' ... (Tagliamonte and Hudson 1999: 165)

This chapter introduces quotation and its major characteristics, while elaborating on the method with which quotatives have been investigated in this study. In the next step, it discusses real-time tendencies attested for innovative *be like* worldwide, while highlighting the theory of grammaticalisation (Ferrara and Bell 1995) as a useful diagnostic measuring the level of the variant's diffusion in each speech community.

## 3.1 Quotation: Definition and some theoretical preliminaries

In this study, I have adopted the following definition of quotation. 'Quotation' is a discourse-pragmatic strategy used to construct dialogue through reporting someone's speech, including code-switched material, as well as thoughts, emotions and attitudes, including gestures and non-lexicalised speech sounds (Davydova and Buchstaller 2015: 441). It is closely associated with narration, although it occurs in other genres as well. Native speakers employ this narrative device routinely and frequently to captivate listeners' attention and render their portrayal of events more vivid and even dramatic. In so doing, they essentially hope to "heighten the performance values of their stories" (Ferrara and Bell 1995: 265). In other words, quotation is a substantially sophisticated means to express evidentiality (Clift 2006; Romaine and Lange 1991). As such, quotation is an integral part of the quotative frame or template, a clause-level structural element. First proposed in Buchstaller (2014: 17) and elaborated on in Buchstaller (2015), the quotative template is illustrated in Figure 2 for convenience.

At the most abstract level, the quotative frame consists of the following syntactic strings: NOUN PHRASE + COPULA VERB/VERBUM DICENDI + (DISCOURSE MARKER) + QUOTE. Because mainstream English is a non-pro-drop variety, the

## 3.1 Quotation: Definition and some theoretical preliminaries

| Noun Phrase | Copula Verb | (Discourse Marker) | Quote |
|---|---|---|---|
| She | 's | all | " ..." |
| He | goes | like | " ..." |
| My mum | feels | kinda | " ..." |
| | Verbum dicendi | | |
| I | say | git | " ..." |
| They | think | totally | " ..." |

**Figure 2:** Quotative template in L1 English (from Davydova and Buchstaller 2015: 452).

slots representing the general category NOUN PHRASE are typically filled with lexical material performing the function of the grammatical subject in various L1 vernaculars. The same is true of the structural string COPULA VERBS/VERBUM DICENDI, which can collectively be called PREDICATION. The slot can be either realised as an actual copula verb such as *be*, or alternatively, it can be filled with various *verba dicendi*, notably *say* and *think*. Note that the realisation of a discourse marker is optional. The quote is a focal point of the quotative template. It is conceptually complete without the main clause containing the quotative marker. In other words, it is semantically and syntactically independent of the main clause. In contrast, the main clause introducing the quote is incomplete both semantically and syntactically without the quoted material. This might explain why we frequently encounter zero quotative markers (see example in (19)) in natural speech but not zero quotes. It is thus quite possible to encounter an utterance of the type, e.g. *and he was standing there and ø, 'What a joy!'* but an utterance of the type, e.g. */? he said, 'ø'* is ill-formed (see also Buchstaller 2014: 37–54).

Grounded in the usage-oriented accounts of linguistic representation and language change (Croft 2001a; Fillmore 1988; Goldberg 1995, 2003, 2006; Langacker 1987; Tomasello 2003; Traugott and Trousdale 2013), the account outlined above proposes that similar to other construction types, the quotative template is productive. The main mechanism through which numerous quotative strategies emerge from the general quotative template is analogical extension. The groups of lexical items that can be recruited into the same slot may have similar meanings (for instance, *ask* and *say*) but they may also be recruited based on some very general semantic-pragmatic properties (for instance, approximation marker *like, kinda*, etc.). In other words, "[c]onstructions tend to expand via local analogies to existing exemplars, motivated by the shared semantic-pragmatic properties of the lexical items in one pragmatic slot" (Buchstaller 2014: 19).

## 3.2 Quotation: The method of study

Most studies looking at the spread of innovative *be like* across the globe are variationist in nature. What this entails is that they comply with the Labovian *principle of accountability* (Labov 1972b) which postulates that language is a highly complex, yet internally organised entity composed of variable subsystems. Each subsystem, in our case quotative marking, in turn, comprises variants competing for the expression of a particular linguistic function. In some cases, a variant might have a zero realisation but still needs to be included into the analysis. The analyst working within the variationist paradigm then needs to account for every single token used for the expression of a linguistic function.

The premise outlined above bears one crucial methodological repercussion for the work with language data. In line with the methodological procedure established in the previous studies (*inter alia* Buchstaller 2014; D'Arcy 2012; Davydova 2015b, 2016a; Davydova and Buchstaller 2015; Tagliamonte and Hudson 1999), the variable context was functionally delineated. In practical terms, it means that I had to extract the data manually to be able to account for each and every instance of quotation in the body of linguistic material that I was working with (see Chapter 5 and 6 for more information on the data sets). Given that quotation is essentially a *re-enactment* of speech, thought or inward emotions, feelings and attitudes (Buchstaller 2014; Davydova 2016b), the parameters that constitute re-enactment must be defined. Following Davydova (2016b: 175), I maintain here that re-enactment or dialogue construction necessarily entails the incorporation of (i) pragmatic cues such as, for instance, discourse markers or hesitation devices, (ii) suprasegmental features, for instance, variations in pitch, speech tempo, varying intonation contours or pauses for dramatic effect, and (iii) paralinguistic elements which encompass gestures, facial and other bodily expressions. While introducing a quote, speakers typically set it off from the rest of speech material with a pause. Crucially, the quote is always oriented deictically towards the person being reported on (Buchstaller 2014: 56–57), as shown in (15) and (16):

(15) ... he is the eldest one so he **is like**, 'Just trust me, just trust me.' ... and he says, 'No, I am not, let's go, let's go!' (HCNVE: IE99)

(16) ... because I **was like**, 'Wow, wow, wow! That's kind of cool, he is a cute guy, he is interesting.' (MaCGE: GE147)

Relying on the definition of the re-enactment presented above, I extracted the quotes containing deictic material that demonstrates unequivocally that the quoted material is inherently oriented towards the experiencer. Secondly, because the suprasegmental component plays such an important role in the construction of a dialogue in discourse (see also Macaulay 2001: 4), I relied on the intonation contours of a phrase by way of delimiting quotation. In other words, "because quotation is usually set apart from the co-text by a pause or other supra-segmental features" and is a "focal intonation unit by itself" (Buchstaller 2014: 54), the patterning of pitch changes served as a cue for delimitation of quoted material in connected speech (Davydova 2016b: 181).

## 3.3 English quotation in real time: A cross-varietal perspective

The variable realisation of quotative marking has been meticulously explored in L1 vernaculars yielding robust intervarietal generalisations. Firstly, we know that back in the late 1970s/early 1980s, the quotative system of North American English began to re-organise (Tagliamonte 2012: 247). A new variant, quotative *be like* (illustrated in (13), (15), and (16)), entered the system and started to compete with other traditional or canonical quotative markers, such as *say*, *think*, and zero quotatives (illustrated in (17) through (19)).[1]

(17)   and she **said**, 'I have never seen anything like that!'

(18)   ... after which I **thought**, 'What a strange coincidence.'

(19)   Then she turned around and, 'Oh my God!'

*Be like* is hypothesised to have originated in California and was originally circumscribed to the Valley Girl Talk, a sociolect associated with promiscuous air-headed (upper-)middle class young females from the San Fernando Valley (Buchstaller 2014: 6, 223). My extended discussions with an over 50 Californian basically confirm this hypothesis. In contrast to other quotative innovations, *be like* was relatively soon picked up by L1 speakers from other geographic locals. To illustrate this point, *be like* was attested at the rate of 13% in speech of young Canadians in 1995 (Tagliamonte and Hudson 1999: 158). In the early 2000s, it becomes a dominant player in the quotative system accounting for as many as 58% of all variants (Tagliamonte and D'Arcy 2004: 501). Similarly, *be like* "become[s] the most frequently used quotative increasing from 10 percent

---
[1] The exact time frame is very difficult to nail down. Most published studies circumscribe the birth of *be like* to the early 1980s (Butters 1982; Macaulay 2001), although my North American informants (one of whom was born in California in the 1950s) notice that this form started surfacing in adolescent speech in the late 1970s.

in 1996 to 68 percent in 2006" among York undergraduates (Durham et al. 2011: 323). It is furthermore attested in 43.3% of all cases in younger people's speech representing a north-eastern English vernacular in 2007–2008 (Buchstaller 2014: 119). In the English of Australian youth, *be like* rose from constituting a mere 8% of the entire system in 1997–1999 (Winter 2002: 10, Melbourne) to the key variant used at the rate ranging between 79.4% and 81.5% in 2011 (Rodríguez Louro 2013: 59, Perth). D'Arcy's (2012: 357) report of New Zealand English informs us that the use of quotative *be like* rises from 4% in 1994–1997 to 21% in 2002–2006. Macaulay (2001: 10) reports the rate of *be like* amounting to 14% in speech of Glasgow adolescents in 1997. Revised from Davydova (2015b: 311), Table 1 documents the incremental spread of innovative *be like* in speech communities all over the world.

**Table 1:** *Be like* across the globe: A real-time perspective (revised from Davydova 2015b: 311).

| (%) | N (quotes) | Variety | Community | Speakers | Year | Source |
|---|---|---|---|---|---|---|
| **Native Englishes** | | | | | | |
| 13.6% | 89/656 | AmE | The USA | younger speakers | 1988–1992 | Buchstaller and D'Arcy (2009) |
| 7% | 92/1314 | BrE | Derby and Newcastle, England | younger speakers | 1994–1995 | Buchstaller and D'Arcy (2009) |
| 6.1% | 38/625 | NZE | Canterbury, Auckland, Taranaki, Nelson, Otago, New Zealand | younger speakers | 1994–1996 | Buchstaller and D'Arcy (2009) |
| 4% | 47/1349 | NZE | Canterbury, New Zealand | younger and older speakers | 1994–1996 | D'Arcy (2012) |
| 13% | 79/612 | CanE | Ottawa, Canada | students | 1995 | Tagliamonte and Hudson (1999) |
| 18% | 120/665 | BrE | York, England | students | 1996 | Tagliamonte and Hudson (1999) |
| 14% | 33/242 | BrE | Glasgow, Scotland | adolescents | 1997 | Macaulay (2001) |
| 8% | 18/218 | AusE | Melbourne, Australia | adolescents | 1997–1999 | Winter (2002) |
| 62% | 114/184 | CanE | St. John's, Canada | preadolescents/ adolescents | 1999–2000 | D'Arcy (2004) |
| 21.2% | 124/586 | BrE | Tyneside, England | younger and older speakers | the 2000s | Buchstaller (2011) |
| 58% | 1198/2058 | CanE | Toronto, Canada | students | 2002–2003 | Tagliamonte and D'Arcy (2004) |

**Table 1** (continued)

| (%) | N (quotes) | Variety | Community | Speakers | Year | Source |
|---|---|---|---|---|---|---|
| 21% | 122/570 | NZE | Canterbury, Auckland, Taranaki, Nelson, Otago, New Zealand | younger and older speakers | 2002–2006 | D'Arcy (2012) |
| 68% | n. d. | BrE | York, England | students | 2006 | Durham et al. (2011) |
| 21% | 124/586 | BrE | Newcastle, England | younger and older speakers | 2007 | Buchstaller (2014) |
| 43% | 171/395 | BrE | Newcastle, England | younger speakers | 2004–2008 | Buchstaller (2014) |
| 72% | 280/385 | AmE | California, USA | younger speakers | 2004–2008 | Buchstaller (2014) |
| 81.5% | 243/298 | AusE | Perth, Australia | young speakers | 2011 | Rodríguez Louro (2013) |
| **Indigenised Englishes** | | | | | | |
| 0% | 0/156 | IndE | Kolhapur, India | younger and older speakers | 1990–1996 | D'Arcy (2013) |
| 3.6% | n. d./496 | SinE | Singapore | younger and older speakers | 1990–1996 | D'Arcy (2013) |
| 4.7% | n. d./213 | HKE | Hong Kong | younger and older speakers | 1990–1996 | D'Arcy (2013) |
| 7.9% | n. d./126 | KenE | Kenya | younger and older speakers | 1990–1996 | D'Arcy (2013) |
| 11.2% | n. d./339 | PhE | Philippines | younger and older speakers | 1990–1996 | D'Arcy (2013) |
| 16% | 55/349 | IndE | New Delhi, India | students | 2007–2011 | Davydova (2015b) |
| **Learner English** | | | | | | |
| 22.7% | 153/674 | GerE | Mannheim, Germany | students | 2014–2015 | Davydova and Buchstaller (2015) |

As Table 1 shows, non-native Englishes lag behind the developmental trends attested in L1 English. *Be like* is rarely recruited as a quotative marker by L2 speakers from India, Singapore, Hong Kong, and Kenya back in the 1990s, although it exhibits somewhat higher rates in the Philippines most probably due to its inherent affiliation with North American English. This finding can be explained both in terms of the 'colonial lag' and 'multilingual inputs'. In Davydova (2015b: 312),

I argue that postcolonial varieties boast unique sociolinguistic ecologies consisting of multilingual inputs. Speakers of indigenised English draw on global but also local resources as they create their distinctive vernaculars (see also Chapter 5 for a detailed discussion). This might explain why global linguistic innovations develop in indigenised Englishes at a slower rate. Notice, however, that *be like* becomes more conspicuous in data pools of indigenised and Learner English recorded between 2007 and 2015 (Davydova 2015b; Davydova and Buchstaller 2015).

The channels through which *be like* spread from one speaker community to the next is a contentious issue in current sociolinguistic research. Two widely discussed conduits of linguistic innovations comprise face-to-face interactions on the one hand (Labov 2007; Tagliamonte, D'Arcy, and Rodríguez Louro 2016; Trudgill 1986) and the global reach of mass media on the other (Androutsopoulos 2014a; Bell and Sharma 2014). Variationist sociolinguists have maintained that the propagation of linguistic variability pertaining to the hardcore levels of linguistic structure (such as morphosyntax but also phonology) requires prolonged interpersonal contact. It is through the process of accommodation or mutual adaptation, so the contention, that such aspects of language are diffused from one speaker community to the next (Labov 2001, 2007; Trudgill 1986, 2014). In contrast, 'superficial' (Chambers 1998) language features "such as new words and idioms, or fashionable pronunciations of individual words, may be *imitated* or *copied* from television or radio (rather than accommodated to)" (Trudgill 1986: 40–41, emphasis in the original). The most recent sociolinguistic undertakings, however, challenge the view that mass media is unlikely to affect the way people speak (Stuart-Smith 2011, 2012; Stuart-Smith et al. 2013). While exploiting advanced methodologies, these studies highlight the importance of 'interactive practices', 'parasocial interaction' and pinpoint the pertinence of speakers' 'engagement with media texts' as well as their motivation (Androutsopoulos 2014b: 16). For instance, Stuart-Smith et al. (2013), which is the most innovative and up-to-date research exploring the impact of television on the use of *th*-fronting and *l*-vocalisation in Glasgow speech, point to a subtle link between mass media viewing habits and linguistic behaviour. It turns out that although linguistic variables are still the strongest predictors for using incoming variants, media influence plays a role in the speech of individuals emotionally involved with the characters of a show. This research thus appears to suggest that mass media might exert a bigger impact on the linguistic behaviour of introverted people because these individuals are more likely to focus their attention inward and spend prolonged periods of time in the imaginary world populated by the characters of the show.

Another strand of research addresses the importance of identity in the propagation of linguistic innovations (Auer and Hinskens 2005; Carvalho 2004; Le Page and Tabouret-Keller's 1985). In this view, speakers will accommodate their linguistic behaviour by way of adjusting to the norms and patterns of a socially attractive group even though this group is not in the immediate vicinity. In fact, this is how researchers account for the processes of dialect levelling in favour of standard language reported for both Anglophone and non-Anglophone world (Ota and Takano 2014; Trudgill 2002). All in all, the current consensus, so it would seem, is that mass media does have at least some impact on the ambient norms of L1 vernaculars, if only indirect.

As far as the spread of innovative *be like* is concerned, earlier studies (Tagliamonte and Hudson 1999) seem to have implicitly assumed that mass media must have played a role in the propagation of the variant, while also emphasising the supremacy of scenarios involving interpersonal communication (see Buchstaller 2014: 93). In his study of quotative *be like* in speech of Glasgow adolescent girls, Macaulay (2001: 17) makes an overt claim that the emergence of the innovative variant is "unlikely to have been through direct contact with young Americans" concluding that the variant "owes something to the media". Macaulay (2001) is probably the only investigation where the role of mass media in the propagation of quotative *be like* is explicitly recognised. Other authors who have tackled the study of the global linguistic innovation seem to vacillate – given current *status-quo* within sociolinguistics – between face-to-face contact and mass media as two possible diffusion channels, acknowledging (but not over-emphasising) the role of television and the media as an additional contributory factor in the propagation of quotative *be like* (see, for instance, Buchstaller 2004, 2008; Buchstaller and D'Arcy 2009; Meyerhoff and Niedzielski 2003). More recently, Tagliamonte, D'Arcy, and Rodríguez Louro (2016) have vigorously argued that *be like* was dispersed to far-distant locales through the global personal connections resulting from worldwide economic expansion and social restructuring that took place from 1945 to the early 1970s. The former was made possible by the introduction of the jet plane in 1958, which subsequently popularised international travel. The latter was accompanied by the emergence of youth (sub-)cultures in industrialised Western societies. Sharing common interests and values, these young individuals were brought together through gap years, the 'overseas experience', or the 'hippie trail' (Tagliamonte, D'Arcy, and Rodríguez Louro 2016: 838–839). And this is how, so the authors, *be like* found its way into new linguistic varieties. Overall, the previous discussion makes clear that the channels through which *be like* was spread around the world remains a hotly debated issue in (variationist) sociolinguistics requiring further investigation.

What is important to understand in the present context is that in contrast to lexical, "off-the-shelf" (Eckert 2003: 395) features, which tend to be short-lived and trivial linguistic phenomena that are also "superficial in terms of [their] penetration into different linguistic varieties" (Trudgill 2014: 216), *be like* is an integral part of a sufficiently complex, "core grammatical" (Sayers 2014: 187) domain of language exhibiting systemic change (Tagliamonte, D'Arcy, and Rodríguez Louro 2016).[2] The relevant question is then whether non-native speakers of English will be able to pick up on the language-internal conditioning underlying its variable realisation in the absence of sustained interpersonal contact with L1 vernaculars. With this said, one of the objectives of this study is to assess the relative role played by the interpersonal contact as well as mass media in the spread of quotative *be like* and its probabilistic grammar to non-native Englishes (see Chapters 5, 6, and 7 for more detail). To put it in Buchstaller's (2006: 375) words, I seek to explore how "globally travelling [linguistic] features" actually travel.

## 3.4 English quotation: Systemic constraints

Perhaps the most important finding stemming from the strand of sociolinguistic research exploring quotative markers is the empirically substantiated contention that while re-enacting dialogue throughout narratives, native speakers do not randomly use various quotative markers; rather their choice can be predicted from a set of language-internal and sociolinguistic constraints. In what follows, I describe what these constraints are, while contextualising them within the theory of grammaticalisation which makes predictions for the incremental spread of *be like* in a speech community (Ferrara and Bell 1995; Tagliamonte and Hudson 1999).

*Mimesis*: The most consistent constraint inextricably linked to quotative marking and the use of *be like* is the one of mimesis (Buchstaller 2014; Buchstaller and D'Arcy 2009; Romaine and Lange 1991; Tagliamonte and Hudson 1999). Mimetic quotes are produced as prosodically marked material and are set off from the rest of the utterance in terms of pitch variations, tempo, and sometimes accent. In contrast, non-mimetic quotes are performed with a normal 'voice' (Bakhtin 1986 [1979]). This fundamental contrast between the two quote types is illustrated in (20) and (21).

(20) ... and I **said**, 'Yeah, well, I am done with my work.' (MaCGE: GE100)

(21) ... she is sitting there and she**'s like** (*mimicking shouting*), 'Stop it!' (MaCGE: GE150)

---

[2] In other words, *be like* is not a mere lexical change in progress (see Blyth, Recktenwald, and Wang1990; D'Arcy 2012).

As demonstrated in these examples, *be like* performs a function of a mimesis marker, similar to zero quotatives. In contrast, *say* and *think* tend to be non-mimetic. When contextualised within the grammaticalisation theory, *be like* can be hypothesised to spread from mimetic to non-mimetic contexts as it evolves as a speech and thought introducer in a speech community (see Buchstaller 2003, 2014: 102).

*Quote type*: Quote type is another major constraint that has been consistently shown to underlie the variable realisation of *be like* and other quotative variants in native English. The overall distinction is between quotes that report mental activities and mental states, as in (23), and those that report outwardly realised speech, as in (22). In addition, some studies looking at non-native English account for the occurrence of the indigenous speech chunks within reported material, illustrated in (24), (Davydova 2015b; Davydova and Buchstaller 2015) because bilingual speakers, as research into language contact shows, employ the quotative frame as a pivot for code-switches (Matras 2009). In this study, I thus draw a distinction between (i) direct speech proper, (ii) thought or inner dialogue, and (iii) quoted material containing indigenous code-switches.

(22) *reported speech*: I did not **say**, 'Hi!' (,) I was there **like**, '(making a gesture and a sound).' (MaCGE: GE151)

(23) *reported thought*: and I **was like**, 'Oh, God I am hating it so much!' (MaCGE: GE150)

(24) *indigenous content*: ... he always **said** in his like funny Dutch accent **like** (imitating the accent), 'Oh, Sie sind so spät. Setzen Sie sich in die erste Reihe, falls Sie so spät kommen.' (MaCGE: GE104)

Earliest descriptions of quotative *be like* report that the variant is preferred with thought over direct speech in L1 English (see *inter alia* D'Arcy 2013; Tagliamonte and D'Arcy 2004, 2007; Tagliamonte and Hudson 1999), and it is, indeed, believed to have come into the English system as a marker of internal thought (Tannen 1986). Later investigations into English quotative marking (Gardner et al. 2013; Tagliamonte and D'Arcy 2007), however, indicate levelling tendencies with *be like* being used profusely with direct speech, albeit still more frequent with thought. As for other quotatives, *say* is closely associated with the reporting of direct speech and *think* with thought (Buchstaller 2014), which is perhaps not very surprising given their semantics. Furthermore, there is evidence pinpointing a close link between quotative *say* and quotes containing indigenous code-switched material (Davydova and Buchstaller 2015: 455).

*Grammatical subject*: There is a substantial amount of sociolinguistic evidence demonstrating that quotative markers tend to ground themselves in the system by developing distinctive functional profiles with respect to the grammatical subject contained in the main clause. Thus, quotative *say* is reportedly preferable in third-person contexts, whereas *think* is more robust with the first-person grammatical subject (see, for instance, Davydova and Buchstaller 2015: 447). Quotative *be like* bears strong associations with the first-person grammatical subject and some studies document the retention of this effect across time (Tagliamonte and D'Arcy 2007: 209). Others, in contrast, report levelling tendencies for this constraint, with *be like* spreading from the first over to the third-person grammatical subject (Buchstaller 2014; D'Arcy 2004; Ferrara and Bell 1995; Sanchez and Charity 1991) as it evolves into a key quotative marker in a speech community. Although analysts disagree whether to include the neuter pronoun *it* into the analyses of quotative variation, the studies that do so report a highly favouring impact of neuter *it* on the occurrence of quotative *be like* (Buchstaller 2014).

*Tense*: The final language-internal factor underlying variable realisation of English quotatives is the tense marking of the quotative verb. Previous research shows that *say* tends to occur with a variety of tense and aspect markers (Buchstaller 2014: 163); *think* vacillates between the past and present tense marking, exhibiting alternate preferences from data set to data set (Buchstaller 2014: 163–186). As for *be like*, it shows unequivocal preferences for the present tense marking, and much of this effect is due to *be like*'s occurrences with Conversational Historical Present (henceforth, CHP), the use of present tense morphology with past time reference, illustrated in (25). This is particularly true of North American English (Buchstaller and D'Arcy 2009; Tagliamonte and D'Arcy 2007). A feature of colloquial English speech, CHP has been reported to collocate well with speech and thought introducers (D'Arcy 2012: 348). With this said, Buchstaller (2014) also reports a favouring effect of the past time marking on *be like* in her British English set.

(25)   … he just said something and we **are like**, 'Wow, wow, wow!' (HCNVE: IE82)

*Gender*: Decades of sociolinguistic research have highlighted the role of women in the advancement of language change. Crucially, women are in the vanguard of linguistic change irrespective of the type of change as they put forward linguistic features that spread both and above and below the level of conscious awareness in a speech community. *Be like* has been described as a socially salient feature that is given much attention in the media (see Buchstaller 2014: 198–244). With this said, it is perhaps not surprising that it is attested far more frequently in female speech as documented by Ferrara and Bell (1995), Singler (2001) for the US; Tagliamonte and Hudson (1999) for England; Macaulay (2001) for Scotland, and Tagliamonte and D'Arcy (2004, 2007) for Canada. Some studies have, however, shown a preference of *be like* in male speech (Blyth et al. 1990; Dailey-O'Cain 2000). Others report no significant effects of speaker sex (Tagliamonte and Hudson 1999 for Canada; Buchstaller 2008 for the US), although in these studies *be like* is still more frequent in the speech of female speakers that it is in that of male speakers.

## 3.5 Quotative *be like* and grammaticalisation theory

Given the results in Table 1, I am operating under the assumption that *be like* is by and large a new incoming variant in ESL/EFL speaker communities, still at the initial stages of its development. Here, I use the theory of grammaticalisation for *be like* as a heuristic device and a suitable benchmark allowing for direct comparisons between ESL and EFL English. My choice to use this theoretical construct rather than an existing L1 corpus of English as a reference point in this study is motivated by the fact that ESL/EFL learners exhibit highly diverse patterns of L1 exposure both through interpersonal communication and mass media. Not a single corpus of native English can do justice to this astounding heterogeneity of linguistic inputs accompanying L2 acquisition of the variable grammar as the language target becomes increasingly shifty in such situations. With this said, the analyst arguably needs a more abstract point of reference overriding variety-specific idiosyncrasies, which are plenty in any form of English. Conceived by Ferrara and Bell (1995) and elaborated on by Tagliamonte and Hudson (1999), the proposed theory is a useful construct that can be used to investigate the developmental tendencies of *be like* and measure the level of its diffusion within and across varieties (Tagliamonte and Hudson 1999: 159). Its main tenets are summarised in Table 2 for convenience. Note that the tenets draw on empirical data obtained from varieties of North American English, which has been claimed to have been developing into a 'hub/hyper-central variety' (Mair 2016: 24) with a great potential influence on the newly emerging forms of English.

**Table 2:** Grammaticalisation of *be like* in a speech community (amended from Tagliamonte and Hudson 1999: 159).

| Measure | Initial stage | Later stage |
|---|---|---|
| mimesis | mimetic quotes | expansion into non-mimetic quotes |
| quote type | thought | expansion into speech |
| grammatical subject | first person | expansion into third person |
| tense | CHP | expansion into other tenses |
| gender | female speech | neutralisation of sex difference |

The premise that allows me to explore and revise the major predictions for the grammaticalisation of *be like* in non-native-speaker communities is the sociolinguistic contention assuming a fair amount of continuity existing between L1/parent varieties and their linguistic offspring, also known as daughter varieties (Collins 2015: 1–3). The linguistic continuity assumption allows the analyst to hypothesise a common English 'core' (Schneider 2000: 205) which characterises *all* the varieties of English irrespective of its varietal type. Previous research furthermore demonstrates that this common core is manifested not only through a similar composition of linguistic variants but also through identical patterns underlying their use (see Davydova 2011, 2016b). To illustrate this point, in a study of the present perfect marking in postcolonial Englishes (Davydova 2016b: 182–183), I show that the linguistic domain is not only composed of largely identical variants, i.e. the *have* perfect and the simple past tense. More importantly, the variable realisation of the *have* perfect is contingent upon semantic-pragmatic context and time adverbial specification.

With this explicated, if the predictions for the way *be like* paves its way into the system could be understood as a general property of English quotative marking (see also D'Arcy 2013: 493; Davydova and Buchstaller 2015: 445–449), we can expect this variant to be favoured with mimetic over non-mimetic quotes, with thought over speech and indigenous content, with first- over third-person grammatical subject, while being marked for the present tense, notably CHP in ESL/EFL communities – at the incipient stages of its development. Because this study accounts for the neuter pronoun *it*, we can furthermore hypothesise a strong link between innovative *be like* and neuter *it*, especially in US oriented ESL/EFL English.

In other words, I seek to discover whether non-native speakers of English are adopting innovative *be like* in alignment with the patterns reported for L1 language users, or whether they are using this variable linguistic feature creatively and in a highly localised manner and if so, exactly how they are doing it. This is by and large an empirical question. If it turns out, for instance, that both ESL and EFL learners largely replicate the patterns attested in the donor varieties, this will strengthen the hypothesis predicting the universal path of language-internal integration of *be like* into the quotative system (Ferrara and Bell 1995) and will call for an explanation in terms of more general cognitive processes (salience, frequency, etc.) shaping non-native English in this domain of the variable grammar. If, on the other hand, non-native speakers develop idiosyncratic patterns of quotative use, this would highlight the importance of the local context and the ensuing need for particularised explanations in the account of World Englishes. Crucially, as I explore the intra-and extralinguistic reality of quotative marking in the ESL/EFL communities, I also attempt to understand the role played by local sociolinguistic ecologies and mass media (TV series and English films) in the process of adaptation of global linguistic innovations. Furthermore, I explore non-native speakers' attitudes as they too contribute to a better understanding of the general mechanisms guiding the evolution of modern English worldwide.

# 4 Tackling non-native speakers' attitudes

Whether a given linguistic feature is borrowed from one linguistic variety into another largely depends on the explicit and implicit attitudes expressed by the speakers of the recipient variety towards the donor variety. Furthermore, it is not unreasonable to surmise that positive attitudes are likely to promote the adoption of linguistic variants, including innovative language forms, whereas neutral or negative attitudes might, indeed, stand in the way of linguistic diffusion, the transfer of features from one speech community to the other (Labov 2007: 347). In a similar vein, the degree to which a linguistic trend catches "might depend on our (subconscious) attitude towards [...] the nation responsible for starting it, in this case, the United States" (Baird 2001: 18).

With this said, the major goal of this chapter is to describe ESL and EFL learners' overt and covert evaluations of the mainstream forms of English, i.e. British English and American English, and to contrast those with their perceptions of non-native Englishes, including their own variety, Indian English and English spoken in Germany/Europe. In so doing, I majorly seek to understand ESL and EFL speakers' perceptions of American English, the epicentre of the spread of *be like*, vis-á-vis other varieties of English. My analyses draw on data obtained from students enrolled in Bachelor's and Master's degree programmes at JNU and UM in the period from 2013 to 2014.

Previous research exploring native speakers' perceptions of L1 English has ascertained that standard British English and Received Pronunciation (henceforth, RP), the supra-local accent spoken on the British Isles, receive high ratings for social status and prestige. In contrast, American English is highly valued for its social attractiveness and the feeling of solidary it evokes in its listeners (Ball 1983; Huygens and Vaughan 1983; Stewart et al. 1985). These results have been corroborated by the existing empirical work investigating the social evaluations of these varieties by non-native speakers (Clark and Schleef 2010; Ladegaard 1998; Ladegaard and Sachdev 2006). At the same time, Bayard et al. (2001) as well as Jenkins (2007) and Kirkpatrick and Xu (2002) highlighted the importance of American English as the prestigious form of English in some native and non-native-speaker communities. Moreover, non-native speakers have been shown to downgrade their own variety in comparison to native English, a phenomenon called 'inferiority complex' (Tan and Castelli 2013).

Given that language attitudes are highly complex, multidimensional, psychological constructs which cannot be observed directly, the pertinent question arises, 'Which methods are best suited for the rigorous study of the phenomenon?' Since the attitudinal structure comprises both the cognitive and the affective component (the way people *think* and the way people *feel*), there are two major approaches to tap into people's perceptions of language and linguistic structure (Garrett 2010: 37–52). The so-called direct approach elicits people's conscious reactions towards a given variety. These are oftentimes elicited through various questionnaire tasks, which are then quantitatively evaluated. Alternatively, people's overt reactions can also be investigated through peer-group interviews, which supply the analyst with a fine-grained qualitative detail, indispensable in interpreting quantitative data. In contrast, the indirect approach tackles speakers' unconscious assessments of a specific form of language. The main technique employed in the study of covert attitudes is the verbal guise test (henceforth, VGT). Here, participants are asked to evaluate audio-taped speakers for various personality traits such as friendliness, education, intelligence, social attractiveness, and so on.

Against this backdrop, this chapter discusses the results of ESL/EFL learners' social evaluations of standard British English, mainstream American English, educated Indian English and educated German/European English and in so doing, provides the data stemming from an attitudinal questionnaire, a VGT and sociolinguistic interviews. The attitudinal survey directly targets learners' beliefs about World Englishes, whereas the VGT taps more subtly into students' feelings regarding those. Finally, sociolinguistic interviews add a qualitative methodological detail to the description of the attitudinal data. The employment of a method mix is important as it allows me to consider the data from complementary, yet related perspectives (Davydova 2015a; Garrett 2010). Crucially, this approach is aligned with a well-established variationist wisdom stating that sociolinguistic knowledge can be procured only through converging evidence obtained from various types of data (Labov 2010[1972a]; Schilling 2013: 66). In what follows, I present contrastive findings stemming from each method and then discuss their implications for the study of language variation and change in indigenised and Learner English.

## 4.1 Attitudinal questionnaire

To tap into ESL/EFL learners' direct evaluations of native and non-native Englishes, I distributed an attitudinal survey in both student communities, sampling an overall total of 200 students (106 for JNU and 94 for UM). The attitudinal survey comprised six statements presented in Figure 3 for convenience. The statements comprised the three fundamental dimensions of the attitudinal structure: (i) social status and prestige (evaluative judgements); (ii) social attractiveness/solidarity (affective judgements); (iii) construction of

---

**Quickly** read the following statements about *British English* and decide to what extent you agree with each statement.

1. I think British English is a high-status variety.

| 1 | 2 | 3 | 4 | 5 | 6 |
|---|---|---|---|---|---|
| strongly disagree | | | | | strongly agree |

2. I think British English is prestigious.

| 1 | 2 | 3 | 4 | 5 | 6 |
|---|---|---|---|---|---|
| strongly disagree | | | | | strongly agree |

3. British English is socially attractive.

| 1 | 2 | 3 | 4 | 5 | 6 |
|---|---|---|---|---|---|
| strongly disagree | | | | | strongly agree |

4. I use British English to express my solidarity with others.

| 1 | 2 | 3 | 4 | 5 | 6 |
|---|---|---|---|---|---|
| strongly disagree | | | | | strongly agree |

5. British English is a form of English that I speak.

| 1 | 2 | 3 | 4 | 5 | 6 |
|---|---|---|---|---|---|
| strongly disagree | | | | | strongly agree |

6. British English is a form of English that I strongly identify myself with.

| 1 | 2 | 3 | 4 | 5 | 6 |
|---|---|---|---|---|---|
| strongly disagree | | | | | strongly agree |

**Figure 3:** The attitudinal survey task.

social identity (evaluative-affective judgements) (see also Davydova 2015a). Respondents in both speech communities were instructed to state to which degree they agreed with each statement for each variety by placing their answer on a Likert scale from one to six.

The collected data was entered into an SPSS spreadsheet, checked for outliers, tested for normality (Wilk Shapiro test) and homogeneity of variance (Mauchly's test of sphericity). Stemming from the within-subjects design, the data were then subjected to repeated measures analyses of variance (ANOVA), which compared judgement means for each statement across the four conditions, i.e. British English, American English, Indian English, and German/European English.

The analyses of JNU data revealed that out of 106 students targeted in the survey, only 49 were able to demonstrate a sufficient level of awareness about Englishes spoken in Europe, including Germany. Given this result, I decided to trim the original data set including only those participants who could pronounce coherent judgements about all four varieties studied here. The procedure resulted in a considerable reduction of the sample but ensured the validity of constructed measurements (see also Baker 1992: 24).

**Table 3:** Repeated measures ANOVAs of survey data comparing mean evaluations of two native and two non-native varieties by Indian students (N 49).

| Statement | Mean Scores | | | | F-value | D.F. | P-value |
|---|---|---|---|---|---|---|---|
| | BrE | AmE | EurE | IndE | | | |
| *Dimension: status/prestige* | | | | | | | |
| 1. I think X is a high-status variety | 4.61 | 3.18 | 3.43 | 2.78 | 24.396 | 2.8, 139.1 | .000 |
| 2. I think X is prestigious | 4.29 | 3.24 | 3.33 | 3.00 | 11.647 | 2.9, 140.0 | .000 |
| *Dimension: solidarity/social attractiveness* | | | | | | | |
| 3. X is socially attractive | 4.14 | 3.88 | 3.29 | 3.29 | 5.561 | 2.7, 127.4 | .002 |
| 4. I use X to express my solidarity with others | 2.59 | 2.51 | 1.63 | 4.12 | 37.327 | 2.6, 122.7 | .000 |
| *Dimension: identity* | | | | | | | |
| 5. X is an English that I speak | 3.12 | 2.53 | 1.51 | 4.53 | 38.151 | 2.6, 117.1 | .000 |
| 6. X is an English that I strongly identify with | 3.08 | 2.27 | 1.45 | 4.35 | 42.780 | 2.4, 115.5 | .000 |

Table 3 reveals that my Indian informants accord high social status and prestige to the standard variety of British English. Englishes spoken in Europe come in second followed by American English, although post hoc pairwise comparisons indicate that the mean ratings between condition two and three are not statistically significant. Of interest is the fact that notwithstanding its status as an "endocentric", norm-developing variety that has begun to be increasingly accepted as part of India's cultural identity (Schneider 2007: 171), Indian English is evaluated rather poorly in terms of its social standing in comparison to other forms of English treated here. Overall, these results echo those reported in Hohenthal (2003) and Bernaisch and Koch (2016). In Hohenthal (2003), 70% of the informants regarded British English as the best model for teaching English in classroom, thereby assigning considerable social power to it. Bernaisch and Koch (2016: 118) similarly demonstrate that British English is rated "in a more favourable light" than Indian English on the dimension of competence, power and status (Bernaisch and Koch 2016: 123).

British English furthermore received the highest rating for its social attractiveness, a finding which sits well with that documented in Kachru (1994) who found that a majority of faculty and graduate students at an Indian university chose British English as their target model. This finding is perhaps not entirely surprising given the history of British English on the Indian subcontinent and its inherent associations with good upbringing and education of the highest quality, upward mobility and economic prosperity, all of which, in turn, contribute to the social attractiveness of a given variety. Interestingly, American English trails in second place and pairwise comparisons reveal that the mean differences between two native-speaker varieties are not statistically significant, setting both native Englishes apart from the two non-native-speaker varieties studied here. What this finding entails is that American English has apparently begun to gain ground as a socially attractive form of English in India and is being widely embraced by the younger generation of speakers.

Importantly, the attitudinal survey also indicates that Indian English is the form of English that JNU students use to express their solidarity with others. It is also the form of English that they think they speak and strongly identify with. Pairwise comparisons point to statistically significant differences that set this variety apart from all the other conditions for all three statements. These findings signal an evolved endonormative attitude indicative of the strong acceptance of Indian English as a legitimate form of English (see Schneider 2007: 48–52).

How do EFL learners evaluate World Englishes including their own variety, what kind of attitudes do they harbour towards American English and how does that compare to ESL learners' attitudes discussed above? Table 4 presents results of repeated measures ANOVAs comparing UM students' evaluations of two native and two non-native-speaker varieties.

**Table 4:** Repeated measures ANOVAs of survey data comparing mean evaluations of two native and two non-native varieties by German students (N 94) (see also Davydova 2015a).

| Statement | Mean Scores | | | | F-value | D.F. | P-value |
|---|---|---|---|---|---|---|---|
| | BrE | AmE | GerE | IndE | | | |
| *Dimension: status/prestige* | | | | | | | |
| 1. I think X is a high-status variety | 4.50 | 3.62 | 2.97 | 2.21 | 70.101 | 2.8, 254.8 | .000 |
| 2. I think X is prestigious | 4.36 | 3.39 | 2.78 | 2.00 | 89.126 | 2.9, 267.9 | .000 |
| *Dimension: solidarity/social attractiveness* | | | | | | | |
| 3. X is socially attractive | 4.00 | 4.39 | 2.87 | 2.06 | 66.598 | 2.9, 268.2 | .000 |
| 4. I use X to express my solidarity with others | 2.30 | 3.58 | 2.56 | 1.29 | 46.075 | 2.7, 252.0 | .000 |
| *Dimension: identity* | | | | | | | |
| 5. X is an English that I speak | 2.78 | 4.25 | 3.22 | 1.14 | 58.545 | 2.2, 202.2 | .000 |
| 6. X is an English that I strongly identify with | 2.55 | 3.75 | 2.37 | 1.47 | 45.820 | 1.9, 181.2 | .000 |

Similar to Indian students, German learners assigned the highest ratings to British English both in terms of prestige and status. Importantly, pairwise comparisons indicate that the differences in ratings were statistically significant for all varietal pairs. This finding patterns well with assessments of this variety by EFL learners from other countries such as, for instance, Denmark (Ladegaard 1998; Ladegaard and Sachdev 2006). American English comes in second followed by German learners' own variety. Indian English receives the lowest ratings for this dimension, a finding which replicates that reported for the ESL English.

These results provoke the following question, 'Why is Indian English downgraded for social status and prestige by both learner groups studied here?' One possible explanation for this finding might be related to the way characters speaking Indian English are portrayed in popular culture, more specifically in American TV series (see also Lippi-Green 1997). To briefly illustrate this point, "The Big Bang Theory", a CBS show quite popular with students in both academic communities, features a character of Indian origin called Raj, who is depicted as a funny, slightly silly and eccentric persona known for his metrosexuality and selective mutism.[1] Such a portrayal certainly contributes to the creation of some highly specific socio-cultural connotations which are then inextricably mapped onto the Indian English accent. The resulting stereotype is then transmitted transnationally through the global flows of popular culture resulting in similar downgrading evaluations by speakers from different local cultures.

Crucially, German EFL learners studied here view American English as socially most attractive, although the mean difference is not statistically significant in pairwise comparisons with British English, which comes in second. Therefore, it is clear that ESL and EFL learners studied here hold both native-speaker varieties in high regard with respect to social attractiveness, while exhibiting slightly different, albeit not significant, trends in their preferences. In other words, JNU students place the British variety above the American one and UM students exhibit their preferences in the reversed direction.

My UM informants furthermore contend that they would use American English in order to express their solidarity with others. More importantly, American English is the form of English that German students believe they speak. They also identify strongly with this linguistic variant. Post hoc analyses reveal that the attitudinal differences are statistically significant for all pairwise comparisons with American English in all three statements. These patterns of evaluative-affective judgements are in stark contrast with those reported for Indian informants, who show a clear preference for their own form of English on the dimension of solidarity and identity.

---

[1] Source: https://en.wikipedia.org/wiki/Raj_Koothrappali, accessed on September 14, 2016.

Summing up the results of the previous analyses, both ESL and EFL learners highly value British English for its social status and prestige, while recognising both British and American English as socially attractive varieties. My Indian informants furthermore explicitly express highly favourable sentiments towards their own variety of English on the dimension of solidarity and sociolinguistic identity. In contrast, German students place American English above all the other varieties on these dimensions. This finding gives rise to the following working hypothesis. Given that my German learners of English are so vested in acquiring American English as their target variety, it is logical to surmise that they will be much better at adopting innovative *be like* and the patterns underlying its variable use and socio-ideological evaluations. In turn, we could also expect – given these results – that Indian students would be more adept at coining their own lexicosyntactic innovations in the domain of quotative marking given their endonormative mindset. I will revisit these issues in this and subsequent chapters.

## 4.2 Verbal guise test

One of the inherent challenges presented by any questionnaire is the social desirability bias, which is the "tendency for people to give answers to questions in ways that they believe to be 'socially appropriate'" (Garrett 2010: 44). To overcome this methodological conundrum, the analyst needs to triangulate the survey data with another type of evidence indicative of speakers' more tacit beliefs. In the next step, I thus seek to discover less explicit attitudes that ESL/EFL learners harbour towards the four distinguished forms of English discussed in this chapter. To this aim, I conducted a VGT in the JNU and UM student communities. Developed in the field of social psychology back in the 1960s (Lambert et al. 1960), the VGT technique is a subtle, yet robust approach allowing for testing covert attitudes under methodologically rigorous conditions.

In Mannheim, 65 students were exposed to four recordings of an identical text passage produced by a native speaker of modern non-regional pronunciation, which is the modern version of RP (Collins and Mees 2003: 5), a native speaker of mainstream American English, or General American, a native speaker of German speaking an advanced form of English, and a trilingual (Marathi/Hindi/English) speaker from India. The recordings were obtained from the website of the International Dialects of English Archive (IDEA).[2] The text was produced by each speaker at roughly the same speech rate. Following the major

---

2 Source: http://www.dialects-archive.com/, accessed on June 1, 2015.

tenets maintained within the VGT framework, all the speakers were matched for demographic characteristics: All four were middle-aged male speakers with the middle-class background. I also attempted (as far as it was possible) to control for the speakers' voice qualities. The speakers chosen for the VGT experiment were tenors with a light timber.

In New Delhi, however, I needed to replace auditory stimuli with visual ones in view of fieldwork-related constraints. This methodological adjustment is mitigated by the findings from previous research into language attitudes, which has convincingly demonstrated that using a category label as a stimulus principally yields the same results as the usage of a concrete speech sample (see Coupland, Williams, and Garrett 1999; Williams, Garrett, and Coupland 1999). With this said, I adopted a technique advocated in Bernaisch (2012), which is a modified version of a classic VGT experiment. In this adjusted approach, respondents get exposed to a visual representation of a category, in this case a linguistic variety, through a symbol best describing the category, i.e. a map or a flag. Here, 49 Indian respondents were exposed to the four flags representing the UK, the US, the European Union and India.

Judges from both student communities were instructed to rate each condition (guise) in terms of bipolar adjectival pairs placed on semantic differential (henceforth, SD) scales, revealing the degree to which subjects sympathised with one form of English over others for each feature. Relying on previous research as well as on results of two pre-studies, I included the following sematic features into the analysis: "awesome/unexciting", "competent/incompetent", "cool/not cool", "disciplined/undisciplined", "educated/uneducated", "formal/casual", "friendly/unfriendly", "home-like/exotic", "intelligent/not intelligent", "modern/old-fashioned", "posh/common", "prestigious/stigmatised", "relaxed/tense", "reliable/unreliable", "serious/funny", "sophisticated/simple", "standardised/colloquial", "trustworthy/untrustworthy" and "unemotional/emotional". I employed a ten-point scale while collecting JNU data. In Mannheim, respondents had to rate the four conditions on a scale consisting of 100 dashes. These data collection differences do not bear any method-related repercussions as both scales use even, as opposed to odd, numbers. Previous research also indicates that the use of scales containing different numbers does not affect results in meaningful ways (Dörnyei 2003; Schleef 2014).

Once collected, the data was entered into an SPSS spreadsheet, and checked for outliers. They were then subjected to the principal component analysis (henceforth, PCA), a data reduction technique that establishes correlational relationships between individual features, thereby revealing the underlying supervariables within a body of data. This procedure allowed me to elicit the main dimensions (or components) in the attitudinal structure in each data set. The dimensions of attitudes were arrived at through a combination of two statistical procedures: (i) a scree test and (ii) an item-on-factor technique (McCroskey and Young 2006: 381). In what follows, I report only those features that were selected as representing attitudinal dimensions by the PCA. Those features that were not chosen by the analysis as relevant for the representation of the attitudinal structure in each data set were removed from the analysis. The data was further subjected to the repeated measures analyses of variance (ANOVA), which compared the means for each feature across the four conditions. In what follows, I report the main effects for repeated measures comparisons, while also commenting on post hoc comparisons, carried out subsequent to the major tests.

Let us consider the VGT results stemming from the JNU data first, presented in Table 5. The PCA procedure revealed that out of the 19 features subjected to the analytical perusal, 15 cluster around the two dimensions accounting for 54.86% of the variance in total. The features "awesome/unexciting", "competent/incompetent", "disciplined/undisciplined", "educated/uneducated", "formal/casual", "intelligent/not intelligent", "prestigious/stigmatised", "reliable/unreliable", "serious/funny", "sophisticated/simple", "standardised/colloquial", and

Table 5: Repeated measures ANOVAs of verbal guise data comparing mean evaluations of two native and two non-native accents by Indian students (N 49).

| Feature | | Mean scores | | | | F-value | D.F. | p-value |
|---|---|---|---|---|---|---|---|---|
| 10 | 0 | BrE | AmE | EurE | IndE | | | |
| *Dimension: status and competence* | | | | | | | | |
| awesome | unexciting | 7.39 | 5.84 | 5.57 | 5.67 | 7.679 | 2.8, 135.6 | .000 |
| competent | incompetent | 7.45 | 5.80 | 5.47 | 6.69 | 9.283 | 2.6, 126.4 | .000 |
| disciplined | undisciplined | 8.00 | 4.63 | 5.48 | 5.69 | 21.719 | 2.7, 125.2 | .000 |
| educated | uneducated | 8.53 | 5.67 | 6.82 | 6.80 | 21.508 | 2.4, 117.5 | .000 |
| formal | casual | 7.88 | 3.90 | 5.71 | 5.25 | 27.535 | 2.7, 127.9 | .000 |
| intelligent | unintelligent | 7.70 | 5.72 | 6.52 | 7.00 | 9.862 | 2.7, 116.4 | .000 |
| prestigious | stigmatised | 7.67 | 5.67 | 5.49 | 4.90 | 24.417 | 2.5, 122.2 | .000 |
| reliable | unreliable | 7.49 | 5.47 | 5.40 | 6.64 | 12.255 | 2.9, 131.8 | .000 |
| serious | funny | 6.45 | 4.29 | 5.16 | 4.29 | 9.592 | 2.9, 141.5 | .000 |
| sophisticated | simple | 7.98 | 4.23 | 5.33 | 4.06 | 35.260 | 2.9, 137.8 | .000 |
| standardised | colloquial | 7.78 | 4.53 | 5.40 | 5.40 | 19.000 | 2.9, 127.7 | .000 |
| trustworthy | untrustworthy | 6.68 | 5.06 | 5.68 | 6.13 | 6.966 | 2.9, 131.7 | .001 |
| *Dimension: social attractiveness* | | | | | | | | |
| friendly | unfriendly | 7.04 | 7.43 | 6.10 | 8.02 | 8.973 | 2.7, 127.6 | .000 |
| home-like | exotic | 4.50 | 6.44 | 4.54 | 7.10 | 15.194 | 2.6, 119.9 | .000 |
| relaxed | tense | 5.88 | 7.76 | 4.86 | 7.27 | 13.703 | 2.9, 138.8 | .000 |

"trustworthy/untrustworthy" represent the principal component labelled 'status and competence'. The second dimension is represented by the features "friendly/unfriendly", "home-like/exotic", and "relaxed/tense" and is best described as 'social attractiveness'.

One-way repeated measures ANOVA tests indicate that British English received the highest scores for social status and competence. It has been evaluated by my Indian respondents as the most "awesome", the most "competent", the most "disciplined", the most "educated", the most "formal", the most "intelligent", the most "prestigious", the most "reliable", the most "serious", the most "sophisticated", the most "standardised", and the most "trustworthy" form of English studied here. Remarkably, my Indian informants accord a sufficiently high status to their local variety. Indian English ends in second place with respect to the features "intelligent/unintelligent", "reliable/unreliable", and "competent/incompetent" and post hoc analyses with a Bonferroni adjustment further reveals that there is no statistically significant difference between the British guise and the Indian guise and both guises differ significantly from American English and European English. These results, in all appearance, reflect a strong (albeit unconscious) tendency towards the endonormative attitude, which has been clearly gaining ground on the Indian subcontinent over the past decades, as Indian English is now embraced as socially prestigious by an increasing number of Indians.

Crucially, it is Indian English that received highly positive rankings for social attractiveness. It is assessed as the "friendliest" and the most "home-like" English that is also considerably relaxed. These findings suggest that English is treated not as a foreign language in India but is readily embraced as part of Indian identity and Indian culture (see also Schneider 2007: 171).

European English comes off as fairly "exotic", especially in relation to the Indian guise. This finding can be attributed to the relatively little exposure on the part of my informants to the European culture. For a conspicuous majority of my informants, direct experiences with Europeans, including the Germans, are restricted to sporadic encounters on the JNU campus, which explains how limited personal knowledge results in the evaluations of the European guise – my informants simply cannot relate to this linguistic variant on a deeper affective level. Note, however, that the guise is not downgraded for any of the features studied here, revealing a generally positive view of the Europeans and the kind of English that they speak.

American English is associated primarily with the semantic values "undisciplined", "casual", "funny", "simple", and "colloquial", while being viewed as the antipode to the British guise by my informants. Simultaneously, American English is quite socially attractive for my Indian informants as it is placed in second position after Indian English for "friendliness" and "homeliness". Post hoc comparisons reveal that the difference in means between the American and the Indian guise is not statistically significant for both features, thereby contradicting the evaluations of the other two guises. Finally, American English is assessed as the most "relaxed" form of English and, here again, the differences between the American and the Indian guise are not statistically significant.

We now turn to the discussion of the VGT results stemming from data obtained from the UM student community, presented in Table 6. The PCA revealed the presence of four components accounting for 71.27% of the variance. Here, features "competent/incompetent", "disciplined/undisciplined", "educated/uneducated", "intelligent/unintelligent", "reliable/unreliable", "trustworthy/untrustworthy" cluster together, thereby representing the principal component labelled 'status and competence'. The adjectival pair "posh/common" is closely linked to the dimension 'superiority'. The adjectival pairs "cool/not cool", "friendly/not friendly", "relaxed/tense" load strongly on the dimension 'social attractiveness'. The features "serious/funny" and "unemotional/emotional" pattern together, giving rise to the dimension labelled 'solidarity'.

**Table 6:** Repeated measures ANOVAs of verbal guise data comparing mean evaluations of two native and two non-native accents by German students (N 65) (see also Davydova 2015a).

| Feature | | Mean scores | | | | F-value | D.F. | $p$-value |
|---|---|---|---|---|---|---|---|---|
| 100 | 0 | BrE | AmE | GerE | IndE | | | |
| *Dimension: status and competence* | | | | | | | | |
| competent | incompetent | 77.82 | 63.45 | 39.71 | 35.34 | 71.410 | 2.5, 163.5 | .000 |
| disciplined | undisciplined | 70.88 | 57.45 | 60.09 | 51.16 | 8.282 | 2.7, 170.5 | .000 |
| educated | uneducated | 78.69 | 61.03 | 51.69 | 41.68 | 41.957 | 2.6, 166.8 | .000 |
| intelligent | unintelligent | 71.48 | 64.51 | 50.87 | 45.89 | 30.158 | 2.7, 171.2 | .000 |
| reliable | unreliable | 73.40 | 64.25 | 54.35 | 44.94 | 23.193 | 2.7, 169.8 | .000 |
| trustworthy | untrustworthy | 70.97 | 66.23 | 55.22 | 43.86 | 22.407 | 2.7, 175.4 | .000 |
| *Dimension: superiority* | | | | | | | | |
| posh | common | 41.05 | 33.09 | 33.48 | 28.51 | 3.225 | 2.7, 175.6 | .028 |
| *Dimension: social attractiveness* | | | | | | | | |
| cool | not cool | 51.40 | 66.83 | 27.77 | 33.63 | 38.39 | 2.6, 169.1 | .000 |
| friendly | unfriendly | 70.60 | 72.08 | 48.97 | 51.89 | 18.719 | 2.7, 176.2 | .000 |
| relaxed | tense | 60.12 | 68.14 | 30.60 | 47.43 | 26.821 | 2.7, 172.8 | .000 |
| *Dimension: solidarity* | | | | | | | | |
| serious | funny | 65.52 | 44.23 | 74.05 | 61.70 | 17.802 | 2.5, 159.5 | .000 |
| unemotional | emotional | 61.45 | 44.58 | 72.05 | 79.56 | 27.018 | 2.4, 149.4 | .000 |

The comparisons of the mean differences in the evaluations of specific features through one-way repeated measures ANOVAs indicate that my informants from Germany identified the British guise as the most "reliable", the most "trustworthy", the most "competent", the most "educated", the most "disciplined" and the most "intelligent", and with the exception of the feature "trustworthy/untrustworthy", the mean values for these character traits significantly contrast with those of the three other guises, as indicated by the post hoc tests with a Bonferroni adjustment. Except for the feature "disciplined/undisciplined", American English ends in second place after the British guise. Thus, similarly to the respondents from India, my German learners accord a high level of social prestige to the British guise. In addition, they also provide highly favourable assessments of the linguistic variety on the dimension 'superiority'. Conversely, EFL learners evaluated the two non-native English guises, including their own, less positively in terms of status and competence.

Subsequently, the American guise was assessed as the most "relaxed", "friendly" and "cool". Note that the British guise is ranked second for all three features representing social attractiveness. Crucially, the mean differences between the American and the British guise are not statistically significant for features "relaxed/tense", and "friendly/unfriendly", and the mean values of both native guises differ significantly from their non-native counterparts. Moreover, the American guise received the highest score for the feature "cool/not cool" and the Bonferroni post hoc tests determined that the difference in evaluations is statistically significant with respect to all the other conditions treated here. Furthermore, the American guise bears close associations with the semantic values "funny" and "emotional". Meanwhile, pairwise comparisons reveal a significant attitude difference for American English vis-á-vis all the other guises for both features.

Importantly, both non-native guises are significantly downgraded by my German students on the dimension of prestige and social attractiveness in comparison to the two mainstream native-speaker Englishes. As a side note, UM students also view the German guise as significantly more "trustworthy" and "educated" by comparison to the Indian guise, which they, in turn, view as significantly more "relaxed" in relation to the German speaker.

Taken together, these findings thus point to a largely exonormative orientation, i.e. a tendency for students to gravitate towards native-speaker norms (Galloway and Rose 2015: 182), and are largely consistent with those reported in Adolphs (2005), Cargile, Takai, and Rodríguez (2006), Gnutzmann, Jakish, and Rabe (2015), Jenkins (2007), Kirkpatrick and Xu (2002), Ladegaard (1998), Ladegaard and Sachdev (2006), and McKenzie (2008a, 2008b), all of which highlight the powerful influence of standard language ideology on the formation of EFL learners' attitudes and stereotypes.

In summary, results stemming from the survey and the VGT data yield the following conclusions. Both the survey and the VGT provide converging evidence that ESL and EFL learners attach highly positive associations to standard British English with respect to social status and prestige, while American English garners strong positive associations on the dimension 'social attractiveness'. Such highly amicable feelings towards American English, the geographic epicentre of the global linguistic innovation studied here, provide us with an indication that very broadly speaking, nothing stands in the way of the globe trotter *be like* in both locales. If learners embrace the donor variety and people who speak it on the affective level, they will, probably, also adopt the linguistic variants that these speakers use.

At the same time, the pieces of quantitative evidence presented in the preceding analyses reveal another important pattern. Whereas my German students' view of World Englishes is shaped by the exonormative mindset, dictating orientation towards (and compliance with) outer (native-speaker) norms, my Indian informants profess a generally positive view of their own variety, strongly identifying with it and cherishing it as a carrier of an important social meaning (i.e. an in-group marker) in daily interactions. These fundamental differences in the ESL/EFL learners' attitudinal mindsets are bound, I argue here, to result in the differences at the micro-sociolinguistic level as well. Following the working hypothesis introduced earlier in this chapter, it is plausible to assume that the endonormative mindset of an ESL learner is more likely to tap into the creative potential of the linguistic brain function and become engaged in construction of innovative forms and structures aligned with the indigenous linguistic ecology, which will then serve as distinctive markers of a new variety. When extrapolated to the domain of quotative marking, the focal point of our attention in this book, these observations entail that in contrast to my target-oriented EFL learners, my ESL learners are likely to demonstrate a richer system featuring not only global, but also, more importantly, local quotative innovations (see Chapter 5). Qualitative evidence stemming from sociolinguistic interviews, to which discussion I now turn, can be further adduced in support of this assumption.

## 4.3 Sociolinguistic interviews

To gain a better understanding of the major attitudinal trends and patterns detected with the help of the quantitative tools of data analysis, I interviewed 24 individuals (48 in total) from each student community in the time period from October 2013 to November 2014. In these interviews, each lasting about an hour, students were encouraged to discuss the role of English in the world and in their own community, to share their personal experiences with English and its various users and to comment on their linguistic identities. In addition, Indian informants were asked to comment on the attitudes towards English in India, whereas respondents in Germany were instructed to provide their opinions concerning the same issue for their home country. Finally, both groups of students were asked to comment on their perceptions of British English and American English and how those relate to their assessments of non-native-speaker Englishes, including their local variety.

Sociolinguistic data largely substantiates the findings obtained through the survey and the VGT. In so doing, it also helps to identify and describe the social images that are triggering sociolinguistic evaluations of speech varieties (Campbell-Kibler 2010: 381). The British variety comes across as "sophisticated", "educated" and "highly prestigious" in both locales, as documented by the statements in (26) through (31):

(26) British English is very fine and neat and clean [...] prim and proper (.) (HCNVE: IE076; IE088)

(27) British English is more official [...] (,) more formal (,) tight upper lip (.) I suppose British English is more refined (.) (HCNVE: IE079; IE087; IE091)

(28) British English sounds more elegant [...] British English is more subtle which is why I appreciate their humour and it's poetic as well (.) (HCNVE: IE080; IE094)

(29) But British English is considered to be this sophisticated (,) better in inverted commas than the American English or any other type or varieties of English (.) (MaCGE: GE002)

(30) But I still believe that British English has its prestige (,) it's a very high prestige [...] it's sophisticated and posh (.) (MaCGE: GE003; GE004)

(31) British English is more official (,) it sounds like they are saying something important (.) (MaCGE: GE020)

Clearly, students from both academic communities attribute considerable social power to the British variety, while pinpointing Great Britain's rich literary, socio-historical and cultural traditions as explanatory factors (see examples (32) and (33)). More importantly, British English still dictates the rules in language classroom in India and in Germany (see examples (34) and (35)), which explains why this linguistic variant largely determines learners' writing norms in both countries and why ESL/EFL speakers associate it with more formal contexts, such as education, and consequently, with more social prestige.

(32) British English is like this pure (,) Queen's English (.) (HCNVE: IE087)

(33) I think it's also linked to literature (,) we think that British English is more literal language (,) and we often connect it with kind of literature like Victorian literature (,) very eloquent literature and for American we think [...] American English developed so late we don't have a culture around it (.) (MaCGE: GE001)

(34) We grew up learning that British English was the right thing and American English was well (,) (in a condescending voice) a variant (.) This is what school teaches us (.) Because we were a colony of Britain obviously there is more influence of British English than American in the way we've learned English (,) the spellings (,) the constructions (.) (HCNVE: IE088)

(35) Maybe both (.) I think it's good that they [kids in school] start with British English (.) I think it may explain why British English is perceived as more educated and intelligent and more high-status more generally (.) This may be because people are exposed to it at schools from very early on (.) This is how that specific evaluation is gradually constructed in the discourse, 'They teach us British English at school; hence it's a more proper form of English.' (MaCGE: GE017)

Subsequent and similar to the findings stemming from the quantitative data, American English evokes positive meanings linked to social attractiveness, as substantiated by the statements in (36) through (43):

(36) and American English is more casual (.) they are very like, 'Here dude!' [...] and Americans are very chilled out kind, 'Yo' all kind!' [...] American English is fun to speak (.) (HCNVE: IE079; IE99)

(37) American English is more day-to-day [...] I think it's a lot more informal (.) It's a way more easy to relate to American English [because of its dominant presence in the global media] (HCNVE: IE080; IE098)

(38) American English very straight (,) they do not curve their language (,) they speak it very straight (,) I find it a little less arrogant than British English (.) (HCNVE: IE082)

(39) American is much more free style (,) much more relaxed [...] it is more free (,) there ain't any strict rules (,) American English gives us more liberty to experiment with the language (.) (HCNVE: IE093; IE096)

(40) Americans (,) usually easy-going (,) like, 'Yeah, we can do that!' and like always really nice (,) it's like their way of treating people (.) (MaCGE: GE103)

(41) When I was a little girl I thought like, 'Wow! You have to go there. All the celebrities live there. And you are gonna be famous when you are there and whatever.' (MaCGE: GE016)

(42) What it stands for the country behind (.) America is still perceived maybe as the new world with countless (,) numerous opportunities (,) it's got everything and so it's the cool country (,) the cooler language (.) (MaCGE: GE006)

(43) And then of course the American accent is more seen like the cool thing because the cool movies (,) cool music (,) and everything comes from the US mostly (.) So I think it's true that it's the cool English [...] (MaCGE: GE023)

Nonetheless, there are also subtle differences in the way my Indian and German informants evaluate the American variety. These differences are mediated by the differences in the channels through which they gain knowledge about the American people and their language. Indian students largely pick up on the stereotypes and cultural memes that are attached to American English through mass media. In contrast, my German students frequently rely on the memories of their personal experiences (in addition to their encounters with the linguistic variety in the media), while constructing narratives about the Americans and the US.

These obvious differences underpinning the acquisition of attitudes towards American English in India and in Germany also account for distinctive varietal evaluations. My German informants regard American English through the prism of more affective, experience-related attitudes. To them, the US is essentially a cool country populated by "very nice", "laid-back", "easy-going", "cool" people whose form of language they aspire to speak, also because of its promotion through mass media.

While lacking any personal experience with the linguistic variant under study, my Indian students, in contrast, focus on the practical, utilitarian aspects of being familiar with American English. They emphasise its essential accessibility coming about as a result of its pre-eminent presence on the international arena and in the global media, and, subsequently, the opportunities it presents to engage in creative endeavours with language (see example (39)). To my Indian informants, American English is, first and foremost, an additional resource upon which these multilinguals draw during their constant language practices in the community.

It's a linguistic resource, one out of many, which my ESL speakers use specifically to signal modernity-related meanings: being up-to-date, young, and hip.

Further differences between the endonormative and exonormative mindsets are revealed by the students' discussions of non-native Englishes including their local variety. As demonstrated in examples (44) and (45), my German informants essentially lament the fact that German English is nothing to emulate as, like other forms of Learner English, their own lect, so my informants, is inherently "less correct" than the standard form of language.

(44) Indian English is just another kind of accent (,) it's just like German English (,) it's nothing to aim at (,) so I don't know that makes a difference probably (,) yeah (.) It's not the ideal (,) I mean (.) (MaCGE: GE019)

(45) I think German people try to follow this perfect English or the English that they would try to learn as well (.) (MaCGE: GE012)

Moreover, some UM students believe that they replicate the norms set out by the standard varieties of English much more closely than their peers living in (South) Asia and in Africa (see example in (46)). At the same time, they acknowledge the fact that the Indian variant of English is also nice and that there are people in India who speak very fluent, standard-like English (47).

(46) I guess it's because we try to put a plane somewhere and say, 'Okay, our English is much better than the Indian English but Indian English is as good as ours' [...] We consider ourselves better in assimilating to the English standards than the Indians. [...] That's the same principle 'we and the other' again (.) (MaCGE: GE007; GE008)

(47) Yes, I also realise that Indian English has some funny timberings and I also laugh (chuckles) but nevertheless they speak fluently and this is the most important thing I think when you speak English and that's also one of the things that I admire when non-native speakers speak in English (.) (MaCGE: GE004)

By and large, the qualitative contentions voiced in (46) and (47) support the VGT results which placed the German guise above the Indian guise in terms of status and competence but made the Indian speaker sound a bit more socially attractive when contrasted with the German guise (see Table 6). While assessing speakers of non-native English, my German informants attempt to navigate (as skilfully as they possibly can) between the two push-pull forces, driving their judgements in the opposite directions. On the one hand, they are eager to be portrayed as individuals speaking the right kind of English, which, in all probability, translates in their minds into success and good social standing. On the other hand, many of them are more than willing to emphasise their respect of and empathy towards other non-native speakers of English by way of expressing their solidarity with them (see also Davydova 2015a). Remarkably, the exonormative orientation of my German learners is also manifested in their attitudes towards German-English code-switching practices (see examples in (48) and (49)), upon which many frown and thereby advocate a monolingual state of mind as their routine linguistic practice (see discussion of the Grosjean's (1998, 2001) model in Chapter 2).

(48) ... in advertisements it's so English sometimes (,) like the words (,) I'm like, 'Seriously, could you not have said that in German?' Sometimes I think that (.) (MaCGE: GE087)

(49) Say it in English or say it in German (!) But don't use one word in English (,) one word in German (,) one word in English (,) one word in German (.) Ph-hui-i (!) [...] That is just stupid (.) (MaCGE: GE088)

JNU students' assessments of their local variety are in stark contrast with those reported for the young individuals studying at UM. Fully realising that they speak a substantially unique version of English, they unanimously endorse their local variety as the linguistic form most appropriate and most suited for everyday interactions (see examples in (50) and (51)). Although my informants are acutely aware of the way Indian English is portrayed in the local and global media, they nevertheless embrace it as a marker of intimacy and an in-group identity (see example (52)).

(50) What comes to my mind is, 'Speak whatever you want to!' Indian English equals to Hinglish and that means Hindi plus English (.) Indian English is the way how we communicate (.) (HCNVE: IE097)

(51) Indian English (,) oh yeah (,) it's good (!) We people (,) when we speak (,) tend to pronounce the word in a very clear way I would say (.) Our pronunciation (,) our enunciation (,) our (,) the way we speak is (*in a whisper*) the best (.) (HCNVE: IE076)

(52) If I go out in the world I do see examples of Indian English (,) the exaggerated ones would be comic parodies on TV where they have either those politicians or those call centre people enacting and thereby exaggerating all those differences in English or I have cases in my own home where my

grandmother very sweetly (*smiling*) when she tries to speak in English (,) I see the difference or the influence of it in her speech (*smiles hugely*) [...] Indian English would be a bunch of colours (,) I say different colours in different places (,) they are so distinct from each other that together they form one work of colours (.) (HCNVE: IE081)

Moreover, JNU students do not denigrate Englishes spoken in Europe. To many, these are viable forms of English, albeit substantially influenced by the native tongues, as statements in (53) and (54) indicate:

(53)  ... beautiful elegant kind of language ... an amalgamation of all European languages (,) an extremely prestigious language more similar to British English (,) prestigious (,) educated (.) (HCNVE: IE092, IE097)

(54)  European accent is heavily laden by people's native language (.) (HCNVE: IE087)

In contrast to their peers from Mannheim, Germany, Indian speakers located in New Delhi, India, readily embrace code-switching practices, which they have adopted as a routine linguistic strategy in their daily intimate interactions with friends and peers, as shown in (55) through (57):

(55)  In a formal setup maybe not (,) but in a casual set up (,) like if you are at a party or somewhere (,) it is (*with emphasis*) absolutely normal (.) [...] It's very normal in India to be in a place where people are switching languages (,) but in a formal setup it's more like you stick to one language (.) (HCNVE: IE087)

(56)  We have corrupted the language [...] We code-mix like crazy people [...] People would be very particular about using the correct forms earlier and now they sort of (,) yeah as I said we own it [Indian English] (,) it's our language (.) (HCNVE: IE088)

(57)  It depends on the setting (,) in an interview and if it's happening in English (,) you'd better stick to English (,) but at the same time people don't really mind if you start speaking in Hindi (,) because all over the country there is this tendency to know how to have some kind of knowledge of Hindi (,) not all over country (,) all over Delhi (,) [...] there is a tendency to constantly switch and people don't really mind (,) or there are some grammar Nazis who have a problem with everything (,) you have to be grammatically correct all the time (,) write properly (,) (HCNVE: IE085)

What is also interesting is that code-switching practices have been primarily adopted by the young generation of speakers (aged 30 and below). In other words, mixing two languages during a conversation seems to be a relatively recent, age-related and urban development that reportedly affected the middle/upper-middle class populating bigger cities of India. Older speakers (aged 50/55 and above) strongly separate both languages, i.e. Hindi and English, throughout conversation, whereas the middle-aged (aged 30/35 to 50/55) are somewhat cautious about code-switching, although they, in all appearance, will not refrain from it in an appropriate situation, for instance, while interacting with their children. In so doing, they would try to create an intimate atmosphere of solidarity and comradeship. All of this is in stark contrast to young adults, to whom code-switching "comes naturally" (HCNVE: IE063). What these ethnographic observations imply is that ever since the 1990s, there has been an emergent shift in speakers' attitudes towards English and the role it occupies in a multilingual context. In contrast to their grandparents (and, to some extent, parents), the young generation of speakers appear to view their spontaneous face-to-face interactions as complex and multi-layered events, in which each language (and its variety) evokes a distinctive meaning. The level of their current dialect-mixing awareness is, indeed, so high that they can provide very coherent metalinguistic associations with each linguistic code in contact: British English is used when one wants to sound "prim" and "proper"; American English triggers modernity-related meanings in speakers' minds and is oftentimes labelled as "carefree", "informal", "colloquial", and "casual". In contrast, the local version of English is an important identity marker, whereas Hindi is construed as the language in which they feel "most at home". "Hindi is the language that we miss so much, so we are happy to use it on every occasion", one informant reports. Overall, the observed change in linguistic practices are arguably diagnostic of a gradual shift from a split, target-oriented mindset dominated by standard language ideologies to an all-embracing view of language, in which speakers' lects exist and re-enforce each other as one dynamic whole, at least in an informal situation.

In conclusion, distinctive attitudinal profiles gleaned from two academic locales highlight the fundamental differences between the endonormative and exonormative orientation, characterising ESL and EFL speaker communities (cf. Galloway and Rose 2015: 47). More specifically, I argue here that the attitudinal mindset (endonormative orientation vs. exonormative orientation) will determine the type of language practices that an L2 speech community is likely to adopt for spontaneous face-to-face interactions. It appears that the endonormative attitude results in the bilingual mode of the psycholinguistic activity promoting code-switching and ultimately cross-linguistic diversity. In contrast, the exonormative attitudinal orientation fosters a monolingual-state productivity, which explicitly bans, or at least restricts severely, the use of multiple codes in the same utterance. Different language practices, in turn, are bound to affect the way language patterns at the micro-sociolinguistic level. Coupled with quantitative findings, the qualitative evidence presented here lends weight to the hypothesis formulated earlier in this chapter that given their overall conformity to the target vernacular norms, German learners will adopt quotative *be like* at a higher rate than ESL speakers and they will also be more adept at replicating the constraints governing the variable use of the innovative variant (see also Davydova and Buchstaller 2015) and its patterns of social evaluations (see also Davydova, Tytus, and Schleef 2017). As they are in tune with their endonormative perceptions of language, young Indians can be expected to rely extensively on a variety of linguistic resources, both local and global, giving rise to a quotative system exhibiting high levels of internal diversification and localisation (see also Davydova 2015b). I will address these issues in the subsequent chapters.

# 5 The nativised ecology of quotation

"More research needs to be done on how global innovations are adopted in local communities of various sizes and how they get transmitted across social space" (Buchstaller 2008: 38). This statement serves well to open a discussion of the local systems of quotative marking in non-native-speaker communities, which also aims to pinpoint the niche occupied by the innovative features, both local and global, within that system. My major goal here is to describe what the quotation marking of Indian English looks like, how it is different from what has been attested for native-speaker varieties, and most importantly, whether the language-internal mechanism triggering the occurrence of innovative *be like* is similar to that reported for native-speaker English and if so, to what extent. In this chapter, I thus explore the distributions of *be like* by several system-intrinsic parameters (introduced in Chapter 3) vis-á-vis other major elements of the quotative system. In so doing, I also account for the ESL sociolinguistic realities and the role they play in the adaptation of vernacular features.

The case study draws on data obtained from 80 young adults (36 males and 44 females), aged 18 to 26, enrolled in Bachelor's and Master's degree programmes at JNU. The data was collected in 2007–2014 with the help of one-on-one sociolinguistic interviews under methodologically similar conditions, each interview taking approximately one hour (see Appendix A). The interviews are part of the HCNVE (see also Davydova 2011). The sociolinguistic interviews were accompanied by a background questionnaire which tapped into various aspects of informants' local sociolinguistic biographies (see Appendix B).

JNU is India's leading educational institution in the field of humanities and social sciences that has been granted the status 'the university with potential for excellence'. Located in the southern suburbs of New Delhi, JNU is a good diagnostic of the ESL setting. It is a home to 8,061 full-time students that come from 30 States and Union Territories. JNU is an ethnically and socioeconomically diverse community with a visible body of international students where English is routinely used on a day-to-day basis during classroom interactions as well as for communication with friends and peers. An overwhelming majority of the international student contingent comes from East and South-East Asia (China, South Korea, Malaysia, Nepal, and Sri Lanka). Moreover, JNU is perhaps best described as the most socialist student community in the entire country, defending the values of equality and social justice, and overtly opposing the heritage of the caste system as well as elitism. It is a politically vigilant campus, actively participating in the all-India student movement. Given JNU's geographic location, a majority of students (about 60%) come from Hindi-speaking areas, the so-called

'Hindi belt' (Allan and Zelizer 2004: 220). These are Hindi dialects, more specifically Rajasthani, Hindi, and Bihari varieties, spoken in north central India. In my analysis, I majorly focus on speakers with Hindi-related background in order to minimise L1 substrate as a possible confounding variable. Other linguistic backgrounds include Assamese (1 speaker), Bengali (2 speakers), Goya Portuguese (1 speaker), Punjabi (3 speakers), Odia (1 speaker), Malayalam (2 speakers), Tamil (1 speaker), and Urdu (3 speakers).

The analyses presented in Chapter 5 and 6 proceed in two stages: I first determine which linguistic elements constitute the system of variable quotative marking. I then investigate the operation of each individual language-internal constraint, i.e. mimesis, quote type, grammatical subject, and tense, on quotative marking (Davydova and Buchstaller 2015: 453), thereby determining the functional niches occupied by the major players within the system. This procedure is a direct replication of the variationist methodology adopted in Buchstaller (2014) as well as in Davydova and Buchstaller (2015), which ensures a rigorous approach to the work with empirical data and replicability of findings. Following the method adopted in these studies, I delineated the variable context on a functional basis, manually extracting every single instance of quotation, as defined in Chapter 3, from the body of language material.

As a first step, let us ascertain which linguistic variants constitute the variable context of quotation in the entire data set comprising the overall total of 80 informants. Table 7 presents results of the overall distribution analysis of variants in the Indian component of the HCNVE.

Overall, the system of Indian English quotation is marked by an exceptional diversity featuring an elevated number of quotative types unattested in

**Table 7:** Overall distribution of quotative markers in Indian English, HCNVE 2007–2014 (N speakers = 80).

| Traditional variants | N | % |
|---|---|---|
| *say* (see example 58) | 501 | 23.7% |
| other verbs of reporting (see example 59) | 207 | 10.2% |
| zero (see example 60) | 289 | 13.6% |
| *think* (see example 61) | 61 | 2.9% |
| other verbs of mental activity and perception (see example 62) | 48 | 2.3% |
| **Variants featuring *like*** | | |
| *be like* (see example 63) | 370 | 17.5% |
| *zero-like* (see example 64) | 109 | 5.1% |
| *say like* (see example 65) | 26 | 1.2% |
| other collocations with *like* (see example 66) | 26 | 1.2% |

**Table 7** (continued)

| Variants featuring *like* | N | % |
|---|---|---|
| *think like* (see example 67) | 6 | 0.3% |
| *feel like* (see example 68) | 3 | 0.1% |
| *know like* (see example 69) | 1 | 0.0% |
| **Variants featuring *okay* (*fine*)** | | |
| *be okay* (see example 70) | 8 | 0.4% |
| *zero-okay* (see example 71) | 51 | 2.4% |
| verb + *okay* (see example 72) | 40 | 1.9% |
| verb + *that* + *okay* (see example 73) | 40 | 1.9% |
| **Variants featuring verb + *that*** | | |
| verb + *that* (see example 74) | 199 | 9.4% |
| verb + *that* + discourse marker (see example 75) | 22 | 1.0% |
| verb + noun + *that* (see example 76) | 2 | 0.1% |
| verb + prep. phrase + *that* (see example 77) | 4 | 0.2% |
| **Other variants** | | |
| copula *be* (see example 78) | 42 | 2.0% |
| dynamic verbs and verbs of motion (see example 79) | 12 | 0.6% |
| *ki* (see example 80) | 27 | 1.3% |
| verbs of achievement (see example 81) | 14 | 0.7% |
| *so* (see example 82) | 10 | 0.5% |
| TOTAL | 2118 | |

native-speaker varieties (cf. Davydova 2015b: 307). Examples below are a selection of tokens illustrating each quotative type.

(58) I **said**, 'No, no, no, I can't arrange for anything!' (HCNVE: IE87)

(59) [...] and she **told**, 'You did that? Why would you do that? [...]' (HCNVE: IE89)

(60) [...] she came to me and I was trembling (,) trembling like this, '(making a gesture)!' – 'Have you caught fever?' – 'No, Mam!' – 'Then why are you trembling?' (HCNVE: IE95)

(61) [...] and I **thought**, 'Seriously? That's what you are saying?' (HCNVE: IE99)

(62) [...] and I **realised**, 'No, no, no! North India is not India!' (HCNVE: IE80)

(63) And if you trying to give them direction (,) then they'll **be like**, 'You know, there'll be a board, right? There'll be a sign board.' (HCNVE: IE32)

(64) I was so scared of Sir (,) **like**, 'What if he sees that?' (HCNVE: IE65)

(65) [...] and they **said like**, 'Let's go to the police station!' (HCNVE: IE59)

(66) [...] and that's when my parents **decided like**, 'Let's start speak in English. Let's start speak in English.' (HCNVE: IE94)

(67) [...] and they were actually **thinking like**, 'We'll beat him. We'll beat the shit out of this guy.' (HCNVE: IE91)

(68) I **felt like** weird kind of thing, 'You see I got through!' (HCNVE: IE92)

(69) [...] they **know like**, 'Okay, someone is speaking something, I may not ((be)) getting this language, must be English.' (HCNVE: IE14)

(70) So it **was okay**, 'I'll go.' [...] so I **was okay**, 'It's too far, let's go this way.' [...] so that used to **be okay** (,) **fine**, 'We are sitting in an English class.' (HCNVE: IE60; IE35; IE08)

(71) [...] she pointed my friend and **okay**, 'You must have seen Mayank's copy.' [...] and she saw the door locked (.) **Okay**, 'Who did this door? Close it!' (HCNVE: IE92; IE08)

(72) [...] and she **called** us **okay**, 'Come here, come here!' [...] a person came (,) started talking and **asked okay**, 'Can I talk to you three?' (HCNVE: IE66; IE81)

(73) I **thought that okay**, 'Door is open; nobody is inside.' (HCNVE: IE81)

(74) [...] so they **tell** me **that**, 'Still you are in our category, you are the special kid.' (HCNVE: IE82)

(75) I **was praying that you know**, 'Show me one silver line and I wanna study there. That's what I wanna do.' (HCNVE: IE90)

(76) [...] they **make** it **a point that**, 'You should pronounce it as a British English ehm, thing.' (HCNVE: IE35)

(77) [...] and we **were laughing on the point that**, 'Why she is laughing? Why he is laughing?' (HCNVE: IE60)

(78) I **was** (making a face and shouting), 'A-a-a!' (HCNVE: IE57)

(79) He **goes** complaining to mum and dad, 'She did this to me, she did that to me!' [...] he **was** still **struggling with**, 'What am I supposed to do with my life?' (HCNVE: IE02; IE35)

(80) [...] so I **thought** [ind] **ki** [/ind], 'Okay, let me go. (...)' [...] so he just took it and **said** [ind] **ki** [/ind], 'Okay, what should I do?' [...] so we are **told like**

[ind] **ki** [/ind], 'You have to speak!' But I didn't go there for a long time (.) ...my father **asked** me [ind] **ki** [/ind], 'Now, you have to go out.' (HCNVE: IE92; IE79; IE60)

(81) [...] people **refute**, 'No, it doesn't work!' (HCNVE: IE31)

(82) [...] so sometime I am to another friend **so**, 'Friend, please, please, come, come, come! And play.' (HCNVE: IE71)

What we notice first and foremost is that the variability in this domain is very robust to the extent that no quotative marker is a dominant element; rather there are cohorts of variants vying for a place in the system. Traditional quotative markers, such as *say* (58), other verbs of reporting (59) and zero-quotatives (60), are leading the way accounting for 47.5% of variation. Innovative *be like* (63) amounts to a mere 17.5% and when counted together with other variants featuring *like*, as shown in (64) through (69), it contributes 24.2% to the system. Overall, these findings are compatible with two previous studies reported in Davydova (2015b) and Davydova (2016a) which investigate the same academic community and rely on the same type of data but draw on much smaller token numbers.

Remarkably, the data set also contains cohorts of variants that have not been reported for other English varieties. These include (i) variants featuring discourse marker *okay* (*fine*), illustrated in (70) through (73), (ii) structures consisting of a verb and the complementiser *that*, illustrated in (74) through (77), and (iii) quotatives featuring the complementiser *ki*, illustrated in (80). In order to be able to understand the cross-linguistic sources of these discourse-pragmatic constructions, we need to consider some important aspects of quotation strategies attested in Hindi.

Firstly, Hindi allows for an expanded inventory of verbs to be used as a quote introducer (Koul 2008: 182), which might explain why Hindi speakers overgeneralise a whole array of English verbs including verbs of achievements, as in (81), and dynamic verbs or verbs of motion, as in (79), to the quotative function. Secondly and most importantly, while introducing quotation in Hindi narratives, speakers recruit constructions that are different from those attested for L1 English (see Figure 2 in Chapter 3). These are illustrated in (83) through (86)[1]:

(83) maine kaha ki, 'aap ka naam kya hai?'
 I said that your name what is
 'I said (politely), 'What is your name?''

---

[1] These examples were elicited from native speakers of Hindi during my fieldwork trip to JNU in March 2016.

(84) maine   kaha,   'aap ka   naam   kya   hai?'
     I       said    your      name   what  is
     'I said, 'What is your name?''

(85) maine   kaha,   matlab,   'aap ka   naam   kya   hai?'
     I       said    DisPrt    your      name   what  is
     'I said meaning, 'What is your name?''

(86) matlab,   'aap ka   naam   kya   hai?'
     DisPrt    your      name   what  is
     'My meaning was, 'What is your name?''

As these examples indicate, there are four major construction types attested in Hindi which vary from each other regarding the degree of formality. A high degree of formality is expressed with the help of the complementiser *ki* (translated into English as 'that') preceded by a *verbum dicendi*, as in (83). When used on its own, a *verbum dicendi* such as, for instance, *say* signals a fairly formal context, as in (84). Young speakers also employ various discourse markers such as *matlab* (literally translated as 'meaning') coupled with a *verbum dicendi*, as in (85), in order to introduce a quote in an informal situation. Other discourse-pragmatic elements include *jaar* (literally translated as 'close friend') and *jaise* (*ki*) (literally translated as 'like'). Crucially, the discourse markers can be used on their own resulting in constructions illustrated in (86). On a more abstract level, these constructions from Hindi fit into two quotative templates, illustrated in Figure 4.

| (Noun Phrase) | (Verbum Dicendi) | (Complementiser) | Quote |
|---|---|---|---|
| maine | kaha | (ki) | "…" |
| I | say | (that) | "…" |
| (Noun Phrase) | (Verbum Dicendi) | (Discourse Marker) | Quote |
| (maine) | (kaha) | (matlab) | "…" |
| I | say | (like) | "…" |

**Figure 4:** Quotative templates in Hindi.

The quotative templates can be conceived of as comprising four schematic slots, i.e. Noun Phrase, Verbum Dicendi, Complementiser/Discourse Marker and a quote. In contrast to the quotative template attested in L1 English (Buchstaller 2014; Davydova and Buchstaller 2015; see also Chapter 3), the first three slots can be variably omitted. This is largely due to the fact that unlike English, Hindi is a pro-drop language (Davydova 2014: 158), allowing for the omission of subjects.

A *verbum dicendi* can either occur on its own (without a subject) or be omitted altogether, leaving a complementiser or a discourse marker to introduce a quote.

These observations regarding Hindi substratum are important as they help us understand the sources of structural variation attested in Indian English quotative marking. It is thus clear that constructions of the type 'verb + that', illustrated in (74) through (77), are derived from the Hindi substrate. Though infrequent, constructions involving the complementiser *ki*, as in (80), are a remarkable example demonstrating L1 influence from Hindi. Examples in (80) show that *ki* frequently occurs with *say* and other verbs of reporting such as *tell*, *ask*, and it also occurs with *think*, all of which is not particularly surprising. What is, however, interesting is that speakers also recruit this linguistic item together with *be like* or they sometimes use it on its own in order to introduce a quote. These strategies are illustrated in (87). What these examples seem to suggest is that the Hindi complementiser *ki* has been developing into a discourse marker in Indian English since it is inserted as a pivot introducing quoted material similarly to other linguistic forms, notably *like* and *okay (fine)*.

(87)   ...we all **were like** [ind] **ki** [/ind], 'Oh, my God! In two hours, we have to write five answers and he is already 20 minutes late.' [...] and I was simply out of you know answers [ind] **ki** [/ind], 'What should I say?' (HCNVE: IE92; IE64)

Speakers of Indian English actively and, in all probability, consciously insert L1 material into the quotative template as they construct dialogue in spontaneous interactions. They do so by way of making a full expression of their multilingual repertoires (Matras 2009: 308). What licences this process is an endonormatively oriented mindset of ESL speakers allowing for the simultaneous use of two or more linguistic codes in informal spontaneous interactions (see also discussion in Chapter 4).

Constructions containing the discourse marker *okay (fine)* is a local innovation not attested in other English vernaculars. There is evidence suggesting that quotatives of this type have been gaining currency in the JNU community (Davydova 2015: 324). What is interesting about this construction type is that it is partially moulded on the English superstrate and is partially derived from the Hindi substrate. Similar to the constructions containing *like*, *okay (fine)* can occur with copula *be*, as in (70), it can modify *verba dicendi*, as in (72), or it can function as a sole quote introducer in zero-*okay* constructions, illustrated in (71). These constructions are thus best analysed as superstrate-induced innovations. *Okay (fine)* furthermore occurs in quotative schemas featuring a *verbum dicendi* and the complementiser *that*, as shown in (73), which is a clear-cut case of a substrate-induced innovation in a situation of language contact. Overall then, the variable system of Indian English quotative marking, as documented in this data set, is perhaps best accounted for in terms of substrate-superstrate interactions (see also Sharma 2009: 170).

Cross-linguistic analysis of quotative markers has ascertained that the origins of a large majority of innovative quotative variants can be traced back to specific lexical items that are particularly well suited as quote introducers by virtue of their original referential, or cognitive, meaning. These include (i) lexical items denoting comparison, similarity or approximation; (ii) lexical items with demonstrative or deictic function; (iii) elements with quantificational semantics; (iv) verbs of motion and generic verbs (Buchstaller 2014: 20–23). As such, *okay* (*fine*) does not fit with any of these categories. In other words, its inclusion into the cohorts of quotative markers cannot be motivated by its general semantic meaning. In Davydova (2016b), I argue that the emergence of *okay* (*fine*) as a quotative marker is best explained in terms of its frequency encountered in spontaneous conversations. It occurs in speech of JNU students far more frequently than any other discourse-pragmatic elements such as, for instance, *well* or *haan*, a discourse particle from Hindi. Table 8 reports normalised frequencies of all three language forms, as encountered in the HCNVE data, 2007–2011.

**Table 8:** *Okay, haan, well*: Frequencies of occurrence in the HCNVE-India, 2007–2011 (from Davydova 2016b: 186).

| Discourse marker | Frequency of occurrence | Word count | Normalised per 10,000 words |
|---|---:|---:|---:|
| *okay* | 500 | 235,806 | 21,2 |
| *haan* | 41 | 235,806 | 1,7 |
| *well* | 263 | 235,806 | 11,1 |

Against this backdrop, I explain the rise of *okay* (*fine*) to the quote introducer along the following lines:

> ...the motivation underlying the recruitment of *okay* (*fine*) into the quotative system can be related to the frequency with which this lexical item is encountered in the IndE input. That said, frequency is not the only factor which may have been responsible for the emergence of *okay* (*fine*) as a quotative marker. Speakers seem to emphasise this element with a specific intonation/stress pattern followed by a short pause before introducing a quote so that *okay* (*fine*) stands out as a quote presenter. It may well be that coupled with frequency, prosody has played at least some role in the emergence of *okay* (*fine*) as a quotative device in IndE as both conditions [may have] made this element more salient, that is easier to notice, in the discourse (see also discussion in Cheshire et al. 2011: 177–178).
>
> Davydova (2016a: 187)

Overall then, it seems that the system of Indian English quotative marking represents some sort of a compromise between substrate- and superstrate-induced innovations on the one hand and traditional variants on the other. But will this picture still obtain once we take the local sociolinguistic ecology into consideration?

Despite its immense progress over the past seven decades (of which JNU is one outstanding proof), India is still, by and large, not an egalitarian society. The different sociolinguistic circumstances accompanying the acquisition of English arguably entail some very real psycholinguistic consequences for its speakers. With this said, the Indian context of L2 English development presents the researcher with a unique opportunity to test the psycholinguistic reality of the L2 speakers' minds (operationalised through the sociolinguistic context) within the linguistic model of variation.

Consistent with observations regarding the sociolinguistic ecology accompanying the acquisition of English in India (see Chapter 2), I have identified three speaker cohorts within the entire data sample that differ from each other in terms of the amount and quality of contact with English. In order to introduce a modicum of methodological rigour, I have explored their individual biographies, relying on the data stemming from sociolinguistic interviews and background questionnaires. These investigations revealed that informants differ from each other with respect to (i) patterns of language use in the family; (ii) medium of instruction; (iii) patterns of language use in informal daily interactions with peers; (iii) onset age of the acquisition of English and (iv) informants' self-reported proficiency in English regarding their writing, speaking, reading and listening comprehension skills. These four variables allowed me to classify my informants into English-dominant, Hindi-dominant and mixed bilinguals. In what follows, I characterise each speaker cohort, also presented in Table 9 for convenience.

Table 9: Indian English speakers by type of bilingualism.

| Type of bilingualism | Number of speakers |
|---|---|
| English-dominant | 11 |
| Hindi-dominant | 25 |
| mixed bilinguals | 44 |
| Overall total | 80 |

English-dominant bilinguals grew up in families where English was a dominant means of communication. These informants report that they use English on a day-to-day basis with one of the parents, typically father, and their siblings. They were also educated through the medium of English in primary and secondary schools.

They furthermore indicated that they were able to speak English fluently by the age of 4 and described the overall level of their proficiency in English as advanced. These speakers come from metropolitan cities, typically New Delhi. In contrast, Hindi-dominant bilinguals grew up speaking a regional language, typically a Hindi-related dialect. They were educated through the medium of Hindi through their primary and secondary education. They also indicated that they speak English once a week or less while communicating with their peers, thereby indicating that their social networks predominantly consist of other Hindi-dominant speakers. They usually described their knowledge of English as intermediate and basic. Most of these students came from smaller towns or rural areas to study at JNU. Finally, mixed bilinguals grew up speaking a regional language; English was introduced as a second language in the family around the age of five or a bit later and was actively promoted in the family by one of the spouses, typically father (but in some cases also mother). Such students were educated through a mix of English and Hindi at school. Similar to English-dominant speakers, they report an extensive use of English in daily interactions. In contrast to English-dominant students, they also report an extensive use of Hindi or other dialects related to Hindi. They furthermore profess (upper-)intermediate knowledge of English and stem from bigger regional cities in northern India. The previous discussion entails the observation that these different sociolinguistic modes of L2 acquisition must bear immediate repercussions for the kind of English that speakers use. In the next step, I explore the frequency of quotative variants by the type of speakers' bilingualism.

Table 10 illustrates that there is a gap between Hindi-dominant speakers on the one hand and English-dominant/mixed speakers on the other regarding the quotes' ratios. The former cohort produces far fewer quotes on average when compared to the other two. As is clear, speakers who put English to use through consistent linguistic practices are also the ones who exhibit the highest rates of quotation. As a discourse device, quotation is thus part of oral narrative skills of those speakers who practise the skill of narration in English on a daily basis. This finding is consistent with previous research into the L2 acquisition of discourse structures (Collentine 2004). Notice also that it is the English-dominant students

**Table 10:** Distribution of quotative markers by the type of bilingualism (N speakers = 80; N quotatives = 2118; N *be like* = 370).

| Bilingualism, type | N (speakers) | N (quotes) | Ratio quotes/speaker | N (*be like*) | Ratio *be like*/speaker |
|---|---|---|---|---|---|
| English-dominant | 11 | 318 | 28.9 | 85 | 7.7 |
| Hindi-dominant | 25 | 365 | 14.6 | 10 | 0.4 |
| mixed | 44 | 1435 | 32.6 | 275 | 6.2 |

who exhibit the highest *be like* per speaker ratio (7.7) followed by mixed bilinguals (6.2). Hindi-dominant speakers, in contrast, lag behind both speaker groups, producing as many as 0.4 *be like*-quotes per speaker. With this ascertained, I explore the variable grammar of quotative marking for each group of speakers in an attempt to ascertain the convergent and divergent patterns in the use of quotative markers across the board. I contextualise these findings within the theory of grammaticalisation for *be like* and triangulate the data, where appropriate, with that obtained for native and non-native varieties.

## 5.1 English-dominant speakers

Let us turn now to the discussion of the variable quotative marking by English-dominant bilinguals. My data base contains 11 speakers complying with the descriptions of this sociolinguistic profile. Table 11 reports the overall distribution of variants within this speaker cohort.

**Table 11:** Overall distribution of quotative markers in English-dominant speakers of Indian English (N speakers = 11).

| Traditional variants | N | % |
|---|---|---|
| *say* | 53 | 16.7% |
| other verbs of reporting | 17 | 5.3% |
| zero | 72 | 22.6% |
| *think* | 8 | 2.5% |
| other verbs of mental activity and perception | 8 | 2.5% |
| **Variants featuring *like*** | | |
| *be like* | 85 | 26.7% |
| zero-*like* | 14 | 4.4% |
| verb + *like* | 8 | 2.5% |
| **Variants featuring *okay* (*fine*)** | | |
| *be okay* | 0 | 0.0% |
| zero-*okay* | 3 | 0.9% |
| verb + *okay* | 4 | 1,3% |
| verb + *that* + *okay* | 4 | 1.3% |
| **Variants featuring verb + *that*** | | |
| verb + *that* | 15 | 4.7% |
| verb + *that* + discourse marker | 7 | 2.2% |

(continued)

**Table 11** (continued)

| Variants featuring verb + *that* | N | % |
|---|---|---|
| verb + noun + *that* | 0 | 0.0% |
| verb + noun + prep. + *that* | 0 | 0.0% |
| **Other variants** | | |
| copula *be* | 8 | 2.5% |
| verbs of motion | 6 | 1.9% |
| *ki* | 0 | 0% |
| verbs of achievement | 4 | 1.3% |
| *so* | 2 | 0.6% |
| TOTAL | 318 | |

Table 11 reveals that these speakers use a very balanced constellation of traditional and innovative variants, while reconstructing dialogue in the discourse. *Be like* is the leading variant in the system accounting for 26.7% of variation. Taken together with other quotative constructions featuring *like*, its contribution to the system amounts to 33.6%. Zero-quotatives and quotative *say* follow suit at the rate of 22.6% and 16.7% respectively. Adolescents and young adults speaking L1 Englishes have been reported to use *be like* at the overall rate ranging between 43% and 72%. Our English-dominant speakers are thus still lagging behind native speakers in terms of variant frequency. Yet this rate is comparable to those attested for German learners with high levels of exposure to North American English and high levels of exposure to mass media (see Chapter 6).

Notice also that the number of contact-induced quotative tokens is, in contrast, extremely low. English-dominant speakers thus rarely use quotative constructions featuring the discourse element *okay* (*fine*). They furthermore sporadically recruit quotative markers consisting of a *verbum dicendi* and the complementiser *that*, while introducing speech and thought. Quotatives featuring the substratum complementiser *ki* are not attested in this set of data. Overall then, the entire system is perhaps best described as L1 vernacular oriented as it exhibits a fairly high degree of conformity with L1 vernacular norms. But what is the role of each individual constraint on the quotative system of English-dominant speakers?

Here and in Chapter 6, I examine the functional allocation of quotative *be like* and its major competitors within the system of quotative marking. The forms considered in the analyses of Indian English data include quotative *say*, *think*, zero-quotatives, 'verb + *that*' and the category 'other' containing other verbs of reporting and perception as well as low-frequency tokens. Following the methodology adopted in Davydova and Buchstaller (2015), I merged zero-*like* and 'verb + *like*' tokens into the category 'template'. I also treated the variants featuring discourse marker *okay (fine)* as a separate category. Aligned with the established variationist practice (Tagliamonte 2006: 192–193), the ensuing analyses will show distributions of variants within each independent factor, thereby highlighting the contribution of a given quotative in a given context relative to other elements in the system. Such an approach will allow me to present a fine-grained view of quotative marking as a variable system. As I navigate through the data analyses, I will be appealing to their horizontal and vertical dimensions. The horizontal perspective considers a contribution of each individual variant relative to the overall composition of an individual constraint (e.g. mimesis). The vertical perspective reveals the relative frequency of occurrence of a given linguistic variant across an independent factor calculated as a fraction of all quotative variants (see also Buchstaller 2014: 120–121; Davydova 2016c: 331–332).

Mimesis is a globally consistent constraint universally triggering the occurrence *be like* in various L1 vernaculars and it is with this constraint that I begin the exploration of quotative marking as attested in speech of English-dominant Indians. Consistent with previous findings, the mimetic function is clearly assigned to quotative *be like* (31.2%) in this data set, as illustrated in Table 12, followed by zero-quotatives (25.3%), which have also been reported to have a propensity to be used with quotes produced with a 'voice' (Bakhtin 1986). *Say* frames non-mimetic quotes (24.7%), which patterns well with the trends attested in previous research into both native and non-native quotative marking (see, for instance, Buchstaller 2014; Davydova and Buchstaller 2015).

Table 12: Distribution of quotatives by mimesis for English-dominant speakers.

|  | be like | template | say | think | zero | okay | V+that | other |
|---|---|---|---|---|---|---|---|---|
| mimesis | 69 (31.2%) | 19 (8.6%) | 29 (13.1%) | 6 (2.7%) | 56 (25.3%) | 5 (2.3%) | 10 (4.5%) | 27 (12.2%) |
| not | 16 (16.5%) | 3 (3.1%) | 24 (24.7%) | 2 (2.1%) | 16 (16.5%) | 6 (6.2%) | 12 (12.4%) | 18 (18.6%) |

The next predictor is to consider is quote type. Previous research has established a close link between quotative *be like* and the reporting of thought across a set of different varieties spoken worldwide. Patterns presented in Table 13 corroborate this hypothesis: From a vertical perspective, *be like* is more frequent with thought (32.7%) than it is with speech (23.1%) profiling itself as an inner-dialogue introducer. When considered horizontally, *be like* is likewise the major variant used by English-dominant speakers to report thought throughout narration. In contrast, *say* is chiefly used to introduce direct speech (22.1%), and zero-quotes are evenly distributed across speech and thought (23.1% and 22.4% respectively). Though

**Table 13:** Distribution of quotatives by quote type for English-dominant speakers.

|  | be like | template | say | think | zero | okay | V+that | other |
|---|---|---|---|---|---|---|---|---|
| speech | 46 | 14 | 44 | 5 | 46 | 2 | 11 | 31 |
|  | (23.1%) | (7.0%) | (22.1%) | (2.5%) | (23.1%) | (1.0%) | (5.5%) | (15.6%) |
| thought | 35 | 6 | 5 | 3 | 24 | 9 | 11 | 14 |
|  | (32.7%) | (5.6%) | (4.7%) | (2.8%) | (22.4%) | (8.4%) | (10.3%) | (13.1%) |
| indigenous | 4 | 2 | 4 | 0 | 2 | 0 | 0 | 0 |
|  | (33.3%) | (16.7%) | (33.3%) | (0.0%) | (16.7%) | (0.0%) | (0.0%) | (0.0%) |

infrequent in the data, indigenous quotes tend to surface with both *say*, *be like*, and also, to some extent, zero-quotatives.

In the next step, I explore the distribution of quotative markers by grammatical subject for English-dominant speakers. There has been reported a close association between quotative *be like* and first-person subjects as it is through this context that *be like* paves its way into the variable system. Results presented in Table 14 support this contention. From a horizontal perspective, *be like* is used most frequently with first-person contexts at 35.4%, thereby outnumbering other major players within the system. Vertically, it is recruited with first-person contexts more frequently than with third-person contexts (35.4% vs. 26.2%), and it also demonstrates a clear propensity to occur with neuter pronoun *it* (68.2%). Interestingly, *say* is evenly distributed between first- and third-person contexts (23.0% vs. 19.2%), which is in contrast to L1 English usage favouring *say* with third-person quotes (Buchstaller 2014: 129–130).

**Table 14:** Distribution of quotatives by grammatical subject for English-dominant speakers.

|  | be like | template | say | think | zero | okay | V+that | other |
|---|---|---|---|---|---|---|---|---|
| first | 35 | 5 | 19 | 3 | 11 | 6 | 8 | 12 |
|  | (35.4%) | (5.1%) | (19.2%) | (3.0%) | (11.1%) | (6.1%) | (8.1%) | (12.1%) |
| second | 2 | 2 | 2 | 2 | 2 | 2 | 0 | 4 |
|  | (12.5%) | (12.5%) | (12.5%) | (12.5%) | (12.5%) | (12.5%) | (0.0%) | (25.0%) |
| third | 33 | 10 | 29 | 3 | 14 | 2 | 11 | 24 |
|  | (26.2%) | (7.9%) | (23.0%) | (2.4%) | (11.1%) | (1.6%) | (8.7%) | (19.0%) |
| it | 15 | 0 | 2 | 0 | 0 | 0 | 1 | 4 |
|  | (68.2%) | (0.0%) | (9.1%) | (0.0%) | (0.0%) | (0.0%) | (4.5%) | (18.2%) |
| NA | 0 | 5 | 1 | 0 | 45 | 1 | 2 | 1 |
|  | (0.0%) | (9.1%) | (1.8%) | (0.0%) | (81.8%) | (1.8%) | (3.6%) | (1.8%) |

But how are the quotative elements distributed across the English-dominant system regards tense marking? Previous research has ascertained a close association between quotative *be like* and CHP in North American English and results shown in Table 15 provide further empirical evidence for this finding. When viewed horizontally, *be like* occurs most often with the CHP form (59.5%). What is also of interest is the fact that *say* is fairly evenly used with a variety of tense markers, i.e. CHP (13.5%), the present tense (22.5%), the past tense (24.0%), and it is also frequently modified by various modal verbs, particularly habitual *will* and *would* (see also Davydova 2016a: 188), at 36.4%. This distributional pattern is reminiscent of that reported by Buchstaller for British English quotative marking (Buchstaller 2014: 185). Back in the 1960s and 1970s, British speakers used to exploit quotative *say* with a variety of tense and aspect markers, habitual *will* and *would* as well as modals and pseudo-modals, a tendency which diminishes in the 1990s. Buchstaller attributes this effect to the "comparatively low formal diversity of ... [the] quotative system" attested back in the 1960s-1970s going on to explain that speakers create diversity within the local system via tense and aspect marking in order to "breathe variability into ... rather monotonous and semantically undifferentiated sequences of *say*" (Buchstaller 2014: 183). Remarkably, English-dominant speakers use the same distributional profile for quotative *say* in a system that looks nothing like a low-level diversity system dominated by one specific variant. In contrast, as demonstrated in Table 11, it represents a well-balanced constellation of traditional and global innovative variants. The latter finding thus begs the question regarding the origin of the distributional profile for quotative *say* illustrated in Table 15. I would like to suggest by way of providing an explanation to this result that the distributional trend attested for quotative *say* might be an historical retention from earlier settler dialects (see Mesthrie and Bhatt 2008: 188–199). This speculation is attractive for two major reasons. Firstly, British English, especially its earlier forms, is a major input variety that exerted a

Table 15: Distribution of quotatives by tense for English-dominant speakers.

|  | be like | template | say | think | zero | okay | V+that | other |
|---|---|---|---|---|---|---|---|---|
| CHP | 22 | 1 | 5 | 1 | 0 | 0 | 4 | 4 |
|  | (59.5%) | (2.7%) | (13.5%) | (2.7%) | (0.0%) | (0.0%) | (10.8%) | (10.8%) |
| present | 26 | 5 | 18 | 2 | 0 | 5 | 7 | 17 |
|  | (32.5%) | (6.3%) | (22.5%) | (2.5%) | (0.0%) | (6.3%) | (8.8%) | (21.3%) |
| past | 31 | 3 | 18 | 5 | 0 | 1 | 8 | 9 |
|  | (41.3%) | (4.0%) | (24.0%) | (6.7%) | (0.0%) | (1.3%) | (10.7%) | (12.0%) |
| modal | 6 | 0 | 12 | 0 | 0 | 1 | 1 | 13 |
|  | (18.2%) | (0.0%) | (36.4%) | (0.0%) | (0.0%) | (3.0%) | (3.0%) | (39.4%) |
| NA | 0 | 13 | 0 | 0 | 72 | 4 | 2 | 2 |
|  | (0.0%) | (13.9%) | (0.0%) | (0.0%) | (77.4%) | (4.3%) | (2.2%) | (2.2%) |

significant influence on the formation of Indian English at large. Secondly, quite a few speakers from this cohort received their education in convents and missionary schools, which traditionally provide a link to earlier English vernaculars spoken on the British Isles (Mesthrie and Bhatt 2008: 194–195).

Overall then, the trends reported for quotative use by English-dominant speakers are perhaps best described along the following lines. Firstly, the English-dominant system represents a well-balanced constellation of traditional and global innovative variants. Secondly, English-dominant bilinguals replicate all the major patterns of use reported for quotative *be like* in native-speaker English. They prefer *be like* with mimetic thoughts, favouring this variant over non-mimetic direct speech reports. Furthermore, they use it far more frequently with the first-person grammatical subject than with the third-person grammatical subject and recruit this variant with CHP marking more often than with any other tense and aspect marking forms. However, these speakers' use of quotative *be like* does not show the levelling tendencies for quote type and grammatical subject reported for young adults' speech in North American localities. What is then means from the perspective of the grammaticalisation theory is that quotative *be like*, as it is attested in speech of English-dominant speakers, is still at the incipient stages of its development in this type of Indian English. In other words, English-dominant speakers have picked on the variant attested in the parent varieties, i.e. North American English and, also to some degree, British English, but they have not adopted it to the extent that native speakers have. What is, however, remarkable is the level of accuracy with which patterns of *be like* use resurface in the contact variety under scrutiny. I will return to this issue in Chapter 7.

## 5.2 Hindi-dominant speakers

In the next step, let us consider the system of variable quotative marking as it is attested in speech of those individuals who grew up with Hindi as their dominant language and use English only occasionally. Relying on the background questionnaire and the information contained in sociolinguistic interviews, I have been able to spot 25 students complying with the requirements for this sociolinguistic profile. Table 16 depicts the overall distribution of quotative markers in Hindi-dominant speakers of English.

The first observation we can make here is that the system is dominated by the traditional variants, such as *say* (34.8%) and other verbs of reporting (9.6%) as well as zero-quotatives (13.7%). Transfer-induced structures including 'verb + *that*' and *ki*-quotatives are attested at 13.9% and 4.4% respectively. The rates of variants featuring *like* are extremely low in this speaker group ranging between

**Table 16:** Overall distribution of quotative markers in Hindi-dominant speakers of Indian English (N speakers = 25).

| Traditional variants | N | % |
|---|---|---|
| *say* | 127 | 34.8% |
| other verbs of reporting | 35 | 9.6% |
| zero | 50 | 13.7% |
| *think* | 9 | 2.5% |
| other verbs of mental activity and perception | 7 | 1.9% |
| **Variants featuring *like*** | | |
| *be like* | 10 | 2.7% |
| zero-*like* | 19 | 5.2% |
| verb + *like* | 6 | 1.6% |
| **Variants featuring *okay* (*fine*)** | | |
| *be okay* | 3 | 0.8% |
| zero-*okay* | 6 | 1.6% |
| verb + *okay* | 7 | 1.9% |
| verb + *that* + *okay* | 2 | 0.5% |
| **Variants featuring verb + *that*** | | |
| verb + *that* | 51 | 13.9% |
| verb + *that* + discourse marker | 0 | 0.0% |
| verb + noun + *that* | 0 | 0.0% |
| verb + noun + prep. + *that* | 1 | 0.3% |
| **Other variants** | | |
| copula *be* | 8 | 2.2% |
| verbs of motion | 1 | 0.3% |
| *ki* | 16 | 4.4% |
| verbs of achievement | 4 | 1.1% |
| *so* | 3 | 0.8% |
| TOTAL | 365 | |

5.2% and 1.6%. Contact-induced innovative variants featuring discourse marker *okay* (*fine*) are likewise rare in this informants' pool. Overall then, the linguistic behaviour of these speakers is quite similar to that of EFL speakers who have never been abroad to an English-speaking country and use *say* together with other verbs of reporting and zero-quotatives as their preferred option to reference dialogue in speech (see Chapter 6). However, Hindi-dominant bilinguals are different from the latter group of speakers in one crucial respect: They make quite an extensive use of substrate-induced quotative schemas, while introducing reported material. This contrasts with low-level naturalistic exposure EFL learners who do not exploit L1-based innovative quotatives in their speech. This phenomenon could be related to the attitudinal differences characterising the ESL and EFL ecologies discussed in Chapter 4. Endonormatively oriented, Hindi-dominant speakers seem to view Hindi, their mother tongue, as a natural linguistic resource designed to support their spontaneous interactions in English, whereas exonormatively oriented learners, as Chapter 6 will show, strive to emulate the reference variety irrespective of their degree of familiarity with the target.

Let us now explore the language-internal organisation of quotative marking in this speaker cohort starting with mimesis. Table 17 reveals that mimetic quotes are introduced by *say* (30.4%), *zero*-quotatives (21.4%), and other (mostly traditional) variants (21.4%). The variable grammar of Hindi-dominant speakers is thus quite different from that of English-dominant speakers in this regard. However, when considered on its own, *be like* occurs exclusively with mimetic quotes (10 out of 10 tokens).

Table 17: Distribution of quotatives by mimesis for Hindi-dominant speakers.

|  | be like | template | say | think | zero | okay | V+that | other |
|---|---|---|---|---|---|---|---|---|
| mimesis | 10 | 9 | 51 | 5 | 36 | 7 | 14 | 36 |
|  | (5.9%) | (5.4%) | (30.4%) | (2.9%) | (21.4%) | (4.2%) | (8.3%) | (21.4%) |
| not | 0 | 16 | 76 | 4 | 14 | 11 | 38 | 38 |
|  | (0.0%) | (8.1%) | (38.6%) | (2.0%) | (7.1%) | (5.6%) | (19.3%) | (19.3%) |

As for quote type reported in Table 18, *say* is clearly leading the system as a major direct speech introducer (40.8%), followed by other verbs of reporting (20.2%), 'verb + *that*' (14.6%) and zero-forms (13.6%). In contrast, thought or inner dialogue is introduced by a variety of different variants including zero-forms (16.7%), the categories 'other' (16.7%), 'template' (15.2%), 'verb + that' (13.6%), and, finally, *think* (12.1%). Notice that *be like* contributes a mere 7.6% to the entire

Table 18: Distribution of quotatives by quote type for Hindi-dominant speakers.

|  | be like | template | say | think | zero | okay | V+that | other |
|---|---|---|---|---|---|---|---|---|
| speech | 4 | 15 | 117 | 1 | 39 | 11 | 42 | 58 |
|  | (1.4%) | (5.2%) | (40.8%) | (0.3%) | (13.6%) | (3.8%) | (14.6%) | (20.2%) |
| thought | 5 | 10 | 5 | 8 | 11 | 7 | 9 | 11 |
|  | (7.6%) | (15.2%) | (7.6%) | (12.1%) | (16.7%) | (10.6%) | (13.6%) | (16.7%) |
| indigenous | 1 | 0 | 5 | 0 | 0 | 0 | 1 | 5 |
|  | (8.3%) | (0.0%) | (41.7%) | (0.0%) | (0.0%) | (0.0%) | (8.3%) | (41.7%) |

context. Importantly, however, *be like* is still more frequent with thought than it is with direct speech proper (7.6% vs. 1.4%). As far as quote type is concerned, the quotative grammar of Hindi-dominant students is in contrast to that attested for English-dominant peers, where, as we saw, *be like* has been encroaching on the territory of *think*, a major traditional introducer of thought in constructed dialogue (Tagliamonte and Hudson 1999: 168).

Perusing the patterns of quotative use with various grammatical subjects, reported in Table 19, reveals that in line with the patterns attested for English-dominant speakers, *say* is evenly distributed across third-, first- and second-person contexts (39.3% vs. 35.9% vs. 33.3%), although it is more frequent with third person subjects. Substrate-induced variant 'verb + that' shows a similar pattern, showing a preference for third-person contexts at 18.2%. *Think*, in contrast, is circumscribed to first person. Despite being extremely rare in this data set, variants featuring *like*, i.e. *be like* and template, still occur more frequently with first- than with third-person grammatical subjects (3.5% vs. 1.9% and 7.0% vs. 6.5% respectively). Note, however, that the neuter pronoun *it* is not clearly circumscribed to quotative *be like* (28.6%), being used with other quotative markers as well, notably categories 'other' (42.9%), 'verb + that' (14.3%), and *okay (fine)* (14.3%). This is in contrast to how English-dominant bilinguals employ this linguistic environment, assigning neuter *it* majorly to quotative *be like*. Overall then, we see that as far as grammatical subject is concerned, the quotative grammar of Hindi-dominant speakers shows some convergent as well as divergent tendencies when compared to the English-dominant bilinguals. Convergent patterns are related the use of quotative *say* with various grammatical subjects as well as the constraint hierarchy for quotative *be like*. Divergent patterns mainly concern the use of neuter *it*.

**Table 19:** Distribution of quotatives by grammatical subject for Hindi-dominant speakers.

|        | be like | template | say     | think  | zero    | okay    | V+that  | other   |
|--------|---------|----------|---------|--------|---------|---------|---------|---------|
| first  | 4       | 8        | 41      | 9      | 13      | 8       | 12      | 19      |
|        | (3.5%)  | (7.0%)   | (35.9%) | (7.9%) | (11.4%) | (7.0%)  | (10.5%) | (16.7%) |
| second | 0       | 0        | 2       | 0      | 1       | 0       | 0       | 3       |
|        | (0.0%)  | (0.0%)   | (33.3%) | (0.0%) | (16.7%) | (0.0%)  | (0.0%)  | (50%)   |
| third  | 4       | 14       | 84      | 0      | 21      | 6       | 39      | 46      |
|        | (1.9%)  | (6.5%)   | (39.3%) | (0.0%) | (9.8%)  | (2.8%)  | (18.2%) | (21.5%) |
| it     | 2       | 0        | 0       | 0      | 0       | 1       | 1       | 3       |
|        | (28.6%) | (0.0%)   | (0.0%)  | (0.0%) | (0.0%)  | (14.3%) | (14.3%) | (42.9%) |
| NA     | 0       | 3        | 0       | 0      | 15      | 3       | 0       | 3       |
|        | (0.0%)  | (12.5%)  | (0.0%)  | (0.0%) | (62.5%) | (12.5%) | (0.0%)  | (12.5%) |

Let us now scrutinise the system of variable quotation produced by Hindi-dominant speakers with respect to tense making. First and foremost, when considered vertically, we notice that quotative *say* occurs with a variety of tense markers and modal auxiliaries, although it is most robust with present tense marking, notably CHP (57.1%). Category 'verb + *that*' is also used with an expanded number of temporal markers although it is most frequent in contexts featuring modals (36.4%). The category 'other' likewise shows the propensity to occur with an expended repertoire of tense markers, although it is most frequent with present tense marking (32.1%). Recall that in the English-dominant data set, *say* also surfaces with a collection of temporal markers. The propensity of *say* to collocate with various tense-aspect distinctions, as documented in both data sets studied so far, is informative and forces the analyst to consider once again the superstratal influence stemming from the earlier (settler) dialects of British English as a possible explanation for this kind of variability. We can recall the data provided in Section 5.1. whereby a very similar pattern has been attested in conservative L1 British vernaculars (Buchstaller 2014: 185–186). The Hindi-dominant bilinguals may have generalised this tendency to the 'verb + *that*' construction, which draws on *say* as its major contributing token, i.e. 'say + *that*', and to the category 'other', which consists primarily of other verbs of reporting that are similar to *say* in their semantics. Unsurprisingly perhaps, template forms and zero-quotatives mainly occur without any tense marking. Remarkably, not a single instance of CHP occurs with quotative *be like*. Though highly infrequent in the data set, the linguistic form surfaces in present and past tense contexts, which is in contrast to the usage attested for English-dominant speakers and their North American peers. This is the area of variable grammar where the two types of Indian English diverge.

Table 20: Distribution of quotatives by tense for Hindi-dominant speakers.

|  | *be like* | *template* | *say* | *think* | *zero* | *okay* | *V+that* | *other* |
| --- | --- | --- | --- | --- | --- | --- | --- | --- |
| CHP | 0 | 1 | 16 | 0 | 0 | 0 | 6 | 5 |
|  | (0.0%) | (3.6%) | (57.1%) | (0.0%) | (0.0%) | (0.0%) | (21.4%) | (17.9%) |
| present | 2 | 1 | 28 | 1 | 0 | 1 | 5 | 18 |
|  | (3.6%) | (1.8%) | (50.0%) | (1.8%) | (0.0%) | (1.8%) | (8.9%) | (32.1%) |
| past | 8 | 2 | 71 | 8 | 0 | 8 | 28 | 40 |
|  | (4.8%) | (1.2%) | (43%) | (4.8%) | (0.0%) | (4.8%) | (16.9%) | (24.2%) |
| modal | 0 | 2 | 11 | 0 | 0 | 3 | 12 | 5 |
|  | (0.0%) | (6.1%) | (33.3%) | (0.0%) | (0.0%) | (9.1%) | (36.4%) | (15.2%) |
| NA | 0 | 19 | 1 | 0 | 50 | 6 | 1 | 6 |
|  | (0.0%) | (22.9%) | (1.2%) | (0.0%) | (60.2%) | (7.2%) | (1.2%) | (7.2%) |

Overall then, the major findings for the Hindi-dominant quotative systems can be summed up as follows: (i) Hindi-dominant speakers utilise traditional and substrate-induced quotative variants far more frequently than any other variants; (ii) both global and local innovative variants are scarce in the data; (iii) patterns underlying the use of infrequent *be like* do not always align with those reported for English-dominant speakers of Indian English and their L1 peers from North America. More specifically, *be like* has not taken on a function as a major mimesis introducer in the system as yet. Furthermore, there is no close correspondence between neuter *it* and the innovative variant. Similarly, *be like* is not closely associated with CHP, which is in contrast to the pattern consistently reported in the previous literature. At the same time, some of the patterns gleaned from the data are consistent with the theory of grammaticalisation. Though very infrequent, *be like* is primarily recruited by Hindi-dominant bilinguals to introduce mimetic thoughts (if it is used at all) and it appears to be favoured in first- over third-person contexts.

## 5.3 Mixed bilinguals

Let us now turn to the discussion of the quotative system as it is attested in speech of mixed bilinguals, i.e. speakers who grew up speaking both Hindi and English, and actively exploit both linguistic codes in their everyday interactions. Unsurprisingly, and given the fact that India is best described as the paragon of multilingualism, my corpus features 44 mixed bilingual speakers, which accounts for 55% of the entire data set. Table 21 presents the overall distribution of quotative markers in this speaker group.

Table 21: Overall distribution of quotative markers in mixed bilinguals of Indian English (N speakers = 44).

| Traditional variants | N | % |
|---|---|---|
| *say* | 321 | 22.4% |
| other verbs of reporting | 155 | 10.8% |
| zero | 167 | 11.6% |
| *think* | 44 | 3.1% |
| other verbs of mental activity and perception | 33 | 2.3% |
| **Variants featuring *like*** | | |
| *be like* | 275 | 19.2% |
| zero-*like* | 76 | 5.3% |
| verb + *like* | 48 | 3.3% |

(continued)

**Table 21** (continued)

|  | N | % |
|---|---|---|
| **Variants featuring *okay* (*fine*)** |  |  |
| be okay | 5 | 0.3% |
| zero-okay | 42 | 2.9% |
| verb + okay | 29 | 2.0% |
| verb + that + okay | 34 | 2.4% |
| **Variants featuring verb + *that*** |  |  |
| verb + that | 133 | 9.2% |
| verb + that + discourse marker | 15 | 1.0% |
| verb + noun + that | 2 | 0.1% |
| verb + noun + prep. + that | 3 | 0.2% |
| **Other variants** |  |  |
| copula be | 26 | 1.8% |
| verbs of motion | 5 | 0.3% |
| ki | 11 | 0.8% |
| verbs of achievement | 6 | 0.4% |
| so | 5 | 0.3% |
| TOTAL | 1435 |  |

Table 21 points to a highly competitive variable system in which traditional mainstream quotative markers *say* (22.4%), other verbs of reporting (10.8%), and zero-quotatives (11.6%) engage in a contest against innovative *be like* (19.2%), which, taken together with other variants featuring *like*, accounts for 27.8% of variation. Substrate-induced quotative templates of the type 'verb + *that*' are likewise respectable opponents contributing an overall of 10.5% to the variant pool. My next observation concerns the local innovative variants featuring the discourse marker *okay* (*fine*). Though relatively infrequent, this quotative type is attested at the rate of 7.6%. As a point of comparison, English-dominant speakers use this variant in 3.5% of all cases and Hindi-dominant speakers do so with the relative frequency of 4.8%. The differences in the use of local innovations across different speaker groups are statistically significant ($x^2$ (2): 9.5, $p$ = 0.01). Overall then, the quotative system, as it is attested in speech of mixed bilinguals, feeds off a variety of different linguistic resources that rise beyond the substrate/superstrate influences to comprise contact-induced local innovations. Here, I argue that it is speakers who operate from a bilingual state activated through daily linguistic practices that are likely to produce more variable or diverse linguistic systems as they draw on expanded linguistic repertoires available to them online. They do not only enrich superstratal linguistic material with substrate-induced variants as they construct dialogue. Remarkably, they attempt to coin innovative means of expression thereby contributing to the 'feature pool' in a newly emerged contact variety (Mufwene 2001). In contrast, Language X-dominant speakers are likely to end up with more homogenous systems. As we saw, English-dominant speakers employ a pool of variable quotative markers largely aligned with that of L1 speakers, comprising both traditional and non-traditional variants. Hindi-dominant speakers, in turn, use quotative strategies that are conformant with those attested in their native language, Hindi.

Examining the distribution of variants across the factor 'mimesis', presented in Table 22, shows that similarly to the patterns attested in the English-dominant cohort, mimesis is majorly introduced by quotative *be like* (25.2%), although the contribution of *say* and other verbs of reporting as well as zero-quotatives is not at all negligible (18.3%, 16.4%, and 15.1% respectively). Overall then, mixed bilinguals exploit the innovative feature in this linguistic context in a fashion similar to that attested for English-dominant bilinguals (who use mimesis with *be like* at the rate of 31.2%). Non-mimetic quotes are clearly circumscribed to *say* (27.6%) and the category 'other' (17.3%), which includes a considerable proportion of other verbs of reporting. From the perspective of grammaticalisation theory, the overall pattern for 'mimesis' is replicated by mixed, and also English-dominant, bilinguals.

Table 22: Distribution of quotatives by mimesis for mixed bilinguals.

|  | be like | template | say | think | zero | okay | V+that | other |
|---|---|---|---|---|---|---|---|---|
| mimesis | 205 | 68 | 149 | 22 | 123 | 50 | 62 | 133 |
|  | (25.2%) | (8.4%) | (18.3%) | (2.7%) | (15.1%) | (6.2%) | (7.6%) | (16.4%) |
| not | 70 | 56 | 172 | 22 | 44 | 60 | 91 | 108 |
|  | (11.2%) | (8.9%) | (27.6%) | (3.5%) | (7.1%) | (9.6%) | (14.6%) | (17.3%) |

Let us now examine the content of the quote, shown in Table 23. From a vertical perspective, mixed bilinguals use *be like* somewhat indeterminately to report both thought and speech, although they use this variant with reported thought more often than with speech (21.8% vs. 18.8%). A horizontal analysis of data, however, reveals much clearer tendencies. *Say* is a major variant introducing reported speech, which mirrors earlier findings on L1 English in the US and in the UK (Buchstaller 2014: 127). *Say* is also linked to the quotes containing pivotal code-switches into indigenous languages, primarily Hindi. This finding is consistent with that reported in Davydova (2016a). Davydova and Buchstaller (2015: 455) explain that "[i]ndigenous content necessarily implies a higher degree of

**Table 23:** Distribution of quotatives by quote type for mixed bilinguals.

|  | be like | template | say | think | zero | okay | V+that | other |
|---|---|---|---|---|---|---|---|---|
| speech | 196 | 85 | 277 | 4 | 116 | 72 | 109 | 184 |
|  | (18.8%) | (8.1%) | (26.6%) | (0.4%) | (11.1%) | (6.9%) | (10.5%) | (17.6%) |
| thought | 69 | 29 | 13 | 38 | 47 | 38 | 40 | 42 |
|  | (21.8%) | (9.2%) | (4.1%) | (12.0%) | (14.9%) | (12.0%) | (12.7%) | (13.3%) |
| indigenous | 10 | 10 | 31 | 2 | 4 | 0 | 4 | 15 |
|  | (13.2%) | (13.2%) | (40.8%) | (2.6%) | (5.3%) | (0.0%) | (5.3%) | (19.7%) |

commitment to the quoted material, while being arguably associated with a more accurate reproduction of quotation. It is, therefore, not surprising that speakers resort to *say* with this quote type [...]". Perusing the distribution of variants across reported thought it becomes immediately obvious that *be like* (21.8%) dominates the reproduction of inner monologue followed by zero-quotatives (14.9%), the category 'other' (13.3%), *okay (fine)* (12.7%) and quotative *think* (12.0%). Overall then, my mixed bilinguals largely replicate the pattern reported for native speakers (admittedly at a lower rate), thereby reaffirming the status of *be like* as a marker of internal thought.

The distribution of quotatives by grammatical subject, presented in Table 24, yields the following picture. The vertical analysis of data reveals a very close association between *be like* and neuter *it*, which is in accordance with the patterns attested for English-dominant bilinguals and their L1 peers in North America. *Be like* is furthermore evenly spread out across first- and third-person contexts, although it is somewhat more frequent with the first-person grammatical subject (21.0% vs. 17.1%). This finding thus provides further support for grammaticalisation theory which links *be like* to first- over third-person subjects. The category 'template'

**Table 24:** Distribution of quotatives by grammatical subject for mixed bilinguals.

|  | be like | template | say | think | zero | okay | V+that | other |
|---|---|---|---|---|---|---|---|---|
| first | 105 | 50 | 113 | 36 | 39 | 31 | 44 | 81 |
|  | (21.0%) | (10.0%) | (22.6%) | (7.2%) | (7.8%) | (6.2%) | (8.8%) | (16.2%) |
| second | 1 | 3 | 7 | 0 | 0 | 3 | 5 | 12 |
|  | (3.2%) | (9.7%) | (22.6%) | (0.0%) | (0.0%) | (9.7%) | (16.1%) | (38.7%) |
| third | 132 | 63 | 200 | 8 | 69 | 65 | 102 | 135 |
|  | (17.1%) | (8.1%) | (25.8%) | (1.0%) | (8.9%) | (8.4%) | (13.2%) | (17.4%) |
| it | 34 | 1 | 0 | 0 | 1 | 4 | 0 | 7 |
|  | (72.3%) | (2.1%) | (0.0%) | (0.0%) | (2.1%) | (8.5%) | (0.0%) | (14.9%) |
| NA | 3 | 7 | 1 | 0 | 58 | 7 | 2 | 6 |
|  | (3.6%) | (8.3%) | (1.2%) | (0.0%) | (69.0%) | (8.3%) | (2.4%) | (7.1%) |

and zero-quotatives are also evenly distributed across the first- and third-person contexts. Interestingly and in contrast to the results reported for L1 vernaculars, quotative *say* shows a propensity to occur with a variety of grammatical subjects instead of being clearly circumscribed to third-person contexts. The same pattern is true for the category 'other', 'verb + *that*', and *okay (fine)*. Finally, *think* is closely linked to first person contexts, which "is to be expected given the fact that the reporter tends to be the only person who has direct access to his/her inner world in $t_{-1}$ before these thoughts are reported in $t_{-0}$" (Buchstaller 2014: 164).

Considering the tense marking of quotative variants, shown in Table 25, *be like* occurs most frequently with CHP (44.5%). This result tallies nicely with that reported for the English-dominant group. More importantly, both speaker cohorts demonstrate linguistic behaviour which patterns well with that reported for North American English, where a close association of *be like* with CHP has been documented. Quotative *say* occurs with a variety of tense markers, although it is most frequent with modal verbs (36.6%). Recall that an identical pattern of use was reported for the English-dominant and Hindi-dominant groups and I attempted at an explanation in terms of the superstratal influence from British English, an earlier input variety. Categories 'verb + *that*' and 'other' follow suit, being used fairly evenly with different tense markers. Analogous to the Hindi-dominant speakers, my mixed bilinguals extend the pattern attested for quotative *say* to 'verb + *that*' and 'other' via analogy (Hopper and Traugott 2003: 50–70). The most frequent verb used in constructions 'verb + *that*' is *say* and a conspicuous proportion of verbs constituting the category 'other' are verbs of reporting, which provides the baseline for the analogical extension of the pattern.

Table 25: Distribution of quotatives by tense for mixed bilinguals.

|         | be like | template | say | think | zero | okay | V+that | other |
|---------|---------|----------|-----|-------|------|------|--------|-------|
| CHP     | 61 (44.5%) | 6 (4.4%) | 34 (24.8%) | 3 (2.2%) | 0 (0.0%) | 2 (1.5%) | 9 (6.6%) | 22 (16.1%) |
| present | 41 (18.8%) | 11 (5.0%) | 64 (29.3%) | 7 (3.2%) | 0 (0.0%) | 15 (6.8%) | 24 (11.0%) | 56 (25.7%) |
| past    | 166 (26.2%) | 25 (3.9%) | 169 (26.7%) | 32 (5.0%) | 0 (0.0%) | 35 (5.5%) | 89 (14.0%) | 118 (18.6%) |
| modal   | 4 (2.8%) | 10 (7.0%) | 52 (36.6%) | 1 (0.7%) | 0 (0.0%) | 13 (9.1%) | 26 (18.3%) | 36 (25.4%) |
| NA      | 3 (0.9%) | 72 (23.7%) | 2 (0.7%) | 1 (0.3%) | 167 (54.9%) | 45 (14.8%) | 5 (1.6%) | 9 (2.9%) |

What generalisations do the analyses of the three data sets yield? Firstly, the three data sets scrutinised here differ from each other with respect to the overall composition of variants. Whereas English-dominant speakers boast a well-balanced system consisting of traditional and innovative variants attested in mainstream parent varieties, their Hindi-dominant peers demonstrate a quotative system heavily dominated by conservative and substrate-induced quotatives. Remarkably, speakers who consistently use and oftentimes mix two (or more) linguistic codes in their daily interactions, mainly English and Hindi, end up with a system that comprises not only traditional and non-traditional quotatives stemming from L1 vernaculars as well as substrate-induced features. More importantly, it is these speakers who introduce new means of linguistic expression which may then evolve into distinctive features of local vernaculars, quotative *okay* (*fine*) being a case in point. Labelled as mixed bilinguals in this study, these speakers are best described as agents of local contact-induced innovations. Here, I would like to argue that such contact-induced innovations are a direct consequence of the specifics characterising speakers' psycholinguistic realities, which are, in turn, fostered by according sociolinguistic practices. In contrast to English- and Hindi-dominant bilinguals who, in fact, predominantly live in a monolingual state of mind (Grosjean 1998), my mixed bilinguals find themselves in a situation of socio-cultural upbringing allowing for prolonged, consistent and simultaneous activation of two (and in some cases more) languages. Supported by the endonormative attitudinal orientation licencing the simultaneous use of several linguistics codes (see Chapter 4), this truly bilingual state of mind then leads to the creation of local linguistic variants (or clusters of variants) that draw on resources available in two languages. If we consider constructions featuring *okay* (*fine*) as an illustration, this discourse marker can occur with copula *be* or in isolation in zero-*okay* constructions, thereby providing clear parallels to the *be like* and zero-*like* variants attested in the English superstrate. Simultaneously, the discourse marker is used in constructions of the type 'verb + *okay*' and 'verb + *that* + *okay*', which is an appropriate strategy for introducing quotation in Hindi.

Secondly, both English-dominant and mixed bilinguals demonstrate similar patterns regarding use of quotative *be like*, while also using the variant at similar rates. To be more exact, (i) they prefer *be like* to other variants while introducing mimetic quotes; (ii) they exploit this variant to introduce reported thought rather than reported speech; (iii) they link *be like* to neuter *it* and use the variant more often with first- rather than third person subjects; (iv) they consistently map *be like* into non-past tense morphology, more specifically CHP. These patterns are consistent with those reported for North American varieties of English. Furthermore, they are aligned with the predictions regarding the internal development of innovative *be like* within the system, reported in Chapter 3.

The patterns presented above are in contrast with those demonstrated by Hindi-dominant speakers. While using *be like* at an extremely low rate (2.7%), this speaker cohort employs quotative *say*, zero-quotatives and other variants in order to introduce mimetic quotes. They likewise heavily rely on variants other than quotative *be like* while introducing inner dialogue. Their speech shows no clear link between *be like* and neuter pronoun *it* and, finally, they do not unequivocally map this variant onto non-past tense morphology. These differences in the variable grammars of quotative *be like* obtaining between English-dominant and mixed bilinguals on the one hand, and Hindi-dominant bilinguals on the other can be arguably traced back to the differences in the sociolinguistic contexts underpinning acquisition of Indian English. Relying on the evidence presented in the preceding paragraphs, it is not unreasonable to conclude that the amount and type of exposure to English in indigenised settings must bear crucial repercussions for resulting variable grammars exhibited by the speakers. This discussion thus raises the question concerning the role of the local sociolinguistic ecology as the major predictor of variation in L2 English. I address this issue in Chapter 7 by way of constructing a model of variation for innovative *be like* incorporating sociolinguistic context as one of the predictors into the analysis.

## 5.4 Exposure to mass media

In the next step, I explore the effect produced by the media operationalised as the amount of exposure to English films and television series. In order to explore this effect, I first of all investigate how speakers with varying levels of viewing habits use quotation in general and, more specifically, how they use quotative *be like* in their speech. Table 26 presents the distribution of quotative markers by amount of exposure to mass media.

**Table 26:** Distribution of quotative markers by amount of exposure to mass media (N speakers = 80; N quotatives = 2118; N *be like* = 370).

| Exposure to the media | N (speakers) | N (quotes) | Ratio quotes/ speaker | N (*be like*) | Ratio *be like*/speaker |
|---|---|---|---|---|---|
| every day | 6 | 339 | 56.5 | 106 | 17.7 |
| two or three times a week | 24 | 681 | 28.4 | 153 | 6.4 |
| once a week | 17 | 409 | 24.1 | 56 | 3.3 |
| less than once a week | 8 | 168 | 21 | 3 | 0.4 |
| never | 15 | 343 | 22.9 | 37 | 2.5 |
| no data | 10 | 178 | 17.8 | 15 | 1.5 |

Table 26 reveals a general trend: Speakers with the most extensive exposure to the media generally produce more quotes (56.5 quotes per speaker on average) and they also exhibit the highest ratio of *be like* (17.7 tokens per speaker). Note that both values show a declining trend as we move from speakers with higher levels of exposure to those demonstrating lower levels of exposure to mass media. In other words, speakers with lower levels of mass media consumption employ quotation as a discourse device somewhat less frequently. They are also much less likely to use *be like* in their speech. Given these results I have decided to split the group into (i) speakers with high levels of exposure to mass media, i.e. individuals who claim they watch television series and films in English two or three times a week and more and (ii) speakers with low levels of exposure to mass media, i.e. individuals who are reportedly exposed to media products once a week or less. In what follows, I explore variable quotative marking in both speaker groups.

### 5.4.1 High levels of exposure to mass media

Let us now peruse the overall composition of variable quotative marking as attested in speech of JNU students with high levels of exposure to mass media, presented in Table 27. My data set contains data from 30 speakers exhibiting such a profile. Notice first and foremost the relatively elevated numbers of variants featuring *like*. *Be like* makes up for 25.4% of the entire data set and when taken together with other quotative constructions featuring *like*, this figure amounts to 34.2%. Unsurprisingly perhaps, the other dominant variants are quotative *say* (18.2%) and zero-forms (14.6%).

Table 27: Overall distribution of quotative markers in speakers with high levels of exposure to mass media (N speakers = 30).

| Traditional variants | N | % |
| --- | --- | --- |
| *say* | 186 | 18.2% |
| other verbs of reporting | 84 | 8.2% |
| zero | 149 | 14.6% |
| *think* | 23 | 2.3% |
| other verbs of mental activity and perception | 17 | 1.7% |
| **Variants featuring *like*** | | |
| *be like* | 259 | 25.4% |
| *zero-like* | 55 | 5.4% |
| verb + *like* | 35 | 3.4% |
| **Variants featuring *okay* (*fine*)** | | |
| *be okay* | 5 | 0.5% |
| *zero-okay* | 26 | 2.5% |

Table 27 (continued)

| Variants featuring *okay (fine)* | N | % |
|---|---|---|
| verb + *okay* | 15 | 1.5% |
| verb + *that* + *okay* | 19 | 1.9% |
| **Variants featuring verb +** ***that*** | | |
| verb + *that* | 94 | 9.2% |
| verb + *that* + discourse marker | 8 | 0.8% |
| verb + noun + *that* | 2 | 0.2% |
| verb + noun + prep. + *that* | 4 | 0.4% |
| **Other variants** | | |
| copula *be* | 20 | 1.9% |
| verbs of motion | 2 | 0.2% |
| *ki* | 8 | 0.8% |
| verbs of achievement | 6 | 0.6% |
| *so* | 3 | 0.3% |
| TOTAL | 1020 | |

Exploring the distribution of the most frequent quotative forms with voice effects, reported in Table 28, pinpoints a connection between mimesis and innovative *be like*. Mimetic quotes occur with *be like* in 31.6% of all possible cases, which is nearly twice as much as the percentages reported for the traditional variants, i.e. zero-forms (17.6%), *say* (15.1%), and 'other' (12.9%). Non-mimetic quotes are, in contrast, clearly linked to *say* (23.2%). My speakers with high levels of exposure to mass media largely replicate the constraint 'mimesis' reported for mainstream parent varieties, notably North American English.

Table 28: Distribution of quotatives by mimesis for speakers with high levels of exposure to mass media.

| | *be like* | template | *say* | think | zero | okay | V+*that* | other |
|---|---|---|---|---|---|---|---|---|
| mimesis | 199 | 55 | 95 | 13 | 111 | 35 | 41 | 81 |
| | (31.6%) | (8.7%) | (15.1%) | (2.1%) | (17.6%) | (5.6%) | (6.5%) | (12.9%) |
| not | 60 | 35 | 91 | 10 | 38 | 31 | 65 | 60 |
| | (15.4%) | (8.9%) | (23.3%) | (2.6%) | (9.7%) | (7.9%) | (16.7%) | (15.4%) |

Considering the distribution of quotatives by quote type from a vertical perspective, we notice in Table 29 that speakers use *be like* indeterminately with both speech and thought (25.4% vs. 25.1%). Remarkably, and in contrast to the findings

**Table 29:** Distribution of quotatives by quote type for speakers with high levels of exposure to mass media.

|  | be like | template | say | think | zero | okay | V+that | other |
|---|---|---|---|---|---|---|---|---|
| speech | 184 (25.4%) | 63 (8.7%) | 172 (23.8%) | 2 (0.3%) | 111 (15.4%) | 45 (6.2%) | 41 (5.7%) | 105 (14.5%) |
| thought | 65 (25.1%) | 20 (7.7%) | 3 (1.2%) | 21 (8.1%) | 37 (14.3%) | 21 (8.1%) | 65 (25.1%) | 27 (10.4%) |
| indigenous | 10 (26.3%) | 7 (18.4%) | 11 (28.9%) | 0 (0.0%) | 1 (2.6%) | 0 (0.0%) | 0 (0.0%) | 9 (23.7%) |

reported in the previous literature, they also use *be like* with indigenous quotes or code-switched material at 26.3%, a function previously reported for quotative *say* (Davydova 2016a). Note, however, also an elevated rate of indigenous quotes with quotative *say* here (28.9%). I interpret this finding as evidence that *be like* has been evolving into a robust quotative marker in this speaker group, having extended its functions from speech and thought reporter to the introducer of indigenous quotes. In other words, the pattern seems to indicate a more advanced stage of grammaticalisation for *be like* here.

Furthermore, Table 30 reveals that the patterning for grammatical subject reported from earlier research is clearly visible in this data: *Be like* is overwhelmingly circumscribed to the neuter pronoun *it*, while being more frequent in first- than in third-person contexts.

**Table 30:** Distribution of quotatives by grammatical subject for speakers with high levels of exposure to mass media.

|  | be like | template | say | think | zero | okay | V+that | other |
|---|---|---|---|---|---|---|---|---|
| first | 102 (30.4%) | 29 (8.7%) | 49 (14.6%) | 19 (5.7%) | 36 (10.7%) | 21 (6.3%) | 35 (10.4%) | 44 (13.1%) |
| second | 2 (9.5%) | 4 (19.0%) | 4 (19.0%) | 0 (0.0%) | 1 (4.8%) | 2 (9.5%) | 2 (9.5%) | 6 (28.6%) |
| third | 124 (22.4%) | 49 (8.8%) | 131 (23.6%) | 4 (0.7%) | 60 (10.8%) | 35 (6.3%) | 66 (11.9%) | 85 (15.3%) |
| it | 30 (78.9%) | 1 (2.6%) | 1 (2.6%) | 0 (0.0%) | 1 (2.6%) | 2 (5.3%) | 1 (2.6%) | 2 (5.3%) |
| NA | 1 (0.7%) | 7 (9.9%) | 1 (0.7%) | 0 (0.0%) | 51 (71.8%) | 6 (8.5%) | 2 (2.8%) | 4 (5.6%) |

Finally, Table 31 examines the distribution of quotative choices by tense marking in the quotative frame. Here, *be like* clearly functions as a narrative CHP marker

**Table 31:** Distribution of quotatives by tense for speakers with high levels of exposure to mass media.

|         | be like  | template | say     | think  | zero    | okay    | V+that  | other   |
|---------|----------|----------|---------|--------|---------|---------|---------|---------|
| CHP     | 63       | 4        | 28      | 3      | 0       | 1       | 7       | 20      |
|         | (50.0%)  | (3.2%)   | (22.2%) | (2.4%) | (0.0%)  | (0.8%)  | (5.6%)  | (15.9%) |
| present | 42       | 9        | 29      | 3      | 0       | 8       | 15      | 32      |
|         | (30.4%)  | (6.5%)   | (21.0%) | (2.2%) | (0.0%)  | (5.8%)  | (10.9%) | (23.2%) |
| past    | 146      | 19       | 100     | 15     | 0       | 20      | 64      | 62      |
|         | (34.3%)  | (4.4%)   | (23.5%) | (3.5%) | (0.0%)  | (4.7%)  | (15.0%) | (14.6%) |
| modal   | 6        | 6        | 27      | 1      | 0       | 5       | 16      | 20      |
|         | (7.4%)   | (7.4%)   | (33.3%) | (1.2%) | (0.0%)  | (6.2%)  | (19.8%) | (24.7%) |
| NA      | 2        | 52       | 2       | 1      | 149     | 32      | 4       | 7       |
|         | (0.8%)   | (20.9%)  | (0.8%)  | (0.4%) | (59.8%) | (12.9%) | (1.6%)  | (2.8%)  |

(50%). My high-exposure speakers follow closely the pattern reported for North American English. Unsurprisingly, *say* and traditional quotatives from the category 'other' occur with a variety of tense markers, although both are most frequent with modal forms.

### 5.4.2 Low levels of exposure to mass media

What does the system of variable quotative marking look like in speech of those students who are reportedly exposed to English-speaking films and television series once a week or less? Stemming from 40 speakers in total, the distributional analysis of the overall composition of variants pinpoints quotative *say* as the prevalent element in the system (29.8%) followed by zero-forms (10.8%), 'verb + that' (10.7%), and other verbs of reporting (10.5%). Table 32 also indicates that the frequency of *be like* plummets down to 10.4%, which is 15 percentage points below the rate reported for JNU students with extensive viewing habits. This is a considerable decline in the use of the worldwide attested variant across the two speaker cohorts ($\chi^2$ (1): 50.5, $p < 0.001$), raising the question concerning the influence of mass media in the spread of global linguistic innovations, a hotly debated topic in current sociolinguistic research (Androutsopoulos 2014a; Bell and Sharma 2014). What is at issue here is, 'Will the low-level exposure ESL speakers be able to replicate the variable constraints underlying the use of quotative *be like* and if so, to what extent? And how does their grammar compare to the grammar of variable quotative marking reported for my high-exposure speakers of Indian English?' The remainder of this chapter will focus on this question.

**Table 32:** Overall distribution of quotative markers for speakers with low levels of exposure to mass media (N speakers = 40).

| Traditional variants | N | % |
| --- | --- | --- |
| *say* | 274 | 29.8% |
| other verbs of reporting | 97 | 10.5% |
| zero | 99 | 10.8% |
| *think* | 30 | 3.3% |
| other verbs of mental activity and perception | 28 | 3.0% |
| **Variants featuring *like*** | | |
| *be like* | 96 | 10.4% |
| zero-*like* | 44 | 4.8% |
| verb + *like* | 20 | 2.2% |
| **Variants featuring *okay* (*fine*)** | | |
| *be okay* | 2 | 0.2% |
| zero-*okay* | 24 | 2.6% |
| verb + *okay* | 23 | 2.5% |
| verb + *that* + *okay* | 21 | 2.3% |
| **Variants featuring verb + *that*** | | |
| verb + *that* | 98 | 10.7% |
| verb + *that* + discourse marker | 12 | 1.3% |
| verb + noun + *that* | 0 | 0.0% |
| verb + noun + prep. + *that* | 1 | 0.1% |
| **Other variants** | | |
| copula *be* | 17 | 1.8% |
| verbs of motion | 5 | 0.5% |
| *ki* | 19 | 2.1% |
| verbs of achievement | 3 | 0.3% |
| *so* | 7 | 0.8% |
| TOTAL | 920 | |

The distribution of quotatives across the factor group 'mimesis', reported in Table 33, yields quite a different picture than that reported for the cohort of students with high levels of media consumption. Attested at the rate of 16.0%, *be like* stands in very strong competition with other elements, notably *say* (25.0%), other verbs of reporting (18.6%) as well as zero-forms (16.0%) as a mimesis introducer. In fact, it is quotative *say* that is recruited by my low-exposure speakers most frequently in order to introduce various voice effects in constructed dialogue. The vertical perspective, however, reveals that *be like* is more frequent with mimetic quotes, whenever my informants choose to use the variant.

**Table 33:** Distribution of quotatives by mimesis for speakers with low levels of exposure to mass media.

|         | be like | template | say     | think  | zero    | okay   | V+that  | other   |
|---------|---------|----------|---------|--------|---------|--------|---------|---------|
| mimesis | 73      | 30       | 114     | 16     | 73      | 25     | 40      | 85      |
|         | (16.0%) | (6.6%)   | (25.0%) | (3.5%) | (16.0%) | (5.5%) | (8.8%)  | (18.6%) |
| not     | 23      | 34       | 160     | 14     | 26      | 45     | 71      | 91      |
|         | (4.9%)  | (7.3%)   | (34.5%) | (3.0%) | (5.6%)  | (9.7%) | (15.3%) | (19.6%) |

Presented in Table 34, the distributional analysis of the tokens by factor 'quote type' shows unequivocally that *be like* is far more frequent with reported thought than it is with speech (16.1% vs. 8.7%), while providing a solid contribution to the construction of inner dialogue overall. Quotative *say* and other verbs of reporting are primarily responsible for the introduction of direct speech proper in constructed dialogue at 36.0% and 20.7% respectively. The propensity of *say* to introduce indigenous speech patterns well with previous findings reported in Davydova and Buchstaller (2015: 455) and, unsurprisingly, *say* is the major variant introducing code-switches.

**Table 34:** Distribution of quotatives by quote type for speakers with low levels of exposure to mass media.

|            | be like | template | say     | think   | zero    | okay    | V+that  | other   |
|------------|---------|----------|---------|---------|---------|---------|---------|---------|
| speech     | 57      | 41       | 237     | 3       | 65      | 40      | 79      | 136     |
|            | (8.7%)  | (6.2%)   | (36.0%) | (0.5%)  | (9.9%)  | (6.1%)  | (12.0%) | (20.7%) |
| thought    | 34      | 20       | 11      | 25      | 31      | 30      | 30      | 30      |
|            | (16.1%) | (9.5%)   | (5.2%)  | (11.8%) | (14.7%) | (14.2%) | (14.2%) | (14.2%) |
| indigenous | 5       | 3        | 26      | 2       | 3       | 0       | 2       | 10      |
|            | (9.8%)  | (5.9%)   | (50.9%) | (3.9%)  | (5.9%)  | (0.0%)  | (3.9%)  | (19.6%) |

As for grammatical subject, patterns attested for *be like* are quite unsurprising. First-person context favours the occurrence of *be like* over third-person contexts, if only very slightly (10.3% vs. 8.6%). The impact of third-person neuter *it* is remarkably consistent in this data set, in that it is, as predicted, invariably linked to *be like* (58.1%). Showing a propensity to occur with self-quotes, *think* is circumscribed to first-person contexts. Nevertheless, it is interesting that *say* and other traditional quotative markers (category 'other' and zero-quotes) introduce not only third-person speakers; they are used with first-person grammatical subjects as well, which contrasts with previous reports in the literature (see Buchstaller 2014: 130).

**Table 35:** Distribution of quotatives by grammatical subject for speakers with low levels of exposure to mass media.

|        | be like | template | say | think | zero | okay | V+that | other |
|--------|---------|----------|-----|-------|------|------|--------|-------|
| first  | 34 (10.3%) | 29 (8.8%) | 105 (31.9%) | 26 (7.9%) | 23 (6.9%) | 23 (6.9%) | 28 (8.5%) | 61 (18.5%) |
| second | 1 (5.0%) | 0 (0.0%) | 6 (30.0%) | 0 (0.0%) | 1 (5.0%) | 3 (15.0%) | 2 (10.0%) | 7 (35.0%) |
| third  | 41 (8.6%) | 28 (5.8%) | 161 (33.6%) | 4 (0.8%) | 35 (7.3%) | 37 (7.7%) | 80 (16.7%) | 93 (19.4%) |
| it     | 18 (58.1%) | 0 (0.0%) | 1 (3.2%) | 0 (0.0%) | 0 (0.0%) | 2 (6.5%) | 1 (3.2%) | 9 (29.0%) |
| NA     | 2 (3.3%) | 7 (11.5%) | 1 (1.6%) | 0 (0.0%) | 40 (65.6%) | 5 (8.2%) | 0 (0.0%) | 6 (9.8%) |

Let us now turn our attention to Table 3 investigating the functional allocation of *be like* and its major competitor variants by tense. In contrast to the pattern documented for students with high levels of exposure to mass media, my low-exposure speakers do not overwhelmingly use *be like* with CHP marking. In fact, it is quotative *say* that is marked for CHP most frequently in the data set at 36.6%. (As a side note, *say* and 'other' quotative markers are used with a host of different temporal forms, which is in line with the previously reported patterns discussed above.) What is, however, important to point out is that whenever speakers from this cohort use *be like*, they map it, first and foremost, on CHP followed by generic present and past tense morphology (26.8% vs. 14.8% vs. 12.0%).

**Table 36:** Distribution of quotatives by tense for speakers with low levels of exposure to mass media.

|         | be like | template | say | think | zero | okay | V+that | other |
|---------|---------|----------|-----|-------|------|------|--------|-------|
| CHP     | 19 (26.8%) | 3 (4.2%) | 26 (36.6%) | 0 (0.0%) | 0 (0.0%) | 1 (1.4%) | 12 (16.9%) | 10 (14.1%) |
| present | 24 (14.8%) | 6 (3.7%) | 58 (35.8%) | 3 (1.9%) | 0 (0.0%) | 11 (6.8%) | 21 (12.9%) | 39 (24.1%) |
| past    | 50 (12.0%) | 9 (2.2%) | 151 (36.3%) | 27 (6.5%) | 0 (0.0%) | 24 (5.8%) | 59 (14.2%) | 96 (23.1%) |
| modal   | 2 (2.1%) | 5 (5.2%) | 38 (39.2%) | 0 (0.0%) | 0 (0.0%) | 12 (12.4%) | 18 (18.6%) | 22 (22.7%) |
| NA      | 1 (0.6%) | 41 (23.6%) | 1 (0.6%) | 0 (0.0%) | 99 (56.9%) | 22 (12.6%) | 1 (0.6%) | 9 (5.2%) |

In sum, the distributional analyses of quotative marking reveal that speakers with higher mass media intake produce significantly more tokens of *be like* ($\chi^2$ (1): 50.5, *p* < 0.001). More specifically, they use *be like* at the overall rate of 25.4% (N 259/1020), which contrasts with the rate produced by students with more moderate mass media consumption habits. Let us recall that such speakers use *be like* in 10.4% of all cases (N 96/920). More importantly, the former cohort features a system of quotative marking in which *be like* has spread substantially into all the relevant contexts. In contrast, we have seen that low-level exposure speakers tend to employ other quotative markers, notably quotative *say*, in the functional niches associated with *be like* in L1 speech of English-speaking young adults.

These findings are informative as they indicate that ESL speakers have adopted an innovative global feature in their speech and those showing higher levels of exposure to mass media are also more adept, at least from a horizontal perspective, at reconstructing the variable patterns of use that go with it. Notice, however, that from a vertical perspective both speaker groups are on a par in that their use of quotative *be like* is largely aligned with the predictions outlined in Chapter 3. Whenever speakers of Indian English recruit *be like* in their speech, it is used more frequently with mimetic quotes, first person grammatical subject, and CHP. Moreover, low-exposure bilinguals prefer *be like* with thought over speech. In turn, high-exposure speakers exhibit a levelled pattern using *be like* to signal inner dialogue and direct speech proper. This tendency indicates a more evolved status of *be like* in speech of this group, well aligned the most recent trends reported for North American English (Gardner et al. 2013; Tagliamonte and D'Arcy 2007). In conclusion, the differences detected between the high- and low-exposure groups raise the question concerning the impact that the media exerts on the propagation of linguistic innovations on the one hand and the linguistic behaviour of its consumers on the other. I will revisit this issue in the next chapter focusing on the variable grammar of quotative marking in Learner English.

# 6 The Learner ecology of quotation

This chapter proceeds with the discussion of the local uses of the major speech and thought introducers, while focusing on an EFL setting comparable to the JNU community described in the previous chapter. My major goal here is to describe the system of variable quotative marking and its language-internal conditioning as it is attested in speech of German students at the UM and to contrast it with those reported for native-speaker Englishes (see Chapter 3) and indigenised English (see Chapter 5). As in the previous chapter, I consider local (EFL) ecologies here in an attempt to describe the sociolinguistic mechanisms shaping the evolution of the newest forms of English.

UM is composed of young individuals completing their Bachelors' and Masters' degrees in the field of humanities and social sciences. Part of Germany's national "Excellence Initiative", the university is renowned for its successful attempts to cross-fertilise the (traditional) social science disciplines, notably business administration, and linguistics. UM boasts a body of 12,000 students, most of whom are native speakers of German and German dialects. UM is a good diagnostic of the EFL environment because it hosts a vibrant international student community, which is an immediate result of the institution's educational policies. English is the language frequently employed during lectures and other courses of instruction, although, in contrast to the ESL setting, English is not the obligatory tool of education at the tertiary level. Depending on the nature of their social networks, German students come into contact with international students, employing English as a default language. German, however, is the language predominant in informal interactions among students. It is the preferred means of every day communication to the extent that even international students seek to acquire at least some working knowledge of German in order to gain fuller benefits from their studies at UM. A further defining feature of the UM student community is its international mobility. It is not unusual for a German speaking UM student to have spent at least several months abroad, oftentimes in an English-speaking environment. The kind of English that these learners end up speaking is then, to a large extent, a function of classroom input and naturalistic exposure to L1 and international English, which is in fundamental contrast to how users acquire and use English in India.

The data for this case study was obtained from the MaCGE, a collection of one-on-one sociolinguistic interviews, approximately one hour in length, recorded in 2013–2015. The interviews were carried out by student assistants and can thus be taken to represent an authentic style of students' speech. The data stems from 97 individuals (41 males and 56 females), aged 18 to 26, all enrolled in Bachelor's and Master's degree programmes at UM. The data employed in this case study was collected under conditions methodologically similar to those applied during the field work at JNU. The student assistants were instructed to cover the topics and the questions listed in the interview schedule guide (see Appendix A), while at the same time providing their informants with enough freedom so that they could relax into the story they were telling and forget about language monitoring. This technique allows the researcher to minimise the infamous *observer's paradox* (Labov 1972b) and obtain the most authentic type of data coming directly from the learner's stream of consciousness and thus devoid of any self-corrections and overtly standardised language. Sociolinguistic interviews were accompanied by a background questionnaire which elicited a wealth of information about speakers' sociolinguistic backgrounds (see Appendix C).

Let us now examine the overall composition of quotative marking in the Learner variety of German English as it is attested in speech of students at UM. It is clear from the data presented in Table 37, one easily notices that the system is

Table 37: Overall distribution of quotative markers in German Learner English, MaCGE 2013–2015 (N speakers = 97).

| Traditional variants | N | % |
| --- | --- | --- |
| *say* (see example 88) | 541 | 36.1% |
| other verbs of reporting (see example 89) | 132 | 8.8% |
| zero (see example 90) | 212 | 14.2% |
| *think* (see example 91) | 101 | 6.7% |
| other verbs of mental activity and perception (see example 92) | 35 | 2.3% |
| **Variants featuring *like*** | | |
| *be like* (see example 93) | 304 | 20.3% |
| *zero-like* (see example 94) | 66 | 4.4% |
| *say like* (see example 95) | 23 | 1.5% |
| other collocations with *like* (see example 96) | 15 | 1.0% |
| *think like* (see example 97) | 8 | 0.5% |
| *feel like* (see example 98) | 6 | 0.4% |
| *know like* (see example 99) | 3 | 0.2% |
| **Other variants** | | |
| copula *be* (see example 100) | 43 | 2.9% |
| *go* (see example 101) | 5 | 0.3% |
| verb + *that* (see example 102) | 2 | 0.1% |
| *okay* (see example 103) | 1 | 0.1% |
| TOTAL | 1497 | |

clearly dominated by traditional variants, notably quotative *say* (36.1%) and, to some degree, zero-quotes (14.2%). *Be like* contributes a solid 20.3% to the entire system, which contrasts with how young speakers of native English recruit this variant while constructing dialogue. The most recent accounts report that in L1 English, *be like* is attested at the rate ranging between 43% and 72% (Buchstaller 2014: 119; Gardner et al. 2013). All structures featuring *like* amount to 28.1% of the entire data set, a finding comparable to that reported in Davydova and Buchstaller (2015). Similar to JNU students, my German learners are still lagging behind the L1 cohort regards the overall use of the innovative feature. What is also of interest is that the Learner quotative system does not feature any local contact-induced innovations. This is, indeed, remarkable given that quotation is an "extraordinary dynamic domain" (Buchstaller 2014: 1) yielding a variety of novel variants across languages and varieties (see also Chapter 3), and we have already seen that the indigenised variety of Indian English is no exception to this pervasive trend. The Learner variety of German English is, however, best described as standard conformant: traditional variants lead the way, while the global linguistic innovation has just begun making inroads into the system.

Listed below are the examples of individual tokens illustrating how quotative markers occur in the EFL data.

(88) They **said** to her, 'I don't have a picture for you.' (MaCGE: GE121)

(89) And they came and they **told** us, 'Yeah, yeah, I am from (mimicking) Edinburgh.' … after that everybody **asked** me, 'Oh, why? What has happened?' (MaCGE: GE88; GE105)

(90) 'I've never been here, I don't know, why can't I enter?' - 'No, you are not allowed.' (MaCGE: GE100)

(91) When I hear identity (,) I **think**, 'Oh, my God! Problem! Who am I?' (MaCGE: GE03)

(92) I **realised**, 'Oh, my God! These are actually real people, not just your professors.' then I **recognised**, 'Oh, I'm just like my parents.' (MaCGE: GE105; GE116)

(93) And we all **were like**, 'Oh, my God! What just happened?' (MaCGE: GE91)

(94) I mean they will probably look at you like in a funny way **like**, '(mimicking).' Giving you the face (.) (MaCGE: GE147)

(95) Then the other first of all **says like**, 'How about dancing?' (MaCGE: GE103)

(96)  He **yelled** at me **like,** 'Hey, you were going to fast. I saw you.' (MaCGE: GE98)

(97)  And I **think like,** 'It's really a lot of crap that they eat!' (MaCGE: GE112)

(98)  I think it was after my Australia trip (,) I **felt like,** 'Okay, I really did it and I did it by myself.' (MaCGE: GE99)

(99)  But when I received the letter from the University of Mannheim (,) I **knew like,** 'Okay, now I can quit my job.' (MaCGE: GE169)

(100) And I **was,** 'No, I've never been to Australia! Okay!' (chuckles) (MaCGE: GE24)

(101) My roommate gave me a real weird look and she **goes,** 'Can I ask you something?' I was like, 'Okay.' (MaCGE: GE97)

(102) They always **say that,** 'If you want something, you have to work for that.' They never give me money (.) (MaCGE: GE117)

(103) **Okay,** 'Fifteen minutes more.' (MaCGE: 121)

Having considered the most general picture of quotative marking in Learner English, I am now seeking to spot those groups of students within the UM community that might be responsible for advancing the global linguistic change on a local basis. Given that international student mobility plays such an important role in the EFL settings of the economically advanced countries of Western Europe, including Germany, I firstly stratify the sample by the amount of exposure to English in naturalistic settings in order to explore the overall ratios of quotative strategies on the one hand and the use of innovative *be like* by individuals on the other.

Table 38 pinpoints two clear trends: Learners with lower levels of naturalistic exposure are also the ones who (i) produce the lowest number of quotation overall

**Table 38:** Distribution of quotative markers by amount of stay-abroad exposure (N speakers = 97; N quotatives = 1497; N *be like* = 304).

| Time abroad | N (speakers) | N (quotes) | Ratio quotes/ speaker | N (*be like*) | Ratio *be like*/ speaker |
|---|---|---|---|---|---|
| up to two months | 34 | 297 | 8.7 | 62 | 1.8 |
| two to six months | 32 | 405 | 12.7 | 68 | 2.1 |
| seven to 11 months | 14 | 418 | 29.9 | 72 | 5.1 |
| more than 12 months | 17 | 377 | 22.2 | 102 | 6.0 |

and (ii) they also use proportionately fewer forms of *be like*. Crucially, an overwhelming majority of quotatives including the innovative variant in this speaker group was produced by informants who had never been abroad but exhibit high levels of exposure to vernacular English through the media, television series, and shows. Consistent with the results of previous research (Davydova and Buchstaller 2015), this finding leads me to the conclusion that the minimum of two months of stay-abroad experience is needed for the quotation device to begin to emerge within the learner grammar. I will return to this issue in Section 6.5.

Against this backdrop and relying on the information contained in the background questionnaire, I decided to draw a distinction between the learners exhibiting higher levels of exposure (two months and more) and those with the minimum amount of exposure (up to two months). The learner samples are presented in Table 39 for convenience.

**Table 39:** German learners by amount and type of exposure.

| Type of exposure | Number of speakers |
|---|---|
| *High-level naturalistic exposure* | |
| dominant exposure to North American English | 21 |
| dominant exposure to UK English | 8 |
| mixed exposure (North America, UK, and Australia/New Zealand) | 22 |
| dominant exposure in lingua franca contexts | 12 |
| *Low-level naturalistic exposure* | |
| high media-exposure learners | 18 |
| low media-exposure learners | 16 |
| Overall total | 97 |

Previous studies have amassed a body of evidence that the study abroad setting has a fostering impact on the acquisition of vernacular features and vernacular grammars by language learners (see *inter alia* Geeslin et al. 2012; Regan 1995, 1996, 2004; Regan, Howard, and Lemée 2009), and so the results reported in Table 38 are not highly surprising. With this said, the major hallmark of the sample tackled in this case study is the heterogeneity of EFL learners' individual exposures to naturalistic English. Inquiry into speakers' biographies as well as careful assessment of background questionnaires revealed that not only did the learner differ from each other with respect to the amount of exposure to naturalistic English; they also contrasted with each other regards the quality of such naturalistic exposure. Given the overall diversity of naturalistic inputs inherent in the sample, I have classified the high-level exposure cohort into (i) learners with the dominant exposure to North American English, (ii) learners with the dominant exposure to UK English, (iii) learners with mixed exposures to North American, UK, and New Zealand/Australian English, (iv) learners with the dominant exposure to English in multilingual settings or lingua franca contexts (i.e. India, Singapore, South Africa, countries of East Asia, Scandinavian countries, and countries of southwestern Europe). In other words, in these settings, my German learners had a chance to speak English while communicating with other non-native speakers for prolonged periods of time. The low-level naturalistic exposure learners were, in turn, subdivided into two further cohorts revealing the amount of contact to L1 English through the media.

Such a stratification of the sample is an important one as it allows me to explore the effect of exposure to North American English, the alleged epicentre of quotative *be like*, by contrasting the variable grammar of US dominant learners to those of UK dominant students as well as mixed exposure learners. Secondly, the research design also allows me to ascertain the extent to which language learners are capable of reconstructing the variable use of quotative marking once they are forced to use English extensively with other non-native speakers. Interactions with other L2 speakers of English in a lingua franca context are becoming increasingly important in the modern world. Such interactions provide important sociolinguistic venues shaping the development of World Englishes. Variationist sociolinguistic research should expand its focus to comprise those contexts as well in order to assess their overall anthropological dynamics and the role they might play in the propagation of global linguistic changes. Crucially, the sociolinguistic information contained in the students' individual backgrounds enabled me to differentiate between two types of learners exhibiting low-levels of naturalistic exposure: (i) learners with extensive mass media viewing habits and (ii) those with very limited ones. Such a distinction is an important one as well as it allows me to explore the effect of exposure to mass media on the formation of the quotative system, while disentangling the confounding effect produced by the exposure to English in naturalistic environments. In what follows, I present and discuss the variable grammars that emerged as a result of these diverse sociolinguistic experiences with English.

## 6.1 North American exposure dominant learners

We begin our exploration of the variable realisation of verbs and verbal structures introducing quotation in Learner English by focusing on speakers exhibiting high levels of exposure to naturalistic English spoken on the North American continent. This learner cohort is represented by 21 students who spent at least three months in the US or Canada. The average amount of stay-abroad exposure amounts, however, to 9.6 months in this learner group.

The overall distribution of forms is provided in Table 40, which pinpoints two competing variants in the pool of speech and thought introducers. These are quotative *say* and *be like*, contributing equal shares to the variability of the data set, 28.9% and 28.6% respectively. If we consider them as a whole, constructions including *like* account for 36.9% of variation. Evidently, this falls well below the cut-off point attested for young speakers from the US and Canada in the 2000s (compare with Table 1 in Chapter 3).

**Table 40:** Overall distribution of quotative markers in North American exposure dominant learners (N speakers = 21).

| Traditional variants | N | % |
| --- | --- | --- |
| *say* | 142 | 28.9% |
| other verbs of reporting | 43 | 8.8% |
| zero | 78 | 16.0% |
| *think* | 18 | 3.7% |
| other verbs of mental activity and perception | 12 | 2.5% |
| **Variants featuring *like*** | | |
| *be like* | 140 | 28.6% |
| zero-*like* | 19 | 3.9% |
| *say like* | 4 | 0.8% |
| other collocations with *like* | 6 | 1.2% |
| *think like* | 5 | 1.0% |
| *feel like* | 4 | 0.8% |
| *know like* | 3 | 0.6% |
| **Other variants** | 16 | 3.2% |
| TOTAL | 490 | |

Let us now scrutinise the system-internal conditioning that governs variable realisation of quotative marking in this learner group. In order to ensure a high level of comparability with the results presented in the preceding chapter and previous studies on L1 English, I focus on the six major variants traditionally treated in this type of analysis (see, for instance, Buchstaller 2014; D'Arcy 2012; Davydova and Buchstaller 2015). These include quotative *say*, *think*, zero-quotatives, and the category 'other', which consists of low-frequency tokens. Quotative *be like* is treated separately from the category 'template' comprising zero-*likes* and collocative constructions featuring *like* (*say like*, *feel like* etc.).

Table 41 shows the distribution of the main variants by the factor group 'mimesis'. Quotes reporting sounds and gestures as well as expressively rendered lexical material are clearly linked to *be like* (33.4%), whereas quotes constructed with a regular speaking voice tend to be introduced by *say* (42.3%). Notice also that zero-forms tend to occur with mimetic quotes, a trend well-established in native Englishes (Buchstaller 2014: 133, 134).

**Table 41:** Distribution of quotatives by mimesis for North American exposure dominant learners.

|         | be like      | template   | say         | think      | zero        | other       |
|---------|--------------|------------|-------------|------------|-------------|-------------|
| mimesis | 118 (33.4%)  | 26 (7.4%)  | 84 (23.8%)  | 13 (3.7%)  | 68 (19.3%)  | 44 (12.5%)  |
| not     | 22 (16.1%)   | 15 (10.9%) | 58 (42.3%)  | 5 (3.6%)   | 10 (7.3%)   | 27 (19.7%)  |

The second system-internal constraint explored here is quote type. Presented in Table 42, it reveals a close association between quotative *say* and direct speech proper (34.5%). *Say* is also unambiguously mapped onto quotes containing indigenous code-switches into German (47.6%). A similar pattern has been ascertained for speakers of Indian English in the previous chapter. Whereas the category 'template' is used with quotes introducing thought more frequently than with those introducing speech (14.5% vs. 6.4%), *be like* is evenly spread out across both linguistic contexts (30.9% vs. 28.7%). This could be interpreted as a sign that German students demonstrating high levels of exposure to North American English have picked up on the most recent levelling tendencies reported for North American English (Gardner et al. 2013), whereby *be like* is used to introduce internal dialogue just as frequently as it is used to introduce direct speech.

**Table 42:** Distribution of quotatives by quote type for North American exposure dominant learners.

|            | be like      | template   | say          | think       | zero        | other       |
|------------|--------------|------------|--------------|-------------|-------------|-------------|
| speech     | 103 (28.7%)  | 23 (6.4%)  | 124 (34.5%)  | 1 (0.3%)    | 59 (16.4%)  | 49 (13.6%)  |
| thought    | 34 (30.9%)   | 16 (14.5%) | 8 (7.2%)     | 17 (15.5%)  | 18 (16.4%)  | 17 (15.5%)  |
| indigenous | 3 (14.3%)    | 2 (9.5%)   | 10 (47.6%)   | 0 (0.0%)    | 1 (4.8%)    | 5 (23.8%)   |

Considering the distributional trends within the system by grammatical subject, demonstrated in Table 43, two important tendencies come to the forefront of the analyst's attention. Firstly, *be like* is clearly circumscribed to the neuter pronoun *it*, leading way in this particular context above all other linguistic variants at 66.7%. Secondly, *be like* is evenly distributed among the first- and third-person contexts, which could be an indication that these learners have acquired the

**Table 43:** Distribution of quotatives by grammatical subject for North American exposure dominant learners.

|        | be like     | template   | say        | think     | zero       | other      |
|--------|-------------|------------|------------|-----------|------------|------------|
| first  | 43 (31.6%)  | 11 (8.1%)  | 41 (30.1%) | 12 (8.8%) | 11 (8.1%)  | 18 (13.2%) |
| second | 2 (6.1%)    | 4 (12.1%)  | 10 (30.3%) | 5 (15.1%) | 2 (6.1%)   | 10 (30.3%) |
| third  | 81 (31.6%)  | 19 (7.4%)  | 89 (34.8%) | 1 (0.4%)  | 30 (11.7%) | 36 (14.1%) |
| it     | 14 (66.7%)  | 0 (0.0%)   | 1 (4.8%)   | 0 (0.0%)  | 0 (0.0%)   | 6 (28.6%)  |
| NA     | 0 (0.0%)    | 7 (15.9%)  | 1 (2.3%)   | 0 (0.0%)  | 35 (79.5%) | 1 (2.3%)   |

levelled system, in which *be like* is used with both first- and third-person grammatical subjects, 31.6% and 31.6% respectively (Buchstaller 2014; D'Arcy 2004; Ferrara and Bell 1995; Sanchez and Charity 1991).

The perusal of distributional trends by tense marking, as revealed in Table 44, demonstrates that *be like* tends to encode CHP in this data set (61.4%), which accords well with the pattern documented for native Englishes (Buchstaller and D'Arcy 2009). In line with previous research, *say* is marked for a host of tenses, although it appears to be more frequent with modals (70.9%), which is again consistent with foregoing research (see also Chapter 5).

**Table 44:** Distribution of quotatives by tense marking for North American exposure dominant learners.

|         | be like    | template   | say        | think     | zero       | other      |
|---------|------------|------------|------------|-----------|------------|------------|
| CHP     | 27 (61.4%) | 2 (4.5%)   | 11 (25.0%) | 0 (0.0%)  | 0 (0.0%)   | 4 (9.1%)   |
| present | 25 (25.8%) | 3 (3.1%)   | 35 (36.1%) | 7 (7.2%)  | 0 (0.0%)   | 27 (27.8%) |
| past    | 88 (39.8%) | 13 (5.9%)  | 74 (33.5%) | 11 (5.0%) | 0 (0.0%)   | 35 (15.8%) |
| modal   | 0 (0.0%)   | 4 (13.0%)  | 22 (70.9%) | 0 (0.0%)  | 0 (0.0%)   | 5 (16.1%)  |
| NA      | 0 (0.0%)   | 19 (19.6%) | 0 (0.0%)   | 0 (0.0%)  | 78 (80.4%) | 0 (0.0%)   |

Summing up, speakers with dominant exposure to North American English demonstrate a system of variable quotative marking dominated by two variants, one of which is traditional (quotative *say*) and the other is innovative (quotative *be like*). As far as the overall frequency of use of *be like* is concerned, my German learners are still lagging behind their L1 peers. Remarkably, however, they replicate the language-internal conditioning underlying the use of the innovative variant with the most precise detail. To be more exact, they link *be like* to mimetic quotes marked for CHP. They furthermore use this linguistic innovation to introduce thought as well as speech, and they use it evenly in first- and third-person contexts, both of which are the most recent levelling tendencies in L1 English.

## 6.2 UK exposure dominant learners

Let us now turn our attention to the discussion of the variable quotative system produced by learners with high levels of exposure to UK English. This learner cohort consists of eight students who spent the minimum of three months, and 7.3 months on average, in one of the countries of the United Kingdom of Great Britain and Northern Ireland. The results produced by this speaker group are treated with caution here due to the relatively low speaker and token numbers (eight speakers producing 85 tokens of quotation). For this reason, they are not included into a general summary of quotative marking across German learners' cohorts reported in Table 71.

To begin with, the overall distributional analysis reveals that quotative *say* clearly dominates the system at 27.1% followed by zero-forms (16.5%) and quotative *be like* (16.5%). Notice that the frequency of *be like* has diminished by

Table 45: Overall distribution of quotative markers in UK exposure dominant learners (N speakers = 8).

| Traditional variants | N | % |
|---|---|---|
| *say* | 23 | 27.1% |
| other verbs of reporting | 9 | 10.6% |
| zero | 14 | 16.5% |
| *think* | 8 | 9.4% |
| other verbs of mental activity and perception | 3 | 3.5% |
| **Variants featuring *like*** | | |
| *be like* | 14 | 16.5% |
| *zero-like* | 5 | 5.9% |
| *say like* | 6 | 7.1% |
| other collocations with *like* | 0 | 0.0% |
| *think like* | 1 | 1.2% |
| *feel like* | 0 | 0.0% |
| *know like* | 0 | 0.0% |
| **Other variants** | 2 | 2.4% |
| TOTAL | 85 | |

12 percentage points when compared to the US exposure dominant cohort. This is not entirely surprising given that the young Brits tend to produce this form at a much lower rate when contrasted with their peers from the US and Canada (see inter alia Buchstaller 2014: 119). Remarkably, German learners mirror this tendency, albeit at a lower rate.

A highly interesting pattern emerges from the perusal of the distributional trends by mimetic content, presented in Table 46. In contrast to the working hypothesis which assigns the mimetic function to the innovative variant, mimetic contexts are allotted in fairly equal shares to quotative *be like* (24.4%), zero-quotes (22.2%), category 'template' (20.0%), various traditional variants from the category 'other' (17.8%) and, finally, quotative *say* (15.6%) when considered from a horizontal perspective. From a vertical angle, *be like* is, however, still more frequent with mimesis than non-mimesis (24.4% vs. 7.5%).

Table 46: Distribution of quotatives by mimesis for UK exposure dominant learners.

|  | be like | template | say | think | zero | other |
|---|---|---|---|---|---|---|
| mimesis | 11 (24.4%) | 9 (20.0%) | 7 (15.6%) | 0 (0.0%) | 10 (22.2%) | 8 (17.8%) |
| not | 3 (7.5%) | 3 (7.5%) | 16 (40.0%) | 8 (20.0%) | 4 (10.0%) | 6 (15.0%) |

Looking at the distribution of variants by quote type, shown in Table 47, one should notice that from a vertical perspective, quotative *be like*, the category 'template', zero-quotatives, and other traditional forms are used quite evenly to introduce both direct speech and inner monologue. Conversely, *say* links directly to the introduction of speech (35.0%), whereas *think* is the major introducer of inner dialogue in this data set (32.0%).

Table 47: Distribution of quotatives by quote type for UK exposure dominant learners.

|  | be like | template | say | think | zero | other |
|---|---|---|---|---|---|---|
| speech | 10 (16.6%) | 9 (15.0%) | 21 (35.0%) | 0 (0.0%) | 10 (16.7%) | 10 (16.7%) |
| thought | 4 (16.0%) | 3 (12.0%) | 2 (8.0%) | 8 (32.0%) | 4 (16.0%) | 4 (16.0%) |
| indigenous | 0 (0.0%) | 0 (0.0%) | 0 (0.0%) | 0 (0.0%) | 0 (0.0%) | 0 (0.0%) |

The percentage frequencies of quotative markers by grammatical subjects, illustrated in Table 48, reveal that, similarly to the category 'template', quotative *be like* is more frequent with third-person grammatical subject (25.6%) than with the first person (14.3%). This pattern is not aligned with the hypothesis regards the use of *be like* with grammatical subject predicting a strong link to first-person

Table 48: Distribution of quotatives by grammatical subject for UK exposure dominant learners.

|        | be like    | template  | say        | think     | zero       | other      |
|--------|------------|-----------|------------|-----------|------------|------------|
| first  | 4 (14.3%)  | 2 (7.1%)  | 7 (25.0%)  | 7 (25.0%) | 0 (0.0%)   | 8 (28.6%)  |
| second | 0 (0.0%)   | 1 (20.0%) | 3 (60.0%)  | 1 (20.0%) | 0 (0.0%)   | 0 (0.0%)   |
| third  | 10 (25.6%) | 8 (20.5%) | 13 (33.3%) | 0 (0.0%)  | 4 (10.3%)  | 4 (10.3%)  |
| it     | 0 (0.0%)   | 0 (0.0%)  | 0 (0.0%)   | 0 (0.0%)  | 0 (0.0%)   | 2 (100.0%) |
| NA     | 0 (0.0%)   | 1 (9.1%)  | 0 (0.0%)   | 0 (0.0%)  | 10 (90.9%) | 0 (0.0%)   |

contexts at the initial stages of grammaticalisation. More importantly, there are no tokens of the neuter pronoun *it* occurring with structures featuring *like*, which again violates the hypothesis that establishes a close association for *be like* with neuter forms. *Say* is fairly evenly distributed across the first and the third person, 25% vs. 33.3% (although it is still more frequent in third-person contexts, as to be expected), whereas *think* is connected to first-person contexts (25.0%).

What can be learned about the variable grammar of quotative marking – as it is attested in speech of individuals exhibiting high levels of naturalistic exposure to English spoken in the UK – by looking at the frequency distributions by the temporal marking? Table 49 sheds light on this issue informing us that even though low in token numbers, *be like* seems to be linked to CHP (50%), a pattern widely attested for native-speaker English. Another point worth making here is that *be like* is quite prominent in its use with past tense morphology (33.3%). Given that the pattern has been demonstrated as the one charactering British English (Buchstaller 2014: 132), it is not unreasonable to assume a British input influence underlying the acquisition of the variable grammar by this learner group.

Table 49: Distribution of quotatives by tense marking for UK exposure dominant learners.

|         | be like    | template  | say        | think     | zero       | other     |
|---------|------------|-----------|------------|-----------|------------|-----------|
| CHP     | 3 (50%)    | 0 (0.0%)  | 1 (16.7%)  | 0 (0.0%)  | 0 (0.0%)   | 2 (33.3%) |
| present | 0 (0.0%)   | 4 (15.4%) | 14 (53.8%) | 1 (3.8%)  | 0 (0.0%)   | 7 (26.9%) |
| past    | 10 (33.3%) | 3 (10.0%) | 5 (16.7%)  | 7 (23.3%) | 1 (3.3%)   | 4 (13.3%) |
| modal   | 1 (20.0%)  | 0 (0.0%)  | 3 (60.0%)  | 0 (0.0%)  | 0 (0.0%)   | 1 (20.0%) |
| NA      | 0 (0.0%)   | 5 (27.8%) | 0 (0.0%)   | 0 (0.0%)  | 13 (72.2%) | 0 (0.0%)  |

While bearing the low token numbers of the data set in mind, one could attempt a summary of the preceding paragraphs along the following lines. Learners with elevated exposure to UK English replicate some of the constraints reported as governing the use of *be like* in L1 English and reorganise the others. On the one hand, they use *be like* to report both thought and speech, a most recent levelling trend, and they seem to couple the innovative variant with CHP, which is also in line with what native speakers do. In addition, they appear to be cognisant of the UK English pattern linking *be like* to past tense morphology. Conversely, they tend to use *be like* in third-person environments far more frequently than in first-person environments and they do not unequivocally link *be like* to quotes produced with various voice effects, both of which contradicts robust and well-documented patterns of native-speaker use. With this said, the results reported for this learner group are preliminary (as they draw on low speakers' number as well as relatively scarce data) and need to be subjected to further investigation in the future.

## 6.3 Mixed exposure learners

What can be said about the system of variable quotative marking produced by German learners exposed to various kinds of L1 English for prolonged periods of time? How well do they reconstruct the patterns underlying the use of *be like* documented for native-speaker English? In order to explore this issue, I focus on 22 students who spent the minimum of two months, with an average of 8.0 months, in a monolingual English-speaking environment. These learners exhibit mixed exposures to North American, UK and/or Australian New Zealand English as they have spent equally long periods of time in the US, in the UK and/ or in the Antipodeans.

Illustrating the distributional frequencies within the overall variable context, Table 50 indicates that *say* has established itself as the most popular form among these learners (35.4%) followed by zero-quotatives (14.5%), and *be like* (13.9%). Notice how infrequent *be like* is in this data set. As a reminder and a point of comparison, the variant is attested at the rate of 28.6% in speech of learners with the dominant exposure to North American English (28.6%), which is closer to the rates of use reported for US English (72% in Buchstaller 2014), UK English (43% in Buchstaller 2014) and for Australian English (81.5% in Rodriguez-Louro 2013). These results appear to suggest that diverse linguistic inputs stand in the way of progressive accumulation of a global variant within the learner grammar. This is, indeed, surprising given relatively high percentage frequencies in all of the donor varieties. I will come back to this issue at the end of this section.

Let us now peruse the language-internal mechanism underlying the variable system of quotation in this learner group. Table 51 reports the distribution of variants by mimesis. One crucial observation is in order here. Although the vertical perspective reveals that *be like* is more frequent with mimetic than non-mimetic quotes (18.4% vs. 7.0%), the horizontal axis shows that this linguistic environment is still largely mapped on quotative *say* (33.2%) rather than *be like* (18.4%),

**Table 50:** Overall distribution of quotative markers in mixed exposure learners (N speakers = 22).

| Traditional variants | N | % |
|---|---|---|
| *say* | 142 | 35.4% |
| other verbs of reporting | 40 | 9.9% |
| zero | 58 | 14.5% |
| *think* | 43 | 10.7% |
| other verbs of mental activity and perception | 7 | 1.7% |
| **Variants featuring *like*** | | |
| *be like* | 56 | 13.9% |
| *zero-like* | 25 | 6.2% |
| *say like* | 6 | 1.5% |
| other collocations with *like* | 3 | 0.7% |
| *think like* | 2 | 0.5% |
| *feel like* | 2 | 0.5% |
| *know like* | 0 | |
| **Other variants** | 17 | 4.2% |
| TOTAL | 401 | |

**Table 51:** Distribution of quotatives by mimesis for mixed exposure learners.

|  | be like | template | say | think | zero | other |
|---|---|---|---|---|---|---|
| mimesis | 45 (18.4%) | 24 (9.8%) | 81 (33.2%) | 24 (9.8%) | 40 (16.4%) | 30 (12.3%) |
| not | 11 (7.0%) | 14 (8.9%) | 61 (38.9%) | 19 (12.1%) | 18 (11.5%) | 34 (21.7%) |

which stands in direct competition with *say*, zero-quotative markers (16.4%), and other traditional variants (12.3%) for the expression of the mimetic function.

Distributional frequencies of the main variants across quote type, reported in Table 52, inform us that, consistent with the grammaticalisation hypothesis, *be like* is more frequent with quotes reporting thought than with those reporting speech (20.7% vs. 11.2%). Nonetheless, it is not nearly as robust as the traditional variants in these linguistic environments. Precisely, it is quotative *say* that dominates the reporting of direct speech at 46.4%, whereas quotative *think* by and large controls the reporting of inner monologue at 36.2%. Overall, *be like* has started to encroach on the functions associated with canonical variants and it does so along the lines predicted for its language-internal development within the system. However, there remains a long way to go in order to become a fully established member within the learner grammar explored here. Note also the

**Table 52:** Distribution of quotatives by quote type for mixed exposure learners.

|            | be like      | template    | say          | think        | zero         | other        |
|------------|--------------|-------------|--------------|--------------|--------------|--------------|
| speech     | 30 (11.2%)   | 25 (9.4%)   | 124 (46.4%)  | 1 (0.4%)     | 38 (14.2%)   | 49 (18.4%)   |
| thought    | 24 (20.7%)   | 11 (9.5%)   | 9 (7.8%)     | 42 (36.2%)   | 17 (14.7%)   | 13 (11.2%)   |
| indigenous | 2 (11.1%)    | 2 (11.1%)   | 9 (50.0%)    | 0 (0.0%)     | 3 (16.7%)    | 2 (11.1%)    |

robustness of quotative *say* with quotes containing code-switches of indigenous (German) linguistic material (50.0%).

The distribution of quotatives by grammatical subject, presented in Table 53, pinpoints a very clear association between *be like* and the neuter pronoun *it* (85.7%), which is consistent with the working hypothesis. Notice also that *be like* is evenly distributed between first- and third-person contexts, albeit at low rates (10.7% and 9.4% respectively). This finding seems to suggest that although my mixed exposure learners have adopted the innovative variant at a low rate, they might have still been able to pick up on the recent levelling trend reported for North American English. Consistent with the working hypothesis, there is a slight preference for *be like* to occur with first- over third-person grammatical subject. Quotative *say* is fairly robust with all persons although, as anticipated, it is most frequent in third-person contexts (47.3%). *Think* is the leading variant in second-person contexts at 42.9%, many of which are generic, as in *But if you think, 'Britain' everybody says, 'London'* (MaCGE: GE15).

**Table 53:** Distribution of quotatives by grammatical subject for mixed exposure learners.

|        | be like      | template    | say          | think        | zero         | other        |
|--------|--------------|-------------|--------------|--------------|--------------|--------------|
| first  | 11 (10.7%)   | 9 (8.7%)    | 36 (34.9%)   | 20 (19.4%)   | 10 (9.7%)    | 17 (16.5%)   |
| second | 1 (3.6%)     | 2 (7.1%)    | 8 (28.6%)    | 12 (42.9%)   | 1 (3.6%)     | 4 (14.3%)    |
| third  | 19 (9.4%)    | 20 (9.9%)   | 96 (47.3%)   | 9 (4.4%)     | 22 (10.8%)   | 37 (18.2%)   |
| it     | 24 (85.7%)   | 0 (0.0%)    | 0 (0.0%)     | 0 (0.0%)     | 0 (0.0%)     | 4 (14.3%)    |
| NA     | 1 (2.6%)     | 7 (17.9%)   | 2 (5.1%)     | 2 (5.1%)     | 25 (64.1%)   | 2 (5.1%)     |

As for the distributional tendencies across temporal markers, we can observe from a horizontal perspective a lack of clear correspondence between *be like* and CHP, one of the defining linguistic environments of the innovative variant in native-speaker English. Indeed, it is quotative *say* that exhibits the most dynamic variability with temporal markers being consistently used with CHP (51.3%), present (42.7%), and past (40.1%) time morphology in addition to being used with different modal (auxiliary) markers (54.8%). From a vertical perspective, we see, however, that *be like* is still more frequent with present tense morphology,

**Table 54:** Distribution of quotatives by tense marking for mixed exposure learners.

|         | be like      | template    | say         | think       | zero        | other       |
|---------|--------------|-------------|-------------|-------------|-------------|-------------|
| CHP     | 8 (20.5%)    | 2 (5.1%)    | 20 (51.3%)  | 2 (5.1%)    | 0 (0.0%)    | 7 (17.9%)   |
| present | 9 (12.0%)    | 3 (4.0%)    | 32 (42.7%)  | 14 (18.7%)  | 0 (0.0%)    | 17 (22.7%)  |
| past    | 35 (21.6%)   | 8 (4.9%)    | 65 (40.1%)  | 21 (12.9%)  | 0 (0.0%)    | 33 (20.4%)  |
| modal   | 4 (9.5%)     | 2 (4.8%)    | 23 (54.8%)  | 5 (11.9%)   | 1 (2.4%)    | 7 (16.7%)   |
| NA      | 0 (0.0%)     | 23 (27.7%)  | 2 (2.4%)    | 1 (1.2%)    | 57 (68.7%)  | 0 (0.0%)    |

including CHP, than with other tense markers. The pattern is aligned with the working hypothesis.

Overall, we can recognise that German learners with the mixed exposure profile have adopted the innovative variant at a somewhat inconspicuous rate, yielding a mere 13.9% of the entire data set. The patterns related to mimesis, quote type, grammatical subject, and tense are by and large consistent with the predictions, although the variant, while being infrequent overall, is also not fully established within the system. This explains why other variants, notably quotative *say*, often perform the functions fulfilled typically by quotative *be like* in the reference variety. So, how can we account for the fact that the learners with multiple L1 exposures do not acquire the variant at a rate similar to the one reported for the learners with a focused L1 exposure to North American English – given fairly comparable frequencies in the input?

In Chapter 5, we saw that local ecologies consisting of multilingual inputs create a sociolinguistic environment that fosters the appropriation of a global linguistic innovation only at a very moderate rate (see also Davydova 2015b: 312). The results presented here add to the picture in that they suggest that dispersed exposures to native English has a detrimental, or at least non-fostering, influence on the rate of adoption of the innovative variant by EFL learners. Overall then, it is very tempting to conclude that the frequency of adoption of a given global feature might stand in direct proportion to the number of inputs that a given learner, both ESL and EFL, has been exposed to. Thus, the working hypothesis predicting a more modest adoption of a global variant in a multiple, as opposed to a single, input scenario can be subjected to further empirical testing in the future.

## 6.4 Lingua franca exposure learners

As discussed in Chapter 2, one notable characteristic of Learner English as it is spoken in the economically developed countries of Western Europe including Germany is that its speakers do not only get a chance to come into prolonged contact with L1 speakers in various parts of the English-speaking world. More importantly, this type of learners also gets an opportunity to sustain fairly extensive interpersonal communication in English through settings where English is not the dominant language of the social environment but rather used as a lingua franca among educated speakers. It is to these learners that we now turn our attention.

The data for this learner profile was obtained from 12 speakers who spent at least three months, and 6.7 months on average, in lingua franca contexts through study-related or work-related experiences in Scandinavia, South/East Asia (India, Singapore, China), South Africa, and South/West Europe (Spain, Italy, Greece). This type of exposure to, and experience of, English is in stark contrast with those obtained in strictly monolingual English-speaking environments. In other words, these speakers have come "to use English more frequently as a contact language among themselves rather than with native English speakers" (Jenkins 2013: 5). Many of these speakers also reported a more-than-once exposure to English in a lingua franca setting. To put it slightly differently, they had been exposed to multiple L2 English inputs by the time the sociolinguistic interview took place. Two issues need to be addressed here, 'What does their system of variable quotative marking look like? And how does it compare to that demonstrated by speakers with a single L1 input and multiple L1 input profiles?' In what follows, I explore the empirical data with an eye on these questions.

Presenting the overall distribution of variants, Table 55 highlights that quotative *say* is by far the most frequent variant in this data set accounting for as much as 50.0% of the variability. Quotative *be like* and zero-quotes follow suit making up for 14.3% and 12.1% of the system respectively. Note that the percentage frequency attested for *be like* (14.3%) in this data set is comparable to that reported for learners with the mixed L1 exposure profile (13.9%). Similar to the latter learner cohort, the lingua franca exposure learners lag behind students with sustained and focused input from North American English, who, as we saw, use the variant in 28.6% of all cases.

Looking at the distribution of the major variants by the factor group 'mimesis', presented in Table 56, one notices, first and foremost, that *be like* is more frequent with mimetic quotes than non-mimetic ones (22.7% vs. 4.8%). At the same time, the horizontal perspective reveals that it is quotative *say* that is a more frequent introducer of performed quotes that quotative *be like* (38.7% vs. 22.7%). Simultaneously, quotative *say* is the major variant speakers turn to while reporting speech and thought without any voice (62.9%). Overall then, these distributional patterns are reminiscent of those reported for learners exhibiting a mixed L1 exposure profile.

**Table 55:** Overall distribution of quotative markers in lingua franca exposure learners (N speakers = 12).

| Traditional variants | N | % |
|---|---|---|
| *say* | 112 | 50.0% |
| other verbs of reporting | 19 | 8.5% |
| zero | 27 | 12.1% |
| *think* | 13 | 5.8% |
| other verbs of mental activity and perception | 5 | 2.2% |
| **Variants featuring *like*** | | |
| *be like* | 32 | 14.3% |
| zero-*like* | 6 | 2.7% |
| *say like* | 4 | 1.8% |
| other collocations with *like* | 0 | 0.0% |
| *think like* | 0 | 0.0% |
| *feel like* | 0 | 0.0% |
| *know like* | 0 | 0.0% |
| **Other variants** | 6 | 2.7% |
| TOTAL | 224 | |

**Table 56:** Distribution of quotatives by mimesis for lingua franca exposure learners.

|  | *be like* | template | *say* | *think* | zero | other |
|---|---|---|---|---|---|---|
| mimesis | 27 (22.7%) | 5 (4.2%) | 46 (38.7%) | 5 (4.2%) | 20 (16.8%) | 16 (13.4%) |
| not | 5 (4.8%) | 5 (4.8%) | 66 (62.9%) | 8 (7.6%) | 7 (6.7%) | 14 (13.3%) |

Reporting the distribution of quotatives by quote type, Table 57 furthermore reveals that although quotative *be like* is far more frequently recruited to introduce inner monologue than it is used to frame instances of actually uttered linguistic material (28.9% vs. 10.9%), the linguistic innovation is still in a very robust competition with the more traditional variant *think* (28.9% vs. 28.9%) as a thought introducer. Unsurprisingly, quotative *say* is primarily exploited to introduce direct speech proper (60.6%) and it is likewise the preferred variant to frame indigenous quotes (75.0%). These patterns again are very much aligned with those reported for learners with multiple exposures to L1 English, indicating an incipient status of the innovative variant in both learner profiles.

Next, I consider grammatical subject, presented in Table 58. Notice a clear link between quotative *be like* and the neuter pronoun *it* (66.7%). From a vertical perspective, *be like* patterns with first-person subjects more frequently than

**Table 57:** Distribution of quotatives by quote type for lingua franca exposure learners.

|  | be like | template | say | think | zero | other |
|---|---|---|---|---|---|---|
| speech | 19 (10.9%) | 6 (3.4%) | 106 (60.6%) | 0 (0.0%) | 21 (12.0%) | 23 (13.1%) |
| thought | 13 (28.9%) | 3 (6.7%) | 3 (6.7%) | 13 (28.9%) | 6 (13.3%) | 7 (15.6%) |
| indigenous | 0 (0.0%) | 1 (25.0%) | 3 (75.0%) | 0 (0.0%) | 0 (0.0%) | 0 (0.0%) |

**Table 58:** Distribution of quotatives by grammatical subject for lingua franca exposure learners.

|  | be like | template | say | think | zero | other |
|---|---|---|---|---|---|---|
| first | 12 (17.1%) | 2 (2.9%) | 30 (42.9%) | 10 (14.3%) | 9 (12.9%) | 7 (10.0%) |
| second | 2 (22.2%) | 2 (22.2%) | 1 (11.1%) | 0 (0.0%) | 0 (0.0%) | 4 (44.4%) |
| third | 14 (10.7%) | 6 (4.6%) | 80 (61.1%) | 3 (2.3%) | 10 (7.6%) | 18 (13.7%) |
| it | 4 (66.7%) | 0 (0.0%) | 1 (16.7%) | 0 (0.0%) | 0 (0.0%) | 1 (16.7%) |
| NA | 0 (0.0%) | 0 (0.0%) | 0 (0.0%) | 0 (0.0%) | 8 (100%) | 0 (0.0%) |

it does with third-person subjects (17.1% and 10.7% respectively), which is consistent with the underlying hypothesis. From a horizontal perspective, it is nevertheless clear that it is quotative *say* that dominates both first- and third-person grammatical subjects at 42.9% and 61.1%. This trend echoes with the patterns reported for mixed L1 exposure learners, where *be like* has been attested at a similarly modest rate.

Introduced in Table 59, the patterns illustrating the distribution of variants by tense marking reveal that learners of the lingua franca profile do not extensively deploy *be like* to signal CHP, although they prefer present tense morphology (25.0%), including CHP (22.7%), over past tense marking (16.0%) with *be like*. Similar to the pattern attested in the speech of learners with the mixed L1 exposure profile, students of the lingua franca profile vigorously endorse the traditional variant, quotative *say*, for a variety of tense markers, including modal

**Table 59:** Distribution of quotatives by tense marking for lingua franca exposure learners.

|  | be like | template | say | think | zero | other |
|---|---|---|---|---|---|---|
| CHP | 5 (22.7%) | 1 (4.5%) | 15 (68.2%) | 0 (0.0%) | 0 (0.0%) | 1 (4.5%) |
| present | 7 (25.0%) | 1 (3.6%) | 9 (32.1%) | 4 (14.3%) | 0 (0.0%) | 7 (25.0%) |
| past | 20 (16.0%) | 3 (2.4%) | 74 (59.2%) | 8 (6.4%) | 0 (0.0%) | 20 (16.0%) |
| modal | 0 (0.0%) | 0 (0.0%) | 14 (93.3%) | 0 (0.0%) | 0 (0.0%) | 1 (6.7%) |
| NA | 0 (0.0%) | 5 (14.7%) | 0 (0.0%) | 1 (2.9%) | 27 (79.4%) | 1 (2.9%) |

verbs (93.3%), CHP (68.2%), past tense (59.2%) and, finally, present tense morphology (32.1%).

Summing up, the previous analyses of data indicate clear parallels in the grammars of variable quotative marking existing between learners with high levels of exposure to English in lingua franca environments and those with extensive experience with L1 English through a mix of monolingual settings. In contrast, the data also reveals that learners with prolonged exposure to a single L1 input, i.e. North American English, are one step ahead in replicating the overall frequency of quotative *be like*. In so doing, they also appear to lead the way in reconstructing the mechanism of variation accompanying the gradual integration of *be like* into the system of speech and thought introducers. Learners dominated by the exposure to North American English exhibit a system of variable quotative marking in which *be like* shows signs of being relatively well-established in the system. While using the innovative variant at a lower rate, learners with mixed and lingua franca exposures frequently use quotative *say* in contexts for which their L1 peers recruit *be like*. It is important, however, to notice that whenever they use the innovative form, they do so in a manner that is highly consistent with the predictions stemming from the theory of grammaticalisation for *be like*, discussed in Chapter 3. Specifically, they choose *be like* in mimetic over non-mimetic contexts; they choose it with reported thought over reported speech; they choose it with first- over third-person subjects, and they use it far more frequently with present tense morphology, including CHP than with other tense markers.

This being stated, which lesson is to be drawn from the obtained results? As far as the acquisition of sociolinguistic competence is concerned, it seems reasonable to suggest that prolonged and focused exposure to a single monolingual input brings more benefits than the same amount of exposure to diverse inputs. To be sure, one should not underestimate the benefits of the intercultural enrichment and increased intercultural awareness that multiple stay-abroad sojourns yield. Yet the appropriation of the relevant variants and their relative frequencies, as well as the language-related patterns governing their use, appears to be facilitated when learners have enriched access to a single L1 input; rather than multiple L1 (and L2) inputs resulting in the same amount of exposure. In other words, a nine-month stay in the US, for example, is apparently of greater benefit to the acquisition of the variable vernacular grammar than a combined exposure to monolingual English in the UK, US, and Australia yielding an overall amount of nine months. This is something that young individuals might want to bear in mind while planning their stay-abroad experiences in English-speaking countries.

## 6.5 Low-level naturalistic exposure learners

This section considers learners with low levels of exposure to naturalistic L1 English. This cohort consists of learners who have either never been abroad or have made shorter trips to the countries around the world, the total exposure not exceeding the overall amount of two months. The preliminary analyses presented in Table 38 reveal that this cohort consists of 34 speakers yielding 297 tokens of quotation in total. Closer and more careful work with naturalistic and questionnaire data furthermore indicated that the informants within this group differed from each other with respect to their English media viewing habits. Thus, in response to the question, 'How often do you watch original TV shows or movies in English?' some informants reported that they do so every day, or at least three or three times a week. Others, in contrast, stated that they indulge in viewing English TV shows and films once a week or less, or never. These very clear differences in English media viewing profiles allowed me to stratify this group into two informants' pools further – while strictly relying on the information provided in the background questionnaire – (i) the one exhibiting high levels of exposure to the English mass media and (ii) the one demonstrating lower levels of that type of exposure. Splitting this learner group in such a way is crucial as it allows me to gauge the effect produced by the media on the emergence of quotation as a discourse device in the learner grammar. The pertinent questions here are these, 'What does the quotative system produced by speakers with low levels of naturalistic exposure but high levels of media exposure look like? Is it comparable to that produced by native speakers? Is it comparable to that produced by learners with higher levels of naturalistic exposure, and if so to what extent?' With that said, let us consider the high media-exposure learners first.

### 6.5.1 High levels of exposure to mass media

This speaker group is represented by 18 speakers who produced the overall total of 233 tokens of quotation during sociolinguistic interviews. These speakers spent 0.5 months (2 weeks) on average in an English-speaking environment by the time the interview took place. At the same time, these learners commit to watching English films and TV series on a very regular basis ranging from two or three times a week to every day.

If we examine the overall composition of quotative marking in this learner group (Table 60), we notice that, perhaps unsurprisingly, *say* is the most robust variant in the system accounting for 36.9% of variation. This is followed by

**Table 60:** Overall distribution of quotative markers for learners with high levels of exposure to mass media (N speakers = 18).

| Traditional variants | N | % |
|---|---|---|
| *say* | 86 | 36.9% |
| other verbs of reporting | 14 | 6.0% |
| zero | 29 | 12.4% |
| *think* | 13 | 5.6% |
| other verbs of mental activity and perception | 5 | 2.1% |
| **Variants featuring *like*** | | |
| *be like* | 57 | 24.5% |
| *zero-like* | 9 | 3.9% |
| *say like* | 3 | 1.3% |
| other collocations with *like* | 6 | 2.6% |
| *think like* | 0 | 0.0% |
| *feel like* | 0 | 0.0% |
| *know like* | 0 | 0.0% |
| **Other variants** | 11 | 4.7% |
| TOTAL | 233 | |

quotative *be like* (24.5%) and zero-markers (12.4%). Note that *be like*'s rate of occurrence closely approximates that reported for learners with the dominant type of exposure to North American English (28.6%). Both are significantly higher than those documented for learners of all the other profiles ($x^2$ (4): 38.9, $p < 0.0001$). The question, however, is, 'Will the learners exhibiting high levels of exposure to mass media be able to replicate the variable patterns of use for *be like* and other quotative markers?' With this in mind, let us consider distributional profiles of the most frequent quotative choices by various language-internal factors.

Similarly to the learners who spent prolonged periods of time in the English-speaking countries on the North American continent, German students with avid mass media consumption habits prefer *be like* over all other quotative markers to signal a performed quote (33.8%), as reported in Table 61. Unsurprisingly, they

**Table 61:** Distribution of quotatives by mimesis for learners with high levels of exposure to mass media.

| | be like | template | say | think | zero | other |
|---|---|---|---|---|---|---|
| mimesis | 46 (33.8%) | 9 (6.6%) | 33 (24.3%) | 7 (5.1%) | 23 (16.9%) | 18 (13.2%) |
| not | 11 (11.3%) | 9 (9.3%) | 53 (54.6%) | 6 (6.2%) | 6 (6.2%) | 12 (12.4%) |

also use *be like* with mimetic quotes far more frequently than with non-mimetic ones (33.8% vs. 11.3%). Quotative *say* is the major linguistic form exploited by the learners to introduce chunks of direct speech and thought performed without any voice effects (54.6%), all of which is consistent with the developmental trajectory predicted by the hypothesis.

Table 62 furthermore shows that *be like* stands in robust competition with quotative *think* for the expression of inwardly realised quotes (31.1% vs. 28.9%). Quotative *say* outperforms all the other variants at 46.1% as a direct speech introducer. Importantly, high-exposure learners employ *be like* for framing inner monologue far more frequently than for reporting sequences of direct speech (31.1% vs. 23.3%).

**Table 62:** Distribution of quotatives by quote type for learners with high levels of exposure to mass media.

|            | be like     | template   | say        | think      | zero       | other      |
|------------|-------------|------------|------------|------------|------------|------------|
| speech     | 42 (23.3%)  | 11 (6.1%)  | 83 (46.1%) | 0 (0.0%)   | 22 (12.2%) | 22 (12.2%) |
| thought    | 14 (31.1%)  | 6 (13.3%)  | 0 (0.0%)   | 13 (28.9%) | 4 (8.9%)   | 8 (17.8%)  |
| indigenous | 1 (12.5%)   | 1 (12.5%)  | 3 (37.5%)  | 0 (0.0%)   | 3 (37.5%)  | 0 (0.0%)   |

Looking at the percentage frequencies by grammatical subjects reported in Table 63, one notices that *be like* is the major variant employed in first-person contexts (29.3%) followed by *say* (22.4%) and other verbs of reporting (20.7%). As predicted by the working hypothesis, *be like* is used in first-person contexts more often than in third-person contexts (29.3% vs. 20.9%), and *say* is overwhelmingly preferred with third-person subjects (48.9%). Note also that *be like* shows a very strong association with neuter *it* in this data set (71.4%). Thus, it appears that my high exposure learners have not picked up on the recent levelling tendency regards grammatical subject, which contrasts with the patterns

**Table 63:** Distribution of quotatives by grammatical subject for learners with high levels of exposure to mass media.

|        | be like     | template  | say        | think     | zero       | other      |
|--------|-------------|-----------|------------|-----------|------------|------------|
| first  | 17 (29.3%)  | 4 (6.9%)  | 13 (22.4%) | 6 (10.3%) | 6 (10.3%)  | 12 (20.7%) |
| second | 0 (0.0%)    | 0 (0.0%)  | 0 (0.0%)   | 3 (75.0%) | 0 (0.0%)   | 1 (25.0%)  |
| third  | 30 (20.9%)  | 13 (9.1%) | 70 (48.9%) | 4 (2.8%)  | 13 (9.1%)  | 13 (9.1%)  |
| it     | 10 (71.4%)  | 0 (0.0%)  | 0 (0.0%)   | 0 (0.0%)  | 0 (0.0%)   | 4 (28.6%)  |
| NA     | 0 (0.0%)    | 1 (7.1%)  | 3 (21.4%)  | 0 (0.0%)  | 10 (71.4%) | 0 (0.0%)   |

attested for German students exhibiting high levels of naturalistic exposure to North American English.

The further analysis presented in Table 64 indicates that from a vertical perspective, students exhibiting high levels of exposure to English mass media map *be like* on present tense morphology, including CHP, more frequently than on other tense markers, which is consistent with the working hypothesis. A horizontal perspective, however, makes clear that it is quotative *say*, not *be like*, that is overwhelmingly robust with CHP at 41.7%. In addition, *say* is used invariably with a variety of tense markers, but most frequently with modal verbs (72.7%).

**Table 64:** Distribution of quotatives by tense marking for learners with high levels of exposure to mass media.

|         | be like     | template   | say         | think      | zero        | other       |
|---------|-------------|------------|-------------|------------|-------------|-------------|
| CHP     | 2 (16.7%)   | 2 (16.7%)  | 5 (41.7%)   | 0 (0.0%)   | 0 (0.0%)    | 3 (25.0%)   |
| present | 8 (24.2%)   | 2 (6.1%)   | 9 (27.3%)   | 9 (27.3%)  | 0 (0.0%)    | 5 (15.2%)   |
| past    | 47 (34.6%)  | 5 (3.7%)   | 61 (44.9%)  | 2 (1.5%)   | 0 (0.0%)    | 21 (15.4%)  |
| modal   | 0 (0.0%)    | 0 (0.0%)   | 8 (72.7%)   | 2 (18.2%)  | 0 (0.0%)    | 1 (9.1%)    |
| NA      | 0 (0.0%)    | 9 (21.9%)  | 3 (7.3%)    | 0 (0.0%)   | 29 (70.7%)  | 0 (0.0%)    |

Having considered the variable grammar of learners with low levels of exposure to L1 English vernaculars but high levels of exposure to English mass media, let us now explore the patterns of variable quotative marking in speech of those students who had a very limited access to L1 English through both face-to-face interactions and media consumption.

### 6.5.2 Low levels of exposure to mass media

This speaker group consists of 16 speakers who contributed the mere 64 tokens to the overall data pool. Notably, three of these speakers did not produce a single quotative token during the entire interview. On average, these speakers spent 0.6 months (2.5 weeks) in an English-speaking environment by the time the interview took place. Moreover, these learners report only very rare occasions of exposure to the English TV shows and films (once a week or less).

Crucially, the low token numbers is not the result of the paucity of the speakers attested in the sample. Table 65 cross-tabulates the frequency of quotation variants with speakers' exposure to the media. When contrasted with a similarly sized cohort of speakers who likewise had limited experiences with naturalistic English but expanded exposure to naturally occurring L1 speech through

**Table 65:** Distribution of quotative markers in a group with low levels of naturalistic exposure by amount of exposure to mass media (N speakers = 34; N quotatives = 297; N *be like* = 62).

| Level of mass media exposure | N (speakers) | N (quotes) | Ratio quotes/ speaker | N (*be like*) | Ratio *be like*/ speaker |
|---|---|---|---|---|---|
| high | 18 | 233 | 12.9 | 57 | 3.2 |
| low | 16 | 64 | 4.0 | 5 | 0.3 |

the media, it becomes obvious that the low media-exposure group lags behind regarding both production of quotative markers and the use of innovative *be like*. A speaker from the high-exposure group produces 12.9 quotes on average, whereas a learner from the low-exposure group resorts to quotation not more than four times throughout the interview. Furthermore, the former produces 3.2 instances of *be like* on average, which is in contrast to 0.3 instances produced by the low-level exposure learner. Overall, learners with low levels of naturalistic L1 and mass media exposure are still in the process of developing quotation as a narrative skill.

Table 66 documents some very general trends in this developing interlanguage system. Quotative *say* is the major variant low-exposure learners resort to if they use quotation at all (56.3%), which highlights once again its status as a

**Table 66:** Overall distribution of quotative markers for learners with low levels of exposure to mass media (N speakers = 16).

| Traditional variants | N | % |
|---|---|---|
| *say* | 36 | 56.3% |
| other verbs of reporting | 5 | 7.8% |
| zero | 6 | 9.4% |
| *think* | 6 | 9.4% |
| other verbs of mental activity and perception | 3 | 4.7% |
| **Variants featuring *like*** | | |
| *be like* | 5 | 7.8% |
| *zero-like* | 2 | 3.1% |
| *say like* | 0 | 0.0% |
| other collocations with *like* | 0 | 0.0% |
| *think like* | 0 | 0.0% |
| *feel like* | 0 | 0.0% |
| *know like* | 0 | 0.0% |
| **Other variants** | 1 | 1.6% |
| TOTAL | 64 | |

traditional discourse-pragmatic device recruited to construct speech and thought throughout narration. This is followed by quotative *think* (9.4%) and zero quotative markers (9.4%). Quotative *be like* contributes a mere 7.8% to the variability of the data set, which contrasts starkly with the rates demonstrated by learners from all the other cohorts studied so far.

Let us now take one step further and consider the distribution of quotative variants by language-internal constraints starting with mimesis. Table 67 reveals that quotative *say* is the major contender of the system reigning in both mimetic and non-mimetic contexts (51.5% and 61.3% respectively). Interestingly, the five instances attested for *be like* are all mimetic, a pattern well aligned with the working hypothesis.

**Table 67:** Distribution of quotatives by mimesis for learners with low levels of exposure to mass media.

|  | be like | template | say | think | zero | other |
| --- | --- | --- | --- | --- | --- | --- |
| mimesis | 5 (15.2%) | 1 (3.0%) | 17 (51.5%) | 4 (12.1%) | 1 (3.0%) | 5 (15.2%) |
| not | 0 (0.0%) | 1 (3.2%) | 19 (61.3%) | 2 (6.5%) | 5 (16.1%) | 4 (12.9%) |

Looking at the distribution of quotative markers by quote type reported in Table 68, we note that quotative *say* is exploited primarily by low-exposure learners in order to introduce direct speech (67.4%). Conversely, thought is framed by a variety of different quotatives including *say* (30.0%), *think* (30.0%), zero-quotes (15.0%), and representatives from the category 'other' (15.0%). Importantly, quotative *be like* is more frequently exploited to report on sequences of events than to construct inner monologue (9.3% vs. 5.0%). This pattern does not align with the hypothesis, thereby suggesting that my low-exposure learners have trouble replicating the variable pattern reported for L1 English, whereby *be like* is more frequent with thought than it is with speech.

**Table 68:** Distribution of quotatives by quote type for learners with low levels of exposure to mass media.

|  | be like | template | say | think | zero | other |
| --- | --- | --- | --- | --- | --- | --- |
| speech | 4 (9.3%) | 1 (2.3%) | 29 (67.4%) | 0 (0.0%) | 3 (7.0%) | 6 (14.0%) |
| thought | 1 (5.0%) | 1 (5.0%) | 6 (30.0%) | 6 (30.0%) | 3 (15.0%) | 3 (15.0%) |
| indigenous | 0 (0.0%) | 0 (0.0%) | 1 (100.0%) | 0 (0.0%) | 0 (0.0%) | 0 (0.0%) |

Table 69 furthermore suggests that quotative *say* is the preferred variant in second- and third-person contexts (62.5% and 65.9% respectively). First-person

Table 69: Distribution of quotatives by grammatical subject for learners with low levels of exposure to mass media.

|        | be like     | template    | say         | think       | zero        | other       |
|--------|-------------|-------------|-------------|-------------|-------------|-------------|
| first  | 1 (7.7%)    | 1 (7.7%)    | 4 (30.8%)   | 4 (30.8%)   | 0 (0.0%)    | 3 (23.1%)   |
| second | 0 (0.0%)    | 0 (0.0%)    | 5 (62.5%)   | 1 (12.5%)   | 1 (12.5%)   | 1 (12.5%)   |
| third  | 3 (7.3%)    | 0 (0.0%)    | 27 (65.9%)  | 1 (2.4%)    | 5 (12.2%)   | 5 (12.2%)   |
| it     | 1 (100.0%)  | 0 (0.0%)    | 0 (0.0%)    | 0 (0.0%)    | 0 (0.0%)    | 0 (0.0%)    |
| NA     | 0 (100.0%)  | 1 (100.0%)  | 0 (0.0%)    | 0 (0.0%)    | 0 (0.0%)    | 0 (0.0%)    |

subjects pattern well with both *say* (30.8%) and *think* (30.8%) followed by the category 'other' (23.1%). *Be like* is used evenly with first and third person, being in addition the sole variant used with the neuter pronoun *it*.

The final factor to consider is temporal marking. Table 70 shows that CHP, a pervasive feature of L1 English vernaculars, is not part of the oral narrative skills of these learners. They tend to employ past tense morphology, which they link almost invariably to quotative *say* (63.6%), while reproducing direct speech events and reconstructing inner dialogue.

Table 70: Distribution of quotatives by tense marking for learners with low levels of exposure to mass media.

|         | be like    | template  | say         | think      | zero       | other       |
|---------|------------|-----------|-------------|------------|------------|-------------|
| CHP     | 0 (0.0%)   | 0 (0.0%)  | 0 (0.0%)    | 0 (0.0%)   | 0 (0.0%)   | 1 (100.0%)  |
| present | 1 (6.3%)   | 0 (0.0%)  | 9 (56.3%)   | 3 (18.7%)  | 0 (0.0%)   | 3 (18.7%)   |
| past    | 4 (12.1%)  | 0 (0.0%)  | 21 (63.6%)  | 3 (9.1%)   | 0 (0.0%)   | 5 (15.2%)   |
| modal   | 0 (0.0%)   | 0 (0.0%)  | 6 (100.0%)  | 0 (0.0%)   | 0 (0.0%)   | 0 (0.0%)    |
| NA      | 0 (0.0%)   | 2 (25.0%) | 0 (0.0%)    | 0 (0.0%)   | 6 (75.0%)  | 0 (0.0%)    |

What generalisations can be made regarding the L2 acquisition of variable grammar of quotative marking, more specifically the use of quotative *be like*, by German learners with differing sociolinguistic profiles? The following section provides a summary of the major findings of this chapter in order to address this question.

Table 71 reveals that learners with extensive exposure to North American English are one step ahead of all the other learner cohorts with respect to the variable use of quotative *be like*. Their grammar is aligned with the most recent developmental trends signalling advanced stages of grammaticalisation reported for North American varieties of English. While using this feature at the rate of 28.5%, German learners with dominant North American exposure exhibit

**Table 71:** The variable grammar of quotative marking across German learners' cohorts: A summary[a]

| Percentages for *be like* | NA<br>28.6% | Mixed<br>13.9% | LF<br>14.3% | HME<br>24.5% | LME<br>7.8% |
|---|---|---|---|---|---|
| **Constraints** | | | | | |
| *Mimesis* | | | | | |
| A close link to mimetic content | *be like* | *say* | *say* | *be like* | *say* |
| *Quote type* | | | | | |
| Thought over speech | – | √ | √ | √ | – |
| Levelled | √ | – | – | – | – |
| *Gram. subject* | | | | | |
| First over third | – | – | √ | √ | – |
| Levelled | √ | √ | – | – | – |
| A close link to neuter *it* | *be like* | *be like* | *be like* | *be like* | *be like* |
| *Tense marking* | | | | | |
| A close link to CHP | *be like* | *say* | *say* | *say* | – |

**Note:** NA: North American exposure; LG: lingua franca exposure; HME: high-levels of exposure to the media (but low levels of naturalistic exposure); LME: low-levels exposure to the media (and low levels of naturalistic exposure). The cohort of learners exhibiting high levels of naturalistic exposure to UK English were excluded from the analysis due to low token numbers.

levelled patterns in the use of *be like* regards quote type and grammatical subject. Meanwhile, this variant is linked clearly to quotes with mimetic content, neuter *it*, and non-past tense morphology reporting past events, all of which are highly consistent with how younger speakers of North American English use this feature in their speech.

Learners with a mixed type of exposure to monolingual L1 inputs, as well as learners demonstrating extensive experiences with English in lingua franca settings, differ in crucial ways from the cohort dominated by the exposure to North American English. While using quotative *be like* at lower rates (13.9% and 14.3% respectively), these learners do not exhibit the levelling in the conditioning factor 'quote type', showing a tendency to use quotative *be like* with quotes containing inner dialogue. Moreover, quotative *say* is very robust with mimetic quotes and CHP morphology, although whenever recruiting *be like* in speech, both learner groups use this variant with mimetic contexts more frequently than with non-mimetic ones, and they also map *be like* on present tense morphology, including CHP, more often than on any other tense marker. With regard to, grammatical subject, mixed exposure learners demonstrate a levelled pattern, whereas learners of the lingua franca profile exhibit a non-levelled trend. In both cases, however, *be like* is used with first-person subjects more frequently than with third-person subjects, and is overwhelmingly preferred with neuter *it*.

Remarkably, learners demonstrating low levels of exposure to naturalistic English but expansive patterns of mass media consumption fall somewhere in between North American exposure learners on the one hand, and mixed/lingua franca exposure learners on the other. To begin with, these learners use quotative *be like* at a rate comparable to that exhibited by students with prolonged exposure to North American English – solid 24.5%. Similarly, they clearly link *be like* to mimetic content. Simultaneously, the variable grammar of students exhibiting high levels of exposure to mass media is aligned with that of learners with mixed and lingua franca profiles along several parameters. Firstly, all three groups prefer *be like* with reporting thought over speech. (In contrast, the cohort dominated by exposure to North American English uses a levelled pattern here, while demonstrating a minute preference for thought over speech with *be like*.) Secondly, quotative *say* retains its position as the variant dominating the context of CHP, although *be like* is still more frequent with present tense morphology, including CHP, than with other tense markers. Finally, high-exposure learners do not demonstrate a levelled pattern of use for grammatical subject, although, importantly, they prefer *be like* with first- over third-person subjects whenever they do use the variant in their speech. Finally, neuter *it* links unequivocally to innovative *be like*.

At this juncture, it is vital to emphasise that even though German learners with the elevated intake of North American English exhibit a system of variable quotative in which *be like* encroaches on a variety of different functions signalling its advanced status as a thought and speech introducer, other EFL learners use the innovative variant in compliance with the predictions for its grammaticalisation, reported in Chapter 3. Indeed, only learners with low levels of both naturalistic and mass media exposure present an exception. They trail behind all the other learner groups investigated here in that they seldom use the innovative variant in the speech and by and large do not replicate the patterns associated with the use of *be like*, as highlighted in Section 6.5.2.

The implications of these findings are as follows. First and foremost, the results obtained from the previous analyses highlight the supremacy of prolonged face-to-face interactions with a single monolingual L1 input over all other sociolinguistic settings in promoting L2 acquisition of variable linguistic features. Secondly and somewhat remarkably, given current consensus in sociolinguistic research, the findings presented here highlight the relevance of exposure to mass media in the absence of sustained personal contact with L1 vernaculars. Indeed, learners with high intake of mass media managed to outperform students exhibiting prolonged but diverse exposures to naturalistic English on two parameters

NA → HME → mixed → LF → LME

**Figure 5:** A hierarchy of learner groups acquiring the variable grammar of quotative *be like*.

(frequency of use and mimesis). Overall, the findings pinpoint some sort of a continuum underpinning the acquisition of the variable grammar of quotative *be like* in Learner English, presented in Figure 5 for convenience.

It follows from this exposition that both face-to-face interactions and extensive exposure to mass media play a beneficial role, albeit to various degrees, in the acquisition of sociolinguistic competence by EFL language learners. We have observed that learners with low levels of exposure to mass media do not, generally, pick on the variant, whereas high-exposure speakers do quite well in adopting the variant in terms of its distributional frequency and the overall direction of constraints, despite not replicating the levelling tendencies reported for *be like* in North American English. Remarkably, these speakers were still able to outperform their peers who acquired English vernacular through multiple/lingua franca naturalistic inputs. Finally, learners with expansive North American English intake have not only done a better job adopting the innovative variant; they also exhibit a variable grammar of quotative marking, whereby *be like* functions as a well-established element in the system.

Having provided detailed analyses of variable quotative marking stemming from EFL speakers with different sociolinguistic profiles, the following question arises, 'How are the findings presented here fit with those reported for ESL (Indian) English in the previous chapter?' Chapter 7 provides a contrastive analysis of both varieties, enabling us to view the bigger picture.

# 7 Quotation in non-native English: Bird's eye perspective

This chapter investigates commonalities and differences in the patterns underlying the variable use of quotative *be like* – a global linguistic newcomer promoted by the younger generation of speakers – in two distinctive sociolinguistic ecologies. Over the course of this exploration, I attempt to pinpoint the mechanisms guiding the adaptation of language innovations in non-native English. Chapters 5 and 6 have ascertained that *be like* has been adopted at the overall rate of 17.5% in the ESL variety of Indian English (see Table 7), whereas the EFL learners living in Germany use this variable feature in 20.3% of all possible cases (see Table 37). Despite trailing their L1 peers, who use the variant with the frequency ranging between 43% and 72% (Buchstaller 2014: 119), both speaker groups have adopted the new variant at a largely comparable rate. It is significant that EFL learners have not adopted *be like* to a conspicuously higher degree despite their target-oriented learner mindset (see also discussion in Chapter 4). This issue will be revisited in Chapter 8.

What yet needs to be determined is whether the structured use of *be like* exhibits essentially similar properties in both types of English or whether its variable realisation has undergone re-organisation, getting aligned with the specifics of the ESL/EFL ecologies. More importantly, how do the variable patterns underpinning the use of *be like* in L2 English compare with those reported for native-speaker English? To this end, I draw on the comparative method employed in variationist sociolinguistics (see also discussion in Chapter 2). This method allows for constructing and comparing models of variation in order explore the simultaneous impact of system-internal and sociolinguistic predictors on the occurrence of innovative *be like* in indigenised and Learner English.

In contrast to Chapters 5 and 6, both of which detail the use of major quotative markers across a set of language-internal parameters by splitting the overall data into individual sociolinguistic profiles, this chapter will consider the variable use of *be like* from the perspective of the whole population group by analysing this feature in the full HCNVE and MaCGE data sets. With the aim of recapitulating the information contained in the previous chapters, the data was obtained with the help of sociolinguistic interviews with students enrolled in Bachelor's and Master's degree programmes in JNU and UM, each interview lasting for about an hour. The JNU data stems from 80 individuals (36 males and 44 females), yielding a total of 2118 quotative markers. Comprising speech samples of 97 informants (41 males and 56 females), the UM data has provided me with an overall amount of 1497 quotative tokens. Chapter 6, however, revealed that German learners demonstrating high levels of naturalistic exposure to UK English are represented by a limited number of speakers (N = 8), especially when contrasted with other subgroups. This fact poses problems for the generalisability of the results stemming from this learner cohort, which at best should be treated with caution. Consequently, I decided to exclude these eight speakers from the analyses reported here. Narrowing down the data pool reduced the token number to 1412 instances of quotation, which were obtained from 89 individuals (39 males and 50 females).

Previous research on native-speaker English has unveiled a number of language-internal constraints underpinning the variable grammar of quotative *be like*. These were detailed in Chapter 3 and are summarised for convenience here. In short, *be like* has been linked to mimetic quotes, i.e. quotes performed with a 'voice' marked by specific intonation patterns and variations in pitch or accent. Furthermore, close associations have been revealed between the variant and quotes that express thoughts and inner dialogue more generally, rather than quotes reporting speech or importing instances of code-switching. However, studies conducted more recently reported levelling tendencies, with *be like* being equally used to report thought and speech in native English (Gardner et al. 2013). *Be like* is also preferred with first-person grammatical subject over third-person grammatical subject and here again, levelling tendencies towards third-person contexts have been reported for L1 English (Buchstaller 2014; D'Arcy 2004). When included in the analysis, the neuter pronoun *it* has demonstrated a highly close association with the innovative variant (Davydova and Buchstaller 2015). Finally, *be like* has been shown to be intimately related to CHP, a rhetoric device allowing speakers to recount past events while using present tense morphology. Against this backdrop, the exciting question to ask is whether ESL/EFL language learners – conceived of in this chapter as two self-contained speaker communities – will replicate the patterns reported for *be like* in L1 speech communities and if so, to what extent? My goal is to uncover those constraints that can be regarded as genuine system-internal predictors rising above idiosyncrasies of individual linguistic behaviour.

The sociolinguistic parameters considered by the models of variation include (i) speaker sex; (ii) the sociolinguistic context of exposure to English; and (iii) speakers' mass media viewing habits. We know from previous research that speakers' sex impacts significantly on the occurrence of *be like*, with female speakers promoting the variant. Will this tendency also be reflected in non-native English?

The second sociolinguistic predictor explores the role of the local sociolinguistic ecology as a viable predictor for the occurrence of innovative *be like*. My ethnographic work has allowed me to stratify the sample of each student community while taking learners' individual experiences with English into account. The ESL community is this classified with respect to the type of bilingualism whereby speakers are divided into English-dominant, Hindi-dominant, and mixed bilinguals. Speakers in the EFL community are stratified into distinctive cohorts revealing their amount of naturalistic exposure to L1 English and English as a lingua franca. My EFL learners are thus divided into those exhibiting a high level of naturalistic exposure to North American English; learners with high levels of mixed exposure to L1 vernaculars; learners whose sociolinguistic experience with English is circumscribed to lingua franca contexts and learners with low levels of naturalistic exposure to English. Because the latter group of learners could be subdivided further into those with high and low levels of exposure to mass media, I decided to retain that distinction with the intention of teasing these two confounding factors (sociolinguistic context vs. exposure to mass media) apart. This procedure allowed me to introduce a modicum of methodological rigour into the statistical modelling of data. The pertinent question here is whether the specifics of the sociolinguistic context underlying the acquisition of English by speakers of indigenised and Learner English, indeed, triggers the occurrence of the innovative variant in each community. Stemming from micro-sociolinguistic data, the results of these analyses might turn out to be helpful in revising the traditional ESL/EFL distinction, while highlighting the role of learner-specific properties in the process of adaptation of global linguistic innovations. I will return to this issue later in this chapter.

Finally, the amount of mass media exposure is tested here with an eye on the question concerning the role of speakers' viewing habits in the spread of vernacular features and their linguistic conditioning. To this aim, my ESL/EFL learners from both student communities were coded as indulging in watching English films and TV series (i) every day; (ii) two or three times a week; (iii) once a week, and (iv) less than once a week.

## 7.1 Modelling the variable grammar for *be like* in nativised and Learner English

Having revised all independent predictors relevant to the occurrence of *be like*, let us now probe their simultaneous impact on the use of this variant. Most studies exploring the variable use of *be like* in native Englishes have exploited fixed-effects logistic regression analyses run in Goldvarb (Sankoff, Tagliamonte, and Smith 2005), the most widespread statistical method employed in variationist analysis. Most recently, this statistical tool has been replaced by generalised mixed-effects models run in Rbrul (Johnson 2009). The latter have been argued to be the ideal tool for handling spontaneous language data as they allow for the incorporation of two types of effects into the statistical model – fixed effects and random effects – thereby enabling the researcher to address the critical relationship between linguistic behaviour demonstrated by the individual on the one hand and the group on the other.

Whereas fixed-effects models have been shown to overestimate the statistical significance of the sociolinguistic predictors, thereby increasing the possibility of Type 1 error, mixed-effects models have been argued to run the danger of failing to recognise external effects (so-called between-subject predictors) that might really exist in the data, thus creating the possibility of Type 2 error (Tagliamonte 2012: 141). In other words, choosing one type of modelling over the other appears to involve an inevitable trade-off between detecting an effect that is not present (Type 1 error) and failing to detect an effect that is, in fact, present in the data (Type 2 error). Given this state of affairs, the practical question arises, 'How should the analyst go about evaluating his or her data?' The position advocated here is that we need to construct both fixed- and mixed effects models of variation and report converging as well as diverging evidence before providing our interpretation of results. This step is a strategic attempt to reconcile the established method, upon which much of the variationist research is based, with a new technique, offering additional tools for data analysis, in order to sustain continuity in our assessment of empirical data.

With this explicated, I made use of both statistical procedures described in the preceding paragraphs. In the first step, I subjected the two data pools to fixed-effects modelling performed in Goldvarb in order to ensure comparability between my data and the data reported in earlier studies on L1 English (*inter alia* Durham et al. 2011; Buchstaller and D'Arcy 2009; D'Arcy 2004, 2012; Tagliamonte and Hudson 1999). I then fitted the data to the mixed-effects modelling in Rbrul, where individual ESL/EFL speakers were introduced as a random intercept. The models are similar in that they report statistically significant effects. Both allow the analyst to make statements concerning the relative impact of each significant predictor on the occurrence of *be like*. Crucially, constructed models reveal the patterning of individual constraints within factor groups, thus enabling the analyst to assess the extent to which patterns of variation in non-native Englishes overlap with those attested in the donor varieties. Such fine-grained diagnostic is helpful in determining the universal and idiosyncratic tendencies in the variable realisation of quotative *be like* in newly emerging varieties of English.

Following the state-of-the-art practices adopted in current variationist research, I report results of the Rbrul output. I also comment on the outcomes of the fixed-effects modelling performed with Goldvarb and presented in Appendix D. In so doing, I pinpoint converging evidence obtained through both types of data modelling, while also attempting to account for diverging results.

## 7.1 Modelling the variable grammar for *be like* in nativised and Learner English — 125

I also triangulate these findings with the data obtained from varieties of North American English, the epicentre of sociolinguistic diffusion of *be like*. It is this empirical data that serves as an L1 benchmark here since it also underpins the major tenets of the theory that explains the evolution of *be like* as a quotative marker in a given speech community (Ferrara and Bell 1995; Tagliamonte and Hudson 1999). The contrastive analyses will highlight the language-internal and sociolinguistic mechanisms at work in the emergence of non-native variable grammars, thereby allowing me to re-evaluate the path of grammaticalisation for *be like*, while relying on data stemming from ESL/EFL English. Crucially, relying on the results from both models will allow me to make statements concerning the role of the sociolinguistic context and media influence in the process of adaptation of variable linguistic features.

Bearing in mind that both Rbrul and Goldvarb require that the data be treated in terms of binominal contrasts, the application value includes *be like* and zero-*like* as a single variant set against all the other quotative forms (see also Davydova and Buchstaller 2015: 459). The outcomes reported here, therefore, show which predictors trigger the use of (*be*) *like* as opposed to all the other competing variants in the system.

Table 72 presents the results of the mixed-effects modelling in the HCNVE data. Table 72 reveals that all four language-internal predictors tested in the model significantly constrain the use of *be like* in the data reported here. Grammatical subject exerts the strongest impact on the use of *be like* (*range 61*) followed by tense (*range 57*). Mimesis and quote type are also relevant to the occurrence of the innovative variant in Indian English spoken by young adults, although their relative impact is substantially weaker (*range 16* and *11*).

As a side note, in an earlier account of Indian English quotative marking stemming from data collected in 2007–2011, Davydova (2016a: 196) reports that grammatical subject is the sole language-internal environment through which quotative *be like* paves its way into the local ecology of indigenous quotation, other linguistic predictors tested in that study (quote type and tense) playing no significant role. It is through this functional niche that *be like* arguably profiled itself as a speech and thought introducer in a new sociolinguistic culture. Interestingly, when the data collected three years later is taken into account, grammatical subject remains the biggest predictor for the occurrence of *be like*, although other linguistic factors are clearly at play as well. I take these findings to mean that in the course of the last years, the innovative variant has expanded its functional scope considerably, developing patterns of highly constrained variability. Such real-time development, in turn, suggests that *be like* has been progressively establishing itself as a robust competitor within the indigenised/ESL system of variable quotative marking.

The independent variables presented in Table 72 are *bona fide* linguistic predictors rising above the level of intraspeaker variability inevitably encountered in large data sets. As far as individual constraints are concerned, my Indian informants highly favour *be like* with the neuter pronoun *it* (FW .902). Importantly, they also prefer this form with first- over third-person grammatical subject (FW .519 and .453). *Be like* is furthermore favoured with CHP (FW .746) and, to some extent, with past tense morphology (FW .546). Furthermore, the use of the linguistic innovation under study is tied to mimetic content (FW .574), and *be like* is also linked to reporting thought (FW .540) over indigenous code-switches (FW .526) and direct speech proper (FW .435).

**Table 72:** Logistic regression analysis of the contribution of language-internal and sociolinguistic constraints to the probability of *be like* in HCNVE, 2007–2014. Rbrul output.

| | | | | |
|---|---|---|---|---|
| Input probability | | | | 0.156 |
| Log likelihood | | | | −887.402 |
| R2 | | | | 0.426 |
| Total N | | | | 479/2118 |
| | Log odds | FW | % | N |
| **1. Grammatical subject** ($p < 1.48\text{e-}18$) | | | | |
| it | 2.221 | .902 | 68% | 52/76 |
| first | 0.077 | .519 | 25% | 179/712 |
| third | −0.187 | .453 | 20% | 225/1114 |
| second | −0.878 | .294 | 9% | 5/53 |
| NA | −1.233 | .226 | 11% | 18/163 |
| range | | 61 | | |
| **2. Tense** ($p < 1.41\text{e-}15$) | | | | |
| CHP | 1.075 | .746 | 41% | 84/202 |
| NA | 0.433 | .607 | 21% | 103/480 |
| past | 0.185 | .546 | 24% | 211/874 |
| present | −0.143 | .464 | 19% | 70/354 |
| modal | −1.551 | .175 | 5% | 11/208 |
| range | | 57 | | |
| **3. Mass media exposure** ($p < 0.0445$) | | | | |
| every day | 0.943 | .720 | 38% | 132/339 |
| two or three times a week | 0.135 | .534 | 26% | 182/681 |
| once a week | −0.166 | .459 | 18% | 75/409 |
| NA | −0.235 | .442 | 14% | 25/178 |
| less than once a week | −0.677 | .337 | 12% | 65/511 |

## 7.1 Modelling the variable grammar for be like in nativised and Learner English — 127

**Table 72** (continued)

| | | | | |
|---|---|---|---|---|
| range | | 38 | | |
| **4. Socio-context** (*p* < 0.00155) | | | | |
| English-dominant | 0.703 | .669 | 31% | 99/318 |
| mixed | −0.004 | .499 | 24% | 351/1435 |
| Hindi-dominant | −0.698 | .332 | 7% | 29/365 |
| range | | 34 | | |
| **5. Gender** (*p* < 0.00973) | | | | |
| female | 0.431 | .606 | 27% | 313/1128 |
| male | −0.431 | .394 | 16% | 166/990 |
| range | | 21 | | |
| **6. Mimesis** (*p* < 8.97e-07) | | | | |
| mimetic | 0.297 | .574 | 28% | 345/1201 |
| not | −0.297 | .426 | 14% | 134/917 |
| range | | 16 | | |
| **7. Quote type** (*p* < 0.0175) | | | | |
| thought | 0.161 | .540 | 28% | 139/489 |
| indigenous | 0.102 | .526 | 22% | 22/100 |
| speech | −0.263 | .435 | 20% | 318/1529 |
| range | | 11 | | |
| **8. Speaker** | | random | std dev. | 0.892 |

**Note:** In each data set, the independent variables as well as individual language-internal and sociolinguistic predictors are reported in the order revealing their relative impact on the occurrence of the linguistic variant under study. The discussion is organised along the same lines. FW stands for factor weights, which report weighted probabilities placed on a scale from 1 to 0. The closer the factor weight is to 1, the more a given context favours the occurrence of *(be) like*. The closer the factor weight is to 0, the more this environment disfavours the occurrence of the variant under study.

Crucially, these findings could be largely replicated by the results stemming from fixed-effects modelling performed with the help of Goldvarb (see Table 89, Appendix D). The only difference between the two types of analysis is related to quote type, which was not selected as a significant constraint in the fixed-effects procedure (see also Davydova 2015b: 320). Interestingly, quote type is the weakest constraint operating on the variable grammar of *be like* when the individual speaker behaviour is taken into account. This is at odds with the results emerging from the research into the variable realisation of *be like* in native-speaker

English, where quote type has been revealed as one of its most important predictors (D'Arcy 2013; Tagliamonte and D'Arcy 2004, 2007).

Taken together, all these pieces of evidence could be adduced in favour of the contention (also argued for in Davydova 2015b: 330) that as a semantic-pragmatic constraint drawing upon a fine-grained distinction between expressive (thought) and narrative (reported speech) content, quote type presents a challenge to ESL learners, who – in the absence of direct, face-to-face contact with L1 speakers – might, indeed, experience difficulties, while trying to acquire it. The argument can be bolstered up by previous research into L2 acquisition, which has demonstrated rather unequivocally that learners do not have that much trouble acquiring overt and explicit aspects of linguistic structure but they do have a hard time trying to master subtle pragmatic, context-based distinctions in their second language (Coppieters 1987: 565) or distinctions that are "more semantically dense" (Collentine 2004: 228).

Our attention turns now to the sociolinguistic factors. All of the three language-external factors tested in statistical modelling were selected as significant in a model that considers all predictor variables simultaneously. Table 72 highlights that exposure to mass media is the strongest sociolinguistic predictor underlying the occurrence of quotative *be like* (*range 38*) followed by the sociolinguistic context (*range 34*), and gender (*range 21*). Thus, speakers watching English-speaking films and TV series on a regular basis are also the most likely users of *be like*. Those who do so every day favour the use of *be like* at .720, and those who indulge in mass media consumption two or three times a week prefer *be like* to other quotative markers at .534. Learners with less exposure to mass media are either fairly indifferent regarding the use of *be like* (FW .459 for 'once a week') or disprefer it altogether (FW .337 for 'less than once a week').

The sociolinguistic ecology is another viable predictor of the variable realisation of the linguistic innovation studied here, with English-dominant speakers embracing the variant at .669 and Hindi-dominant speakers disfavouring it in their speech (FW. 332). The former group of young individuals grew up speaking English in a largely monolingual fashion using it for communication with one of the siblings and/or one of the parents, or while interacting with their peers. The latter group of speakers grew up with Hindi as their major language, having acquired only some working knowledge of English for glaringly rare occasions of communication with outsiders. The third cohort of ESL learners, also called mixed bilinguals here, are fairly neutral with respect to the use of quotative *be like* (FW .499). Having grown in upwardly mobile middle class Indian families, these individuals have used English as an additional language alongside Hindi (and sometimes other dialects) since their mid-childhood starting around the age of five. The major reason for their relative reserve regarding the use of the globally innovative variant is the fact that, as we saw in Chapter 5, their system of variable quotative marking draws on a plethora of different linguistic resources including the innovative local variant *okay (fine)*. Nevertheless, the sociolinguistic differences underlying acquisition of English in India and resulting psycholinguistic realities are, indeed, striking. Crucially, they underpin the adoption and subsequent adaptation of a new linguistic form in a local speech community. As diverse as these sociolinguistic backgrounds are, they nevertheless stand the test of the mixed-effects modelling rising above the variability caused by the linguistic behaviour of individual speakers. This finding has important implications for the modelling of World Englishes, suggesting that sociolinguistic peculiarities of indigenised ecologies require some very careful consideration as they allow the researcher to pinpoint the agents and promoters of linguistic innovations. More generally, the finding substantiates and illustrates the variationist claim that "sociolinguistic factors, particularly social psychological ones, come to the fore in influencing the adoption or non-adoption of linguistic forms" (Kerswill and Williams 2002: 83). In so doing, it adds to the empirical research highlighting the importance of the local sociolinguistic setting, which has been shown to constrain not only phonological (Labov 2010[1972a]) and discourse-pragmatic (Tagliamonte and Denis 2010) variation but also patterns of code-switching (Poplack 1987).

Consistent with the earlier findings reported in Davydova (2015b) and Davydova (2016a), gender was selected as a genuine sociolinguistic predictor for the occurrence of quotative *be like* in the JNU data, with female speakers favouring the occurrence of *be like* at .606 and male speakers using it quite sparingly at .394. This finding provides support for the hypothesis postulating a link between the innovative variant and linguistic behaviour exhibited by women. Crucially, it highlights the role of women as leaders of language change (Labov 1990). Previous sociolinguistic research has accrued evidence that women not only actively participate in ongoing linguistic developments in native-speaker communities; more often than not, they advance those changes as well (D'Arcy 2005; Chambers 1992; Labov 1990; Nevalainen 2002; Raumolin-Brunberg and Nurmi 1997). Lange (2012) furthermore showed that Indian women profiled themselves as linguistic innovators in their local ESL communities. Results reported in Table 72 substantiate one of the major sociolinguistic findings, while providing further data obtained from indigenised English. Notice here also that the results obtained for the sociolinguistic predictors via mixed-effects model run in Rbrul were corroborated by the fixed-effects modelling performed with the help of Goldvarb. The two models converged both in terms of selected constraints as well as their direction (see Table 89, Appendix D).

What does the variable grammar of quotative marking look like in EFL English? Which systemic and language-external constraints operate on the variable use of *be like*? And how does that system compare to the system of quotative marking reported for ESL English? Table 73 presents results of the logistic regression analysis estimating contribution of four language-internal and three sociolinguistic predictors to the probability of occurrence of quotative *be like* in the MaCGE data.

**Table 73:** Logistic regression analysis of the contribution of language-internal and sociolinguistic constraints to the probability of *be like* in MaCGE, 2013–2015. Rbrul output.

| | | | | |
|---|---|---|---|---|
| Input probability | | | | 0.125 |
| Log likelihood | | | | −632.955 |
| R2 | | | | 0.441 |
| Total N | | | | 351/1412 |
| | Log odds | FW | % | N |
| **1. Grammatical subject** (*p* < 2e-19) | | | | |
| it | 2.344 | .912 | 75% | 53/70 |
| first | −0.118 | .470 | 26% | 100/380 |
| third | −0.370 | .409 | 22% | 173/774 |
| NA | −1.095 | .251 | 16% | 17/106 |
| second | −0.761 | .319 | 9% | 8/82 |
| range | | 66 | | |
| **2. Tense** (*p* <1.87e-09) | | | | |
| CHP | 0.958 | .723 | 35% | 42/118 |
| past | 0.575 | .640 | 28% | 195/677 |
| NA | 0.518 | .627 | 22% | 58/263 |
| present | −0.073 | .482 | 20% | 51/249 |
| modal | −1.978 | .122 | 4% | 5/105 |
| range | | 60 | | |
| **3. Mimesis** (*p* < 2.94e-14) | | | | |
| mimetic | 0.620 | .650 | 31% | 277/885 |
| not | −0.620 | .350 | 14% | 74/527 |
| range | | 30 | | |
| **4. Quote type** (*p* < 0.00977) | | | | |
| thought | 0.483 | .619 | 31% | 105/336 |
| speech | −0.048 | .488 | 23% | 237/1024 |
| indigenous | −0.435 | .393 | 17% | 9/52 |

## 7.1 Modelling the variable grammar for *be like* in nativised and Learner English — 131

**Table 73** (continued)

| | | | | |
|---|---|---|---|---|
| range | | 23 | | |
| **5. Socio-context** (*p* > 0.05) | | | | |
| North American exposure | 0.364 | [.590] | 32% | 159/490 |
| low-level naturalistic & high-level mass media | 0.003 | [.501] | 28% | 66/233 |
| mixed exposure | 0.033 | [.508] | 20% | 81/401 |
| lingua franca exposure | −0.039 | [.490] | 16% | 38/224 |
| low-level naturalistic & mass media | −0.361 | [.411] | 4% | 7/64 |
| range | | – | | |
| **6. Gender** (*p* > 0.05) | | | | |
| female | 0.283 | [.570] | 29% | 229/787 |
| male | −0.283 | [.430] | 19% | 122/625 |
| range | | – | | |
| **7. Mass media exposure** (*p* > 0.05) | | | | |
| two or three times a week | 0.433 | [.607] | 26% | 151/567 |
| every day | 0.081 | [.520] | 25% | 114/441 |
| once a week | −0.068 | [.483] | 25% | 54/208 |
| less than once a week | −0.446 | [.390] | 16% | 32/196 |
| range | | – | | |
| **8. Speaker** | | random | std. dev | 1.082 |

Table 73 reveals that four language-internal factors are at work in the corpus of German learners' English. Grammatical subject is the biggest predictor for the occurrence of *be like* (*range 66*), with neuter *it* highly favouring the innovative variant at .912. German learners also choose first- (FW .470) over third- (FW .409) person grammatical subject while using *be like* in their speech. Tense is the second strongest predictor (*range 60*), with CHP demonstrating a strong association with the variant under study (FW .723). Similar to HCNVE data, past tense morphology is also preferred with *be like* at .640. Mimesis is also implicated in the occurrence of the innovative form under analysis (*range 30*) and the constraint hierarchy is consistent with the prediction related to this factor group. Mimetic content shows a clear preponderance for *be like* (FW .650), and non-mimetic content is disassociated with the variant (FW .350). Last but certainly not least, quote type is at play in this data set (*range 23*), with quotes framing thought and inner dialogue favouring *be like* (FW .619) over quotes reporting speech (FW .488) and code-switches (FW .393). Remarkably, the fixed-effects modelling of this data set provides converging evidence for the results reported here. It does so not only in terms of the language-internal variables selected as significant and their relative impact exerted on the occurrence of quotative *be like* but also in terms of the ordering of specific constraints (see Table 90, Appendix D).

As for sociolinguistic predictors, none reached the statistical significance threshold when analysed via mixed-effects modelling with Rbrul. This means that neither of these factors was "strong enough to rise above the inter-speaker variation" (Johnson 2009: 365). This result is, however, in contrast with that stemming from the fixed-effects analysis of data run with Goldvarb. The latter indicates that, when individual linguistic behaviour is not taken into consideration, two sociolinguistic variables – sociolinguistic context and gender – are identified as significant for the variable realisation of *be like*. In alignment with the working hypothesis, female learners are more inclined to use quotative *be like* (FW .565), whereas male learners appear to be fairly neutral regarding its choice (FW .419, see Table 90, Appendix D).

Table 90 (Appendix D) furthermore reveals that the type of sociolinguistic contact with English in face-to-face interactions is relevant to the occurrence of quotative *be like* in the EFL data studied here. The constructed fixed-effects model indicates that German students with the dominant type of exposure to North American English are also the most probable users of *be like* (FW .595), as supported by the findings reported in Chapter 6 (Table 71). German learners exhibiting low levels of naturalistic exposure to L1 English but high levels of exposure to the English mass media trail in second place (FW .532). This learner group is followed by peers with mixed L1 inputs (FW .457) and with the dominant exposure to English in lingua franca contexts (FW .393). Learners with the low levels of naturalistic and mass media exposure are also least likely to use the innovative variant in their speech (FW .303).

Remarkably, these findings concur with the conclusions emerging from detailed analyses of the distributional patterns reported in Chapter 6 (Figure 5). Chapter 6 presented evidence that learners dominated by North American English approximate the grammar of quotative *be like* more closely than other learners, both in terms of relative frequencies as well as the most recent levelling tendencies reported for North American English (see Table 71). These are followed by learners exhibiting low levels of naturalistic exposure but high levels of contact with vernacular-like English through mass media (films and TV shows). The latter cohort resembles the North American group in that it uses *be like* at a compatible rate and maps *be like* on mimetic content far more frequently than on other quotative markers. Learners with the mixed type of L1 exposure and the lingua franca exposure learners fall behind both speaker groups on these parameters. Finally,

German learners demonstrating low levels of naturalistic and mass media exposure contrast with all the other learner groups as they use the innovative variant only very sparingly, and largely do not reconstruct the patterns reported for *be like*. With this said, the constraint hierarchy reported in Table 90 (Appendix D) provides independent evidence for the conclusions arrived at through consistent perusal of cross-tabulated patterns reported in Chapter 6 and summarised here for convenience.

The implications of these sociolinguistic findings stemming from the EFL English data are twofold. First and foremost, they highlight the primary importance of *prolonged face-to-face interactions* with a native-speaker community over other types of contact for the acquisition of vernacular patterns of variation. Secondly, they invite the analyst to re-assess the role played by mass media outlets in the propagation and ultimate adaptation of linguistic innovations by EFL learners. A hotly debated issue in current sociolinguistic thinking (see Androutsopoulos 2014a), mass media is largely believed to be subordinate to interpersonal contacts with respect to the role that it plays in the propagation of linguistic changes (Labov 2007; Trudgill 1986). Two pieces of EFL evidence can be brought forth to support this view. To begin with, the variable reflecting the amount of mass media consumption was not selected as a significant predictor in either fixed-effects or mixed-effects modelling of the EFL data. As far as this data pool is concerned, there is a lack of clear and unambiguous correlation between the use of the innovative variant on the one hand and media consumption behaviour on the other. This parameter comes to the fore of the analyst's attention only when operationalised through the sociolinguistic setting underlying L2 acquisition that reveals itself as a potential predictor of innovative *be like*. Moreover, learners with dominating exposure to North American English outperform all the other learner groups including those with elevated media consumption habits (see also Chapter 6).

Conversely, the very fact that German learners with high levels of media consumption managed to outperform learners with multiple and lingua franca exposures is informative. It suggests that the role played by mass media in the adoption of new linguistic features and their underlying patterns of use might not be as negligible as traditionally assumed (see Tagliamonte, D'Arcy, and Rodríguez Louro 2016; Trudgill 2014). Supported by the fact that 'mass media' is a significant predictor overriding intraspeaker variability in the ESL data set, the finding provides empirical support for the contention that *be like* and its system-internal conditioning floats globally not only through real space, but also through sustained media engagement practices (compare claims in Buchstaller 2004: 289–290, 2008: 19; Buchstaller and D'Arcy 2009: 293–294).

From a more general sociolinguistic perspective, we can safely draw the following conclusion relying on the pieces of evidence obtained from fixed- and mixed-effects modelling in both data sets. Sociolinguistic context and exposure to mass media are two potent predictors of occurrence of *be like* in ESL English but less so in Learner English, where individual intraspeaker variability overrides sociolinguistic constraints. What might explain the differences in the way the two sociolinguistic variables operate in the indigenised and Learner data? First and foremost, introduced during the colonial era by the citizens of the British Empire, English boasts a 400-year-old history on the Indian subcontinent and is, by and large, shaped by constant linguistic practices in various speech communities scattered throughout the country. Since in these speech communities English is put to use on a day-to-day basis, local sociolinguistic ecologies get to play a prominent role in the process called 'group [second-language] acquisition', resulting in 'in-group vernaculars' (Winford 2003: 242). Because English has been around in India for such a long period of time, it has taken sociolinguistic roots. Effectively this means is that the local linguistic micro-climate, to which English has naturally adapted over four centuries, actively shapes the structured variation attested in ESL English and the resulting local outcomes. In Germany, similar to other countries of Western Europe, the situation is somewhat different. On the one hand, English began to play an important role as a means of (international) communication only in the second half of the 20th century, accompanied by the emergence of the US as the world's leading political and socioeconomic power.[1] In other words, the time span that has been allotted to English for sociolinguistic adaptation in the EFL countries is much smaller. Conversely, unlike ESL communities, EFL learner groups do not exploit English for inter-group communication, using it for communication with outsiders instead. The local setting in which English is put to use is, therefore, very different. The language is encountered in academic halls; it is heard on TV, YouTube, and other social media platforms. Yet rarely is it a means of interpersonal contact within a living community. This is, of course, not to deny the importance of EFL learners' biographies, which might lead, as we saw in Chapter 6, to differing linguistic outcomes. These differences in individual experiences of the EFL learners, however, operate on a different level than the differences accounting for the individual experiences

---

[1] In Germany, English began to make inroads into the social system towards the end of the 18th century, when commercial schools with provisions of modern languages were established in Hamburg and Berlin. The early 19th century saw the introduction of school reforms which made provisions for modern languages, including English, in the final years of the grammar school and in the *Realschulen* [secondary modern schools] (see Linn 2016: 15).

of the ESL learners. They are not much of a predictor when intraspeaker variability is taken into account in EFL English but they are always at work in ESL English. This micro-sociolinguistic finding pinpoints a chasm existing between the two varietal types in the sense of Kachru (1985) and McArthur (1998). On the whole, linguistic practices adopted by different social groups play a much bigger role in indigenised English actively shaping its formation to the extent that these individual differences can be construed as various aspects of the sociolinguistic reality permeating ESL speakers' life. In other words, individual experiences with English are different but constitutive facets of an ESL speech community as a whole. In contrast, EFL learners are, indeed, just learners; English is not an inherent part of their community life. Consequently, constraints revealing different experiences with English are not sufficiently robust to override linguistic variability caused by individual speakers.

Similarly, the variable 'exposure to mass media' operates differently in the two types of English. The reason why media-viewing habits play such a critical role in an indigenised setting may be related to the fact that speakers of Indian English do not, as a rule, have an opportunity to travel the world and experience English-speaking cultures firsthand. For German learners, watching films and TV series in English is a viable but not an exclusive option to gain the latest knowledge about the Anglo-Saxon world. In contrast, young Indians are dependent to a greater extent on media consumption. Consuming products of English-speaking television and film-making industry allows them to participate in the mainstream culture of the globalising world in ways that are not accessible otherwise. It is for this reason that young ESL speakers from India might be far more eager to attend, and consequently be more psychologically attuned, to the linguistic and cultural input encountered in various types of English-speaking media. For them, it is the sole means of making contact with the wider English-speaking reality. In line with the notion of 'engagement with the media texts' (Androutsopoulos 2014b: 16), I propose the existence of two socio-(psychological) tendencies in attending to the platforms of culture dissemination which ultimately underpin viewing habits of ESL/EFL learners. One tendency is characterised by a complete alignment with, and perhaps in some cases even an immersion in, the cultural product being consumed. The other tendency essentially lacks such a profound tuning into the linguistic and cultural material offered by the media of mass communication. In the case of ESL English, the propensity for greater psychological attachment to the global media products shows up as a significant predictor in the variationist analysis rising above intraspeaker variability. In the case of EFL English, it does not for reasons upon which this section has elaborated on.

## 7.2 Acquiring a variable grammar

Let us now take one step back and try to see a bigger picture emerging from the results presented so far. Considering all the evidence, the previous discussion yields one vital observation: There are striking similarities in the language-internal mechanism underpinning the use of quotative *be like* in ESL and EFL English. These are evidenced by (i) the relative frequency with which the variant is encountered in the data; (ii) the significance and relative impact of language-internal predictors and (iii) the ordering of specific constraints. These are summarised for convenience in Table 74.

**Table 74:** Language-internal constraints underlying the variable use of quotative *be like* in HCNVE, 2007–2014 and MaCGE, 2013–2015: A summary.

|  | HCNVE | MaCGE |
|---|---|---|
| **Percentages** for *be like* | 17.5% | 20.3% |
| **Constraints** | | |
| *Gram. subject* | | |
| First over third | √ | √ |
| Levelled | – | – |
| A close link to neuter *it* | *be like* | *be like* |
| *Tense marking* | | |
| A close link to CHP | *be like* | *be like* |
| *Mimesis* | | |
| A close link to mimetic content | *be like* | *be like* |
| *Quote type* | | |
| Thought over speech | √ | √ |
| Levelled | – | – |

Table 74 reveals that, when considered as a whole speech community, both ESL and EFL learners use *be like* at a comparable rate. Grammatical subject is the biggest predictor for the occurrence of quotative *be like* in both indigenised and Learner data, with *be like* being highly favoured by neuter *it*. Notice also that *be like* is consistently favoured with first over third person grammatical subjects in both varieties. Tense is the second significant predictor for the occurrence of *be like* in Indian and German Learner English. Relying on data provided in Table 72 and Table 73, we can also recognise the close ties between *be like* and CHP, and to some degree past tense morphology, in both speaker communities. Mimesis is the third language-internal constrained that reached statistical significance threshold in both speaker groups, and, here again, *be like* consistently encodes quotes containing mimetic content. Finally, when constructed via mixed-effects modelling, quote type is a pertinent predictor in both varieties, with inwardly realised mental activities consistently favouring the use of *be like* over outwardly realised material in both types of English.

These findings overhaul the hypothesis formulated in Chapter 4, which predicted improved adoption and adaptation of the innovative variant by EFL learners given their generally exonormative (pro-US English) mindset, yet allow me to draw two major conclusions. Firstly, though alive and well, *be like* is by and large an incipient variant, undergoing an early stage of grammaticalisation in both varietal types. Outlined in Chapter 2, the grammaticalisation theory predicts the incremental spread of the incipient variant into an increasing number of contexts (Ferrara and Bell 1995; Tagliamonte and Hudson 1999). Following this logic, the more robust a given variant is across different linguistic environments, the more evolved it can be assumed to be in the system as a whole.

The preceding analyses show that overall rates of use of *be like* lag behind those documented for native-speaker English. Further evidence supporting the contention that *be like* is at an early stage of development in ESL/EFL English stems from language-internal diagnostics. Firstly, *be like* has preserved a link to first person grammatical subject. Moreover, it is largely circumscribed to CHP and has not yet covered generic present tense morphology or modal verb marking. Thirdly, *be like* has not spread to the reporting of non-mimetic content in both ESL and EFL English. Finally, *be like* is far more robust with quotes reporting thought, and has only started to encroach on the function of direct speech reporting, including code-switched content.

With this said, how come that both ESL and EFL language learners have generally adopted the incoming variant to only a modest degree? In Davydova (2015b), I argued that in a local endonormatively oriented socio-ecology, a newly imported vernacular feature stands in direct competition with other language forms for the expression of a particular linguistic function. Subject to further selectionist pressures, this "feature pool" (Mufwene 2001) emerges as a consequence of multilingual inputs, including speakers' L1 and contact-induced innovations recruited both locally and globally. Because a borrowed linguistic innovation is forced to vie for a place in a highly competitive system (see also Chapter 5), it is adopted at a modest rate. Though not implausible, this explanation is incomplete as it tells us nothing about the mechanism of feature adoption in an EFL socio-ecology, where, as we have seen, the overall composition of the feature pool is substantially reduced and primarily limited to the variants of the donor variety. Moreover, this explanation does not tackle the possible sociopsychological pressures underpinning the process of feature adoption in a local speech community. Yet, whether or not a globally available linguistic item is subsequently adopted by a local group largely depends on speakers' social evaluations of the feature in question. Chapter 8 will examine attitudes harboured by ESL and EFL learners towards quotative *be like*. In so doing, it will assess the role played by learners' perceptions in the process of appropriation of global linguistic resources.

Secondly and perhaps even more importantly, we have also seen that *be like* has systematic and parallel linguistic patterning in both learner communities. These patterns of use mirror those reported for L1 English, particularly North American English, the epicentre of this global linguistic innovation. Crucially, this finding suggests that, when a birds' eye perspective is taken into account, the functional evolution of *be like* must have been following a very similar trajectory or pathway of development in indigenised and Learner English.

This is quite remarkable given the fact that variationist studies exploring the adaptation of variable linguistic features in different speech communities around the world report the re-organisation of the language-internal conditioning in recipient varieties during the process of linguistic diffusion. Initially, the previous literature documents that when a linguistic item enters a new sociolinguistic ecology, it begins to interact with the local structures within an established system. Subsequently, it is "integrated into pre-existing norms and practices" (Buchstaller and D'Arcy 2009: 114), which might result in the readjustment of linguistic patterns in comparison with the donor variety. The result is thus "local not universal outcomes" (Britain 2002: 617).

The re-organisation of the language-internal conditioning has also been reported for situations of language contact. Meyerhoff (2009) explores the reconstruction of the language-internal predictors underlying the overt marking of subjects and objects in a contact linguistic variety called Bislama. Drawing on variationist comparisons between two local languages, Bislama (the recipient variety) and Tamambo (the donor variety), Meyerhoff (2009: 309–310) demonstrates that grammatical constraints operating on the variable realisation of subjects and objects gets only partially replicated in the recipient variety of Bislama: some significant constraints in the donor variety lose their impact in the recipient language. Furthermore, for some independent variables, the individual constraint hierarchies get reversed.

Moreover, the readjustment of language-internal constraints relative to the donor variety has been documented and discussed in variationist studies dealing with second-language acquisition of sociolinguistic variation. The studies conducted by Adamson and Regan (1991), Bayley (1994), Blondeau and Nagy (1998, 2008), Davydova (2011, 2013), Dewaele (2004), Howard, Lemée, and Regan (2006), Knaus and Nadasdi (2001), Meyerhoff and Schleef (2012, 2013), Mougeon, Rehner, and Nadasdi (2004), Regan (1996), Rehner and Mougeon (1999), Rehner,

Mougeon, and Nadasdi (2003), Sankoff et al. (1997), Schleef (2017), Schleef, Meyerhoff, and Clark (2011), Sharma (2005), Sharma and Sankaran (2011), Wolfram (1985), and Young (1991) focus explicitly on the acquisition of sociolinguistic competence by second language learners (see also Labov 2007 and Trudgill 1986: 35–36 for the acquisition of a second dialect). The overall result stemming from this strand of sociolinguistic research is that while L2 learners oftentimes manage to approximate (Selinker 1972) the patterns of variation set out by native speakers, they seldom reconstruct these with precise detail. In what follows, I present and briefly describe a selection of case studies from the domains of phonology and morphosyntax illustrating how this is the case.

Turning our attention to phonological variables, Schleef, Meyerhoff, and Clark (2011) studied the acquisition of the well-known variable (ing) by Polish-born teenagers living in Edinburgh and London. The variable (ing) refers to the alternative realisation of the alveolar and velar nasal allophones – [ɪn] vs [ɪŋ] – in unstressed syllables. Employing the variationist method of contrastive analysis, the authors show that Polish learners of English adopt the vernacular variant at much lower rates than their locally-born peers from Edinburgh and London. Whereas Edinburgh natives use the non-standard [ɪn] at the rate of 68% in their speech, Polish teenagers have appropriated the variant to a less conspicuous degree, using [ɪn] in 33% of all cases. A very similar picture could be gleaned from Schleef et al.'s London data, where the native population uses the vernacular variant more often than young migrants from Poland (24% and 14% respectively). Mixed-effects multiple regression furthermore revealed that two language-internal variables, grammatical category and the number of syllables, were selected as significant constraints on the variation of (ing) in both speaker groups living in Edinburg. However, the internal weightings of individual predictors show idiosyncratic patterning, suggesting that Polish-born teenagers struggle with the adoption of native-like patterns of use. In London, the picture of acquisition is even less complete since Polish-born adolescents managed to reconstruct only one constraint on the variation of (ing) attested in the native-speaker data – the phonological segment preceding the variable item. The findings reported in Schleef, Meyerhoff, and Clark (2011) echo those documented in Adamson and Regan (1991), who examined the variable realisation of (ing) among Vietnamese and Cambodian learners of English living in Philadelphia and Washington, D.C. Here, the authors showed that although grammatical category was a significant predictor in both native and non-native data, the favouring and disfavouring effects of individual grammatical categories (nouns, adjectives, verbs, gerunds, etc.) differed across L1 and L2 groups.

Schleef (2017) examines the acquisition of the variable glottal replacement of (t) in mid-word and final positions (for instance, *water*/wɔːtə/vs./wɔːʔə/and *what*/wɒt/vs./wɒʔ/) by Polish-born adolescents living in London. In this longitudinal study, the author explores the impact of six language-internal predictors on the probability of occurrence of the vernacular glottal variant across three learner groups differing from each other with respect to the amount of time spent in the target sociolinguistic environment. Using speech produced by London-born teenagers as an appropriate L1 benchmark, Schleef demonstrates that (1). following context, (2). grammatical category, (3). preceding context, and (4). lexical frequency are the significant predictors for the glottal variant used in the middle of the word, while (1). following context, (2). preceding context, and (3). lexical frequency underlie the realisation of the word-final glottal replacement in L1 English. None of these constraints was documented as relevant to the word-medial realisation of the glottal stop in speech of Polish-born teenagers who have lived in London between seven and 23 months, and two predictors, i.e. grammatical category and lexical frequency, operate on the variable use of glottal replacement word-finally. Notice that grammatical category was not chosen as a significant constraint for the word-final glottal replacement in native English. In other words, Polish learners seem to realise that grammatical category is relevant to the variable realisation of the glottal stop but they assign it to a different speech segment (word-final instead of word-medial). This constraint continues to operate on the word-final (t) in speech of Polish-born teens who have spent more than three years in London indicating a re-allocation of language-internal conditioning in the learner interlanguage. Further details aside, Schleef (2017) concludes that "[w]hile some constraints are replicated completely, there is also evidence that some are altered, some are rejected and some are re-interpreted, resulting in new constraints".

With regard to the domain of morphosyntax, Rehner and Mougeon (1999) explored the language-internal and language-external conditioning on the omission of the preverbal negator *ne* in speech of Anglophone students enrolled in immersion programmes in Canada. The authors report that the independent variable 'post verbal negators' (*pas*, *plus*, *rien*, etc.) is a significant predictor for the deletion of *ne* by L2 learners. More specifically, most post verbal negators show a favouring effect for *ne* deletion (FW .77) with the exception of the post verbal *pas*, which is associated with the retention of *ne*. At first glance, it seems logical since the two-pronged pattern of negation '*ne* + MAIN VERB + *pas*', e.g. *je ne sais pas*, is the default strategy to build negative sentences in standard French, to which all learners are exposed in classroom. However, the authors argue that the effect of post verbal negators is not attested in Canadian French spoken in Quebec and Ontario. In these French vernaculars, the rates of *ne* deletion have reached such high rates that the effect of post verbal negators as a systemic factor is no longer evident. Being primarily exposed to the standard usage promoting the simultaneous occurrence of *ne* and *pas* in a negation structure, Anglophone learners of French fail to pick up on the levelling tendency attested in the ambient language of L1 speakers (see also Rehner and Mougeon 1999: 147).

Davydova (2013) explored the variable realisation of the *have* perfect marking in Singapore English, which is a recipient variety and a product of L2 acquisition, and compared it to that of the 19th century Irish English. The latter is one of the input varieties that contributed historically to the development of English in Singapore. Many teachers recruited into Singaporean missionary schools in the 19th century were Irish Catholics. These Catholic schools, in which teachers from Ireland have been a prominent element, are still highly regarded in Singapore (see Davydova 2013: 198). The study tested the effect of five language-internal predictors: (1). semantic-pragmatic context, (2). transitivity, (3). negation, (4). time adverbial specification, and (5). verb semantics on the occurrence of the structure featuring auxiliary *have* followed by a past participle of the main verb. The use of the *have* perfect is typically mastered by language learners in a classroom setting and this feature was thus a good diagnostic tool allowing to explore the extent to which Singaporean learners of English were able to master the variable use of the *have* perfect attested in the input of the Irish missionaries. The study showed that the same factor groups were chosen as statistically significant constraints on the variable in both varieties (1 through 4). The ordering of these factor groups, however, differed in relation to each other alongside the favourable impact of individual constraints. Thus, whereas semantic-pragmatic context, transitivity, negation, and time adverbial specification are all significant predictors for the occurrence of the *have* perfect, they operate somewhat differently in these historically related Englishes. In the input variety of Irish English, the semantic-pragmatic force of the context in which the variant occurs has the strongest impact on the *have* perfect followed by negation, transitivity, and, finally, time adverbial specification (1–3–2–4). In the ESL variety of Singapore English, the tested predictors follow a slightly different ordering with negation taking the lead followed by transitivity, pragmatic context, and time adverbial specification (3–2–1–4). Moreover, some individual constraints function differently in each variety. Whereas copula *be* has a huge favouring impact on the occurrence of the *have* perfect in the recipient variety (FW .81), it has no visible favouring effect in the input variety (FW .42), a finding suggesting that second language learners in Singapore have re-analysed some of the functions of the L2 form through developing new, previously non-existing uses. The phenomenon is well described in the literature dealing with the acquisition of a second language (see, for instance, Slobin 1993: 239–252).

It follows from previous discussion that the non-adoption, partial replication and re-allocation of the native-speaker variability are very common, indeed pervasive, scenarios in the L2 acquisition of sociolinguistic competence. In such situations of language contact, language learners "either produce a different version of native speakers' variable grammar by re-ordering the internal hierarchies of existing constraints or they create novel constraints that are not attested in speech of native speakers" Schleef, Meyerhoff, and Clark (2011: 225).

With this said, how can we account for the fact that language-internal conditioning on variation tends to get re-organised in situations of language and dialect contact as well as second-language acquisition? In an attempt to provide a broad explanation of the phenomenon of systemic restructuring, Meyerhoff (2009: 313) suggests that the re-organisation of language-internal patterning is quite normal as "the process of transferring – or replicating more generally – patterns from the model to the replica language may be sufficiently cognitively demanding that speakers cannot replicate (or perhaps do not care if they replicate) the linguistic detail of the model in the replica language". She surmises that there must be a general cognitive principle, "transformation under transfer" (Meyerhoff 2003), which prevents speakers in contact from reconstructing the variable grammar in full detail. Meyerhoff (2009) does not explicitly say what underpins this principle leading to such a "creative" transformation of systemic constraints. Given what we know about cognitive processes involved in language processing, it seems plausible to suggest that the phenomenon must be grounded in the constraints related to the limited capacities of the human working memory and relatively reduced attentions spans in online processing both of which might exacerbate speakers' ability to extract complex, probabilistically organised pieces of information from the incoming language material.

Furthermore, the re-structuring of the language-internal mechanism governing variation can be brought into a slightly different light when the actual mode of acquisition is taken into consideration. This is how Schleef, Meyerhoff, and Clark (2011: 226) describe it:

> L1 learners [internalise] variable input [...], replicating stable variation or advancing changes in progress, based on a very rich diet of sociolinguistic information from birth. L2 learners (especially those in their teens or adulthood) in a situation of language contact do not have access to the same depth and breadth of information about the nature of a variable than an L1 learner does. Perhaps this is because the plasticity of adolescents' and adults' language faculty is reduced due to physiological changes, or perhaps it is simply because they get much less exposure to the language than little children do before they (must) start producing. This is surely an important question. One possibility is that [i]t can be seen as collateral damage in the complicated and challenging business of identifying 1) variants, 2) the independent factors constraining those variants, and 3) the ordering of specific constraints in those factors. It requires highly detailed levels of linguistic analysis which may be more than L2 learners are exposed to, or that they can take the time to replicate.

The "plasticity of [the] language faculty" evoked by Schleef and colleagues might be attributed to the process of neural recruitment (Lakoff 2013a), which is the natural ability of the human brain to build ties between neural circuits, called synaptic connections, eventually resulting in highly complex neural structures, the sum of which is called connectome. Modern neuroscience informs us that each individual is born with 100 billion neuro cells, or neurons, and each of them has 10.000 connections, inputs and outputs, resulting in a quadrillion of synaptic connections. Half of them die by the time a child becomes five years old. This fact suggests that the first five years are crucial for the linguistic and cognitive development of a newly born (Lakoff 2013b). The building of new neural connections is still possible after that age although it does not seem to take place at the same rate or with the same intensity (see Lakoff 2013a for more detail).

Apart from the neurological distinctions underpinning the process of L1 and L2 acquisition, there are other factors, linguistic and socio-psychological, that might affect acquisition of patterns of language use. Linguistic factors include L1 transfer, universal L2 learning strategies (Davydova 2011) as well as constraint complexity (Meyerhoff and Schleef 2013), typological proximity of the languages in contact, and relative frequency with which a given variant is used in speech. The socio-psychological determinants comprise the amount of stay-abroad exposure (Davydova and Buchstaller 2015); the thorny concept of learners' linguistic identities (Regan and Ní Chasaide 2010), their attitudes towards the speakers of the donor variety and the incoming variants (Sharma 2005; Schleef, Meyerhoff, and Clark 2011) and, finally, the social salience of a variable involved in L2 acquisition (see also Schleef 2017).

Supported by a preliminary study reported in Davydova and Buchstaller (2015), the pieces of evidence presented in this chapter pinpoint a fairly accurate replication of the variable grammar by language learners. Surprisingly, given previous research, both Indian and German learners do a fine job replicating patterns of variation even though, as we have seen, *be like* is, by and large, an incipient variant in both types of English studied here, adopted at a noticeable, yet moderate rate. It is also striking that an accurate replication of the patterns of variation has taken place in two highly distinctive sociolinguistic ecologies (see also Chapters 2, 5, and 6). Furthermore, Chapter 6 detailed that EFL learners who had reported stays-abroad exposure spent an average of seven to nine months in the preferred naturalistic environment. (Recall that in Schleef's (2017) study, the target-like acquisition of the glottal replacement is not entirely complete even after three years of exposure to the L1 vernacular.) The main finding of this chapter, i.e. a generally wholesale replication of the language-internal constraints on variation of quotative *be like* by ESL and EFL speakers, is, therefore, an important one and requires an explanation. Which factors might have contributed to a successful acquisition of the structured variation that governs the occurrence of one variant (quotative *be like*) as opposed to the others? Having briefly introduced the major linguistic and socio-psychological determinants of L2 acquisition and language/dialect contact, the preceding paragraph has made clear that this is a complex issue with a host of potentially competing explanations. In the remainder of this book, I will discuss these contributing factors in more detail. Specifically, I will elaborate on social evaluations of the incoming variant by ESL/EFL speakers, frequency, and salience, as these phenomena do not only appear to play a highly fostering role in the L2 acquisition but are also important to our understanding of how language varies and how it ultimately changes over time.

# 8 Non-native speakers' perceptions and adaptation of global linguistic innovations

The preceding chapters have explored the ways in which ESL and EFL speakers have adopted quotative *be like* by investigating the language-internal and sociolinguistic factors underpinning the mechanism of L2 acquisition of linguistic variation. We have discovered that overall, learners from both student communities have adopted the linguistic innovation at a relatively moderate rate hovering around 20%, which is in stark contrast to the rates with which their L1 peers use this form. Simultaneously, Chapter 7 presented evidence demonstrating that the language-internal conditioning that governs the use of *be like* is remarkably uniform across both speaker groups. Crucially, these patterns of use are highly consistent with those documented for native English users. Against this backdrop, the following question arises, 'How come that L2 learners do so well replicating the variable grammar of *be like* and yet, do not adopt the variant at a noticeably high rate in their speech? How can one possibly explain this apparent discrepancy?'

In order to find an answer to this remarkable yet puzzling fact, I set out to explore the social meanings that language learners attach to *be like* and contrast them with those reported for their L1 peers. This is because "there is a strong need to view individual linguistic features more explicitly and carefully in terms of their social embedding and evaluation (to use Labov's terms)" (Kerswill and Williams 2002: 91). This chapter will therefore place emphasis on the exploration of the evaluative side of L2 linguistic structure, which is pivotal to our understanding of the major mechanisms underpinning the evolution of language (Garrett 2010: 179).

Chapter 2 highlighted the fact that language users may exploit different linguistic items in order to signal a particular social meaning. For instance, while using a linguistic item X, a person may want to communicate, however implicitly, that she is a sophisticated language user, a rebel, a school geek, or a cool girl. In order to understand better why ESL/EFL learners use quotative *be like* the way they do, we need to explore which socio-cultural meanings are attached to the variant in the target speech communities. We also need to ascertain whether language learners evaluate *be like* along similar lines or whether they have developed new, idiosyncratic meanings in their interlanguage. Discovering whether and to what extent ESL/EFL learners are able to identify how *be like* is evaluated in the target speech community is important and this procedure might, in turn, allow us to make plausible predictions regarding the likely developmental trajectory of the innovative variant in non-native English. This issue is also interesting from the perspective of second-language acquisition as it helps us understand the extent to which language learners are capable of acquiring indexical information as well as the factors mediating this process.

While embarking on the investigations of perceptions of *be like*, it is important to bear in mind that as a feature of vernacular speech, *like* surfaces in three major functions: (1) *like* as a non-contrastive focuser or a discourse particle (henceforth, DisPrt), (2) *like* as a discourse marker and (3) *like* as a part of the quotative template, the focal point of our attention. As a DisPrt, *like* may occur in front of a verb, a noun phrase, a prepositional phrase, an adjective or an adverb, as illustrated in (104) through (107). As a discourse marker, *like* is typically placed at the beginning or at the end of a clause, as illustrated in (108) and (109) (Levey 2003: 25). In contrast to the quotative use of *like* dating to the late 1970s/early 1980s, the first two uses are not recent innovations in vernacular style. In fact, previous research suggests that as a DisPrt, *like* has been around for about a century, and even longer than that in its function as a discourse marker (Romaine and Lange 1991: 270). Furthermore, in contrast to quotative *be like*, the origin of both non-quotative uses cannot be unequivocally circumscribed to the US. As a marker, *like* is attested in the British literary sources of the 19th century (D'Arcy 2007: 401). As a particle, it has been documented in speech of elderly speakers from New Zealand whose parents had emigrated to New Zealand from England, Ireland and Scotland, not from the US (D'Arcy 2007: 401). These observations are relevant because ESL/EFL English learners encounter both quotative and non-quotative uses of *like* in their input. This being stated, it is clear that the acquisition of ideological and social meanings attached to innovative *be like*, as opposed to other related forms, may not be an entirely straightforward task for an L2 learner. Moreover, most native speakers with no training in linguistics tend to believe that there is just one vernacular use of *like*, yet they claim they see the difference between the quotative and non-quotative uses once it is pointed out to them (Dailey-O'Cain 2000: 70). A pertinent question is whether or not non-native speakers of English will also exhibit the same kind of sociolinguistic awareness with respect to the major vernacular uses of *like*.

(104) He **like** went there for **like** a whole month. (before a verb and a noun phrase)

(105) It was **like** under covers. (before a prepositional phrase)

(106) She was **like** pretty. (before an adjective)

(107) They moved **like** slowly. (before an adverb)

(108) **Like** they began putting things together. (before a clause)

(109) They were all tired **like**, and wanted to go home. (at the end of a clause)

Previous research also informs us that the recent rise and subsequent spread of innovative *be like* has been accompanied by overt and fairly mixed commentaries voiced on the Internet, in the press and expressed by a more general public in the English-speaking world (Buchstaller 2014: 198–244). A vernacular feature involved in an ongoing language change, *be like* has been fully endorsed by some speakers and countered by others. These vast differences in opinions are largely due to the fact that discussions surrounding the spread of vernacular innovations tend to be couched in terms of standard language ideologies, which pursue the sole goal of retaining the 'pure' form of language and, therefore, resist any incoming variants, particularly those associated with the spoken register. A noticeable feature of vernacular style, *be like* has been shrouded in a plethora of deeply entrenched beliefs. D'Arcy (2007: 388) reports that popular beliefs about *(be) like* include the following (i) it is meaningless and lacks articulacy, (ii) characterises female speech, (iii) originated in the Valley Girl Talk, and, by this token, evokes associations with (upper-)middle class, and (iv) is associated with young people speech, particularly adolescents.

Against this backdrop, it is not entirely surprising that *be like* has acquired a full range of connotations, both positive and negative, in those speech communities where English is spoken as a native idiom (Buchstaller 2006, 2014; Dailey-O'Cain 2000; D'Arcy 2007). On the one hand, *be like* has been embraced as a socially attractive feature of informal style performing "important and palpable functions in face-to-face interactions" (D'Arcy 2007: 395). Ever since the 1980s, *be like* has been "gain[ing] prestige as a trendy and socially desirable way to voice a speaker's inner experience" (Tagliamonte and Hudson 1999: 212). On the other, *be like*-users are assigned considerably less social status and prestige. Extrapolated from Buchstaller (2014: 213, 216), Table 75 details how UK and US speakers rate *be like*-users in terms of personality judgements.

**Table 75:** Native speakers' personality judgements for *be like* (extrapolated from Buchstaller (2014: 213, 216) in Davydova, Tytus, and Schleef (2017: 7)).

| *Be like* use is associated with the speaker seeming more | |
|---|---|
| extroverted | UK and US |
| fashionable | UK and US |
| British | UK |
| cheerful | UK |
| excited | UK |
| good sense of humour | UK |
| popular | UK |
| urban | UK |
| American | US |

(continued)

**Table 75** (continued)

| Be like use is associated with the speaker seeming less | |
|---|---|
| articulate | UK and US |
| intelligent | UK and US |
| pleasant | UK and US |
| professional | UK and US |
| reliable | UK and US |
| responsible | UK and US |
| successful | UK and US |
| ambitious | UK |
| educated | UK |
| honest | UK |

Whether and to what extent a given language form is likely to make further advancements in a given speech community, including learner speech communities, depends crucially on speakers' implicit and explicit perceptions of that linguistic variant. Sociolinguistic theory informs us that "for innovative forms to be taken up and advanced, they need to be positively connotated, be it with attractive social attributes or with social groups that are perceived as fashionable or worth emulating" (Labov 2001; Mesthrie et al. 2000; Silverstein 2003, cited in Buchstaller 2014: 207). With this in mind, I carried out an attitudinal survey in both student communities described in the preceding chapters. The data collection took place in JNU and UM in the time period from 2015 to 2016. In Mannheim, the data was collected and evaluated in collaboration with Agniezska Ewa Tytus (University of Mannheim) and Erik Schleef (University of Manchester) (see also Davydova, Tytus, and Schleef 2017).

The data was collected from students' who were currently enrolled in Bachelors' and Masters' degree programmes. Three respondents were doctoral students (one from New Delhi and two from Mannheim). Importantly, there were no trained linguists in both samples. In JNU, a total of 147 participants (65 (44%) males and 82 (56%) females) provided their responses to the questionnaire, and in Mannheim, the number of participants amounted to 196 (70 (36%) males and 126 (64%) females). The mean age of JNU participants is 24.23 (SD = 3.2), whereas the mean age of UM participants is 23.34 (SD = 3.6). All JNU participants were Asians, born and raised in India. All UM participants were Caucasian, born and raised in Germany.

Most respondents in both student communities claimed they were able to speak English fluently since they were 16 years old. In addition, most Indian students reported either advanced (N = 44, 30%) or (upper-)intermediate (N = 92, 62%) proficiency in English. In turn, most German students assessed their knowledge of

**Table 76:** JNU and UM samples by stays abroad in an English-speaking country.

| Number of times | JNU sample N (%) | UM sample N (%) |
|---|---|---|
| four times and more | 2 (1%) | 85 (44%) |
| three times | 3 (2%) | 20 (10%) |
| twice | 4 (3%) | 38 (19%) |
| once | 5 (3%) | 29 (15%) |
| never | 133 (91%) | 24 (12%) |
| Total N | 147 (100%) | 196 (100%) |

English as either advanced (N = 124, 63%) or (upper-)intermediate (N = 71, 36%). In JNU, 17 (12%) respondents claimed they were native English speakers, 45 (31%) students thought they were learners of English, whereas a majority (N = 82, 56%) expressed a belief that they were L2 English speakers. In Mannheim, a vast majority of respondents (N = 162, 83%) considered themselves to be English learners. Furthermore, a big majority of JNU students (N = 93, 63%) stated that they speak Indian English, whereas in Mannheim, young adults seem to believe that they speak either American (N = 57, 29%) or British English (N = 44, 22%) or a mixture of both dialects (N = 40, 20%). A relatively small number of students are of the opinion that they speak German English (N = 30, 15%). The final point of comparison for sociodemographic characteristics of both speaker groups concerns the amount of time spent in an English-speaking environment. Once again, differences are rather dramatic between the two student communities, as reported in Table 76. In JNU, an overwhelming majority of the sample (N = 133, 91%) reports that they have never visited an English-speaking country. This is in contrast to my German students' travelling habits: 85 (44%) informants report four and more sojourns in an English-speaking state, and 87 (44%) students claim to have visited an English-speaking country with a frequency ranging from one to three occasions.

The survey is a replication of Buchstaller's (2014) study of British and American speakers' perceptions of quotative *be like*, with some moderate, study-specific adjustments. The results reported in Buchstaller (2014: 198–244) serve as a suitable L1 benchmark against which the ESL/EFL data can be evaluated and interpreted. It consisted of a VGT task exploring learners' intuitive judgements and implicit beliefs about *be like* followed by a task tapping into learners' overt attitudes and was accompanied by a background questionnaire eliciting informants' age, sex, ethnicity, academic degree, their self-reported proficiency in English, linguistic identity and the length of residence in an English-speaking country (see also Appendix E).

The VGT task comprised two texts presented for convenience in Figure 6. Both texts were tested for regional neutrality and nativeness, and both texts feature no non-standard spellings, regional morphosyntactic features or regional lexical material (see Buchstaller 2014: 211). Both texts represent naturally occurring data and are similar in that each comprises 12 lines and contains six quotative variants. The crucial difference between the two conditions was that in Excerpt 1 Speaker A produces innovative *be like* three times, whereas Speaker X from Excerpt 2 introduces reported speech material via *say*. In this construction, the test exhibits a relatively high level of sophistication and methodological rigour. However, one still cannot exclude the possibility of the text material functioning as a possible confounding variable in the research design of the study since it is next to impossible to devise two texts that would evoke exactly the same associations. In order to solve this methodological problem and following Buchstaller's (2014) lead, I had half of my informants in each speech community fill in a survey in which *be like* tokens were contained in Excerpt 1. Subsequently, half of the informants were given a survey in which *be like* tokens were now contained in Excerpt 2. The stimuli (quotative *be like* and quotative *say*) were retained in their initial positions, i.e. Speaker A was linked to *be like* and Speaker X to *say* irrespective of the carrier material. Swapping the texts this way allowed me to achieve independence of the stimuli, i.e. quotative markers, from the speech excerpts in which they are contained.

Excerpt 1

A: I really like nuts but I am allergic to them.
At first I was sceptical about seeing a doctor.
I thought "how can a doctor help me with this?"
But finally I went to see this doctor.
I said "when I eat nuts I feel as if I have a heart attack"
and she was like "you will have to follow a special diet and I will do a blood test".
She said "we need to be sure that you are not reacting to anything else".
B: This is really interesting.
A: I was like "do I have to cut out nuts completely?"
and she was like "yes you do. When you feel better
you can reintroduce them gradually."

Excerpt 2

X: Coffee does not agree with me.
When I smell it I think "oh I will just have a little one"
and then I can feel my heart burning.
Y: I do love the smell.
X: So I went to the doctor and had a food allergy test
and the doctor said "do you know if there is anything
you are allergic to?"
I said "I definitely think I am allergic to coffee"
and she said "it might not be the coffee. It might be what you put in it".
So she tested milk and just coffee without the milk
and she said "you are right".
She said "please do not drink any caffeine".

**Figure 6:** Verbal guise texts (from Buchstaller 2014: 211).

Respondents thus had to read the two texts positioned next to each other and then were prompted to rate Speaker A and Speaker X on a variety of personality traits placed on a five-point SD scale. The following personality traits were employed in Buchstaller (2014) and thus adopted in this case study: "calm/excited", "old-fashioned/fashionable", "common/posh", "educated/uneducated", "annoying/pleasant", "unreliable/reliable", "intelligent/not intelligent", "unsuccessful/successful", "unprofessional/professional", "responsible/irresponsible", "articulate/inarticulate", "urban/rural", "cheerful/not cheerful", "hesitating/fluent", "unpopular/popular", "American/not American", "extroverted/introverted", "dishonest/honest", "not ambitious/ambitious", and, finally, "good sense of humour/not a good sense of humour". In addition to Buchstaller's catalogue of adjectival pairs, I decided to test some new features in order to ascertain whether learners have developed additional associations with the linguistic variant under study, those that may be guided by standard ideologies (to which speakers from both sociolinguistic ecologies are exposed) as these represent a very powerful means to hamper the propagation of vernacular forms on the rise. These additionally tested features include the adjectival pairs "casual/formal", "careful to speech/not careful to speech", "polite/impolite", and "clear/not clear". Furthermore, respondents were requested to assess both speakers with respect to their age, sex, ethnicity, social standing, occupation, and country of origin.

The second part of the survey taps into explicit beliefs that ESL and EFL learners harbour towards the two vernacular uses of *like*. In this task, respondents were presented with two short speech excerpts highlighting the DisPrt and the quotative function of *like*, illustrated in Figure 7.

---

Please consider the uses of **like** in the example below:

B: This is really interesting.
A: I said "do I have to **like** cut out nuts completely?" (Use 1)
   She was **like** "yes you do and when you feel better (Use 2)
   you can reintroduce them gradually."

---

**Figure 7:** Task eliciting overt evaluations of the two vernacular uses of *like* (from Buchstaller 2014: 293).

Students were asked to differentiate between the two uses of *like* before classifying both uses with respect to age, sex, social class, ethnicity, level of education, likely profession of its user, and geographic location. Furthermore, respondents were requested to report the frequency with which they used *like*. The survey culminated in three open-ended questions inquiring into learners' general opinions of *like*, from where they thought it emerged, and, finally, in what type of speech it tends to appear (e.g. gossip, news broadcasting, jokes, sermons or arguments).

The survey has a mixed research design, including both within-subjects and between-subjects comparisons (Laerd Statistics 2013). The dependent variable is ESL/EFL speakers' subjective reactions measured with the help of SD scales. Students' reactions were assessed across two independent conditions, i.e. Speaker A (*be like* condition) and Speaker X (*say* condition), while simultaneously controlling for an independent between-subjects factor, i.e. speech material featured in Excerpt 1 and Excerpt 2.

Conditions of the continuous variables, i.e. personality traits and age, were compared via the mixed ANOVA. This statistical analysis tested within-subjects comparisons (i.e. Speaker A and Speaker X), simultaneously controlling for the effect produced by the text (between-subjects factor). Here, I report the effects of only those within-subjects comparisons that did not interact significantly with the text type, thereby ruling out the possibility that the reported effects could be in any way related to the "carrier material" (Buchstaller 2014: 211). In the next step, a test was conducted to ascertain whether statistically significant within-subject effects co-vary with respondents' individual characteristics. These comprise

a. informants' age, gender, ethnicity as well as their place of residence between three and 17;
b. their academic degree;
c. their self-identification in terms of speaker status (native speaker/L2 speaker/English learner);
d. age at which they thought they were able to speak English fluently;
e. their self-reported proficiency;
f. time spent abroad in an English-speaking country;
g. reported affiliations with English varieties including their own (British English, American English, Indian English, German English);
h. special feelings harboured towards an English-speaking country.

Statistically significant, informative interactions are reported in Figures (8) through (12). The chi-square tests were employed as an appropriate tool of analysis, while testing for the associations of *like* across social categories (speaker sex, class, ethnicity, etc.). There are two variants of this statistical procedure, the first of which assesses whether frequency differences within nominal categories differ between nominal categories (the chi-square test of independence). The second variant can be implemented to determine whether frequencies differ between nominal categories (the chi-square goodness-of-fit test). Implemented in the VGT task, the chi-square test of independence established if the proportion of responses assigned to Speaker A and Speaker X differed across the categories of gender, social class, occupation, ethnicity, and origin. Likewise, the overt attitudes task determined whether the evaluations of the two vernacular uses of *like* differed significantly across the social categories. This application is relevant for those informants who could, indeed, differentiate between the two uses of *like*. The chi-square goodness-of-fit ascertained if the nominal responses obtained from the metalinguistically less informed cohort varied significantly across social categories. Finally, goodness-of-fit tests were performed to ascertain the differences in the self-reported uses of *like*. Let us now consider the results of the statistical analyses of data.

## 8.1 Verbal guise test

As a first step, we examine students' implicit judgements of *be like* and *say* users. In India, 13 traits – out of the overall 24 – achieved significance and are reported in Table 77. Similar to their L1 peers, my Indian informants evaluated *be like* guise as more "extroverted", more "cheerful", more "popular", and as having "a better sense of humour" than the speaker using *say*. In contrast, the use of *like* made the speaker sound less "pleasant", less "professional", less "reliable", and less "successful".

Table 77: Personality judgements for *be like* by Indian students (responses: 147).[a]

| Trait | $F(1, 146)$ | $p$-level |
|---|---|---|
| *Be like* use is associated with the speaker seeming more | | |
| extroverted | 4.839 | <0.029 |
| cheerful | 11.810 | <0.001 |
| good sense of humour | 8.438 | <0.004 |
| popular | 3.775 | <0.054 |
| American | 20.085 | <0.000 |
| *casual* | 12.913 | <0.000 |
| *Be like* use is associated with the speaker seeming less | | |
| pleasant | 6.869 | <0.010 |
| professional | 9.813 | <0.002 |
| reliable | 6.055 | <0.015 |
| successful | 6.255 | <0.045 |
| *careful to speech* | 15.831 | <0.000 |
| *polite* | 7.237 | <0.008 |
| *clear* | 5.056 | <0.026 |

**Note:** Added features, not tested in Buchstaller (2014), are presented in italics.

A similar picture, comprising both positive and negative associations, emerges once the German data is taken into account, reported in Table 78. Out of 24 tested adjectival pairs, 17 reached statistical significance. Similar to speakers in India and L1 peers, my German learners judge the *like*-guise as more "extroverted", more "fashionable", more "cheerful", more "excited", more "popular", and having a "better sense of humour". Simultaneously, German students are unanimous in viewing the speaker using *be like* as less "articulate", less "intelligent", less "pleasant", less "professional", less "reliable", less "responsible", less "successful", less "ambitious", and less "educated". Similar to Indian informants, my German learners view the *like*-guise as significantly more "American" than the *say*-guise. This evaluation contrasts with that reported for native speakers, who tend to view the use of *be like* as part of their own dialect (see Table 75). Overall, it can be concluded that relying on previous analyses that both Indian and German students manage to interpret the ideological meanings attached to *be like* in the donor varieties without reversing the patterns of evaluations.

**Table 78:** Personality judgements for *be like* by German students (responses: 196), from Davydova, Tytus, and Schleef (2017: 16).[a]

| Trait | $F(1, 194)$ | $p$-level |
|---|---|---|
| *Be like* use is associated with the speaker seeming more | | |
| extroverted | 86.162 | <0.001 |
| fashionable | 38.017 | <0.001 |
| cheerful | 50.789 | <0.001 |
| excited | 73.636 | <0.001 |
| good sense of humour | 60.73 | <0.001 |
| popular | 23.684 | <0.001 |
| American | 102.246 | <0.001 |
| *casual* | 149.465 | 0.000 |
| *Be like* use is associated with the speaker seeming less | | |
| articulate | 25.106 | <0.001 |
| intelligent | 26.124 | <0.001 |
| pleasant | 33.282 | <0.001 |
| professional | 111.568 | <0.001 |
| reliable | 35.120 | <0.001 |
| responsible | 13.049 | <0.001 |
| successful | 27.682 | <0.001 |
| ambitious | 8.510 | 0.004 |
| educated | 44.182 | <0.001 |

**Note:** Added features, not tested in Buchstaller (2014), are presented in italics.

Nevertheless, significant differences are found in the way ESL and EFL speakers evaluate the *like*-guise. Note that Indian students replicate only 8 features from the native-speaker catalogue reported in Table 75, whereas German students replicate as many as 15 associations attached by native speakers to quotative *be like*. This finding suggests that the German learners are one step ahead in reconstructing the social meanings of the innovative variant in their interlanguage, thereby approximating the native-speaker evaluations more closely. Indian students, in contrast, seem to have developed a collection of additional (idiosyncratic) meanings rooted in standard language ideologies because they view the *like*-guise as more "casual", but also less "careful to speech", less "polite", and less "clear".

Which factors are mediating the process of acquisition of sociolinguistic meanings in ESL and in EFL English? Analyses of co-variation between personality traits and individual characteristics of JNU students reveals that 'place of residence between three and 17', 'speaker status' as well as 'feeling a special connection to an English-speaking country' interact in meaningful ways with features "casual/formal", "clear/not clear", and "impolite/polite", all of which are newly developed meanings not reported for EFL or L1 English. As illustrated in Figure 8, respondents who grew up in metropolitan and big regional cities are more confident in their judgements of Speaker A as more "casual" and speaker X as more "formal". In contrast, respondents stemming from small towns and villages give identical ratings for both guises, which results in a weakly significant contrast across groups ($F$ (2, 144) = 2.949, $p$ = 0.056). This finding is symptomatic

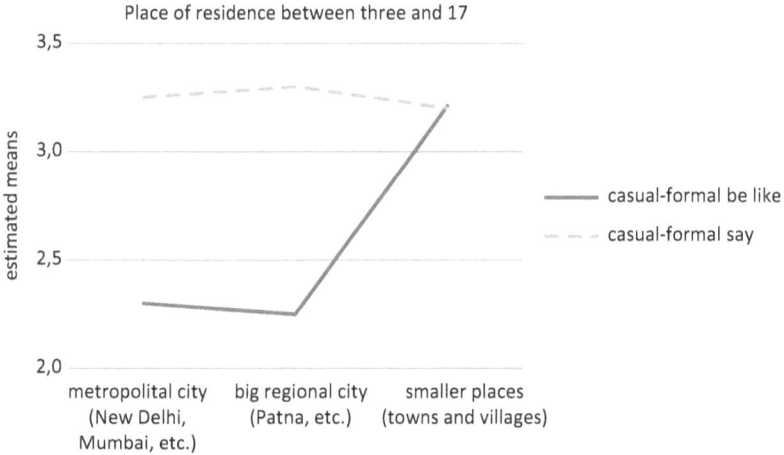

**Figure 8:** Co-variation between mean evaluations provided by Indian students of feature "casual/formal" and place of residence between three and 17 years old.

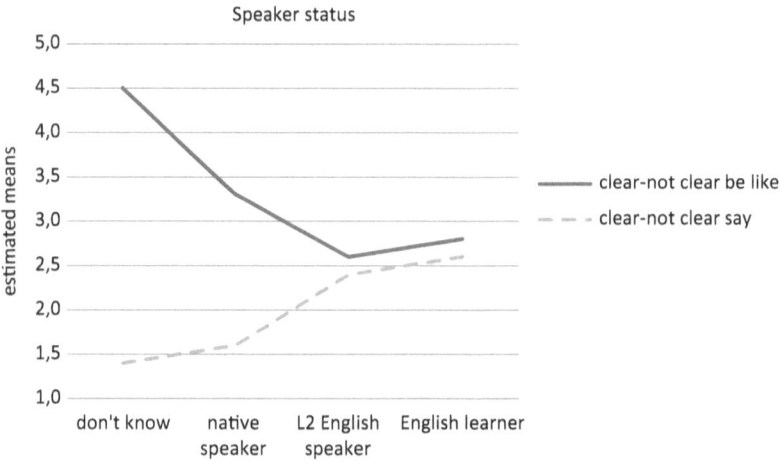

**Figure 9:** Co-variation between mean evaluations provided by Indian students of feature "clear/not clear" and speaker status.

of the major urban/rural divide characterising modern India with most proficient speakers of English stemming from urban areas.

Figure 9 reveals that Indian students assessing themselves as native speakers of English give more pronounced judgements on the feature "clear/not clear" in comparison to students who regard themselves as either L2 English speakers or English learners. The self-professed native speakers of Indian English, thus, rate the use of *be like* as less "clear" and the use of *say* as more "clear" in comparison to the other two groups, which provide very similar ratings for both guises ($F(3, 141) = 3.301$, $p = 0.022$). Finally, Figure 10 indicates that whether or not a JNU student feels a special connection to an English-speaking country has an impact on his or her evaluations of the feature "impolite/polite" ($F(3, 143) = 4.066$, $p = 0.008$). The general pattern that can be detected here is that students feeling certain emotional attachment to an Anglophone country also provide more distinctive, and also more accurate, judgements than students feeling no connection to the English-speaking world at large. The latter, in fact, provide almost identical ratings for both guises.

German learners, conversely, seem to acquire meanings of *be like* following what appears to be a different path. The analysis of co-variation reveals that two learner-related variables are at work in the German data: 'proficiency in English' and 'stay-abroad exposure'. Careful examination of within-subjects contrasts across individual-related predictors indicates that the effects attested for the adjectival pairs "calm/excited", "annoying/pleasant", and "articulate/inarticulate"

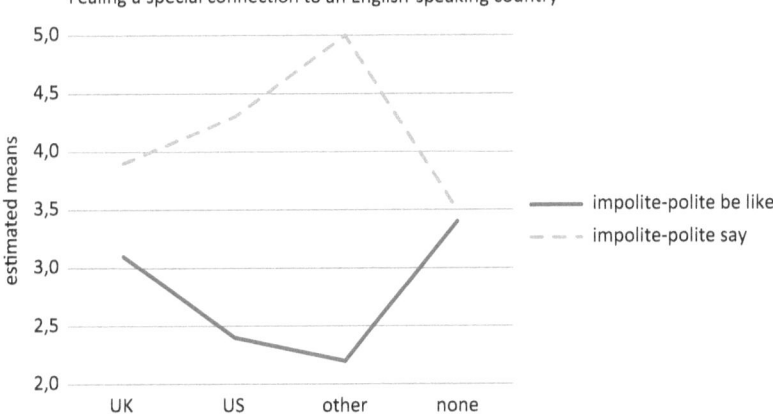

**Figure 10:** Co-variation between mean evaluations provided by Indian students of the feature "impolite/polite" and feeling a special connection to an English-speaking country.

are related to informants' self-reported proficiency in English. In contrast to less proficient students, advanced learners evaluated the *like*-guise as much more "excited" and the *say*-guise significantly "calmer" ($F(1, 194) = 47.860, p = 0.000$). These learners also view the *like*-user as more "annoying" in contrast to the speaker using *say*, who, they agree, is far more "pleasant" ($F(1, 194) = 7.802, p = 0.039$). Finally, it was the most proficient students who pronounced the *like*-guise more "inarticulate" ($F(1, 194) = 4.656, p = 0.077$). These dramatic differences in the mean evaluations of the two guises reveal a tendency to reduce gradually as we move from the advanced through upper-intermediate to intermediate levels of self-reported proficiency, as illustrated in Figure 11. Note also that students exhibiting basic proficiency in English display very incoherent judgements of both guises that are not in alignment with the rest of the learner group although this category is represented by an admittedly insufficient number of respondents.

Further analyses of variation indicated that the effects obtained for features "old-fashioned/fashionable" and "annoying/pleasant" correlate in meaningful ways with the amount of experience with naturalistic English through stay-abroad exposure. Figure 12 highlights the differences in evaluations, indicating that the higher levels of stay-abroad exposure result in learners' more confident judgements of both guises pinpointing a heightened awareness of social values attributed to *be like* by native speakers. Contrary to all other groups of learners, learners who spent more than a year in the US rate the *like*-guise as extremely fashionable and the *say*-guise as highly old-fashioned ($F(1, 88) = 13.39, p = 0.000$). What is remarkable is that these ratings are similar but not as pronounced in speakers with less exposure to US English. Similarly, German students who reported a more-than-a-year sojourn in the UK judge both conditions in extreme terms for pleasantness. Consistent with the native-speaker pattern of evaluation, they assign a high score for "annoying" to the *like*-user. In turn, the *say*-user comes off as very "pleasant" ($F(1, 157) = 3.91, p = 0.05$). Learners with lower levels of naturalistic exposure provide similar evaluations for both guises but they demonstrate less security in pronouncing their opinions and thus rate the two speakers with more moderate values.

What insights can be gleaned from the perusal of co-variation patterns? First and foremost, what, I think, is fairly clear is that in both communities, it is students with higher levels of general 'communicative competence' (Hymes 1966, 1972) in English who are also better judges of the social meanings attached to *be like*. In contrast to the strict definition of proficiency tapping into learners' knowledge of the standard variety and its major linguistic properties, which is typically measured through formal testing methods including aptitude, achievement, norm-referenced, criterion-referenced tests, etc. (see Allison 1999: 77), communicative competence is conceived by anthropologically oriented sociolinguists and applied linguists as a function of regular informal interactions in the target language (Canale 1983; Canale and Swain 1980). In this interpretation, communicative competence comprises individual knowledge, both conscious and unconscious, about language as well as "the ability to function in a truly communicative setting that is, in a dynamic exchange in which linguistic competence must adapt itself to the total informational input, both linguistic and paralinguistic, of one or more interlocutors" (Savignon 1972: 8).

Of particular interest is the fact that communicative competence, as defined in the preceding paragraph, emerges and follows a different path in each variety. A traditionally agricultural country that has been undergoing rapid economic growth, India has been marked by considerable disparities existing between the rural and the urban areas resulting in differential wages, occupation rates as well as achievement in education (Deaton and Dreze 2002; Pal and Gosh 2007). Although there is empirical evidence suggesting that the rural-urban divide has been diminishing (see Hnatkovska and Lahiri: 2012), the locus of socioeconomic prosperity is still located in the urban centres of the country. Given that the fluent command of English, oftentimes approximating native-speaker competencies, is one of the major signs of high social standing and financial stability in India, it is not entirely surprising that the most communicatively proficient speakers of English tend to grow up in metropolitan cities. As discussed in Chapter 2, metropolitan cities are also home to native speakers of Indian English. Against this backdrop, the plausible conclusion is that communicative fluency is primarily a function of a place of birth in India. In the EFL

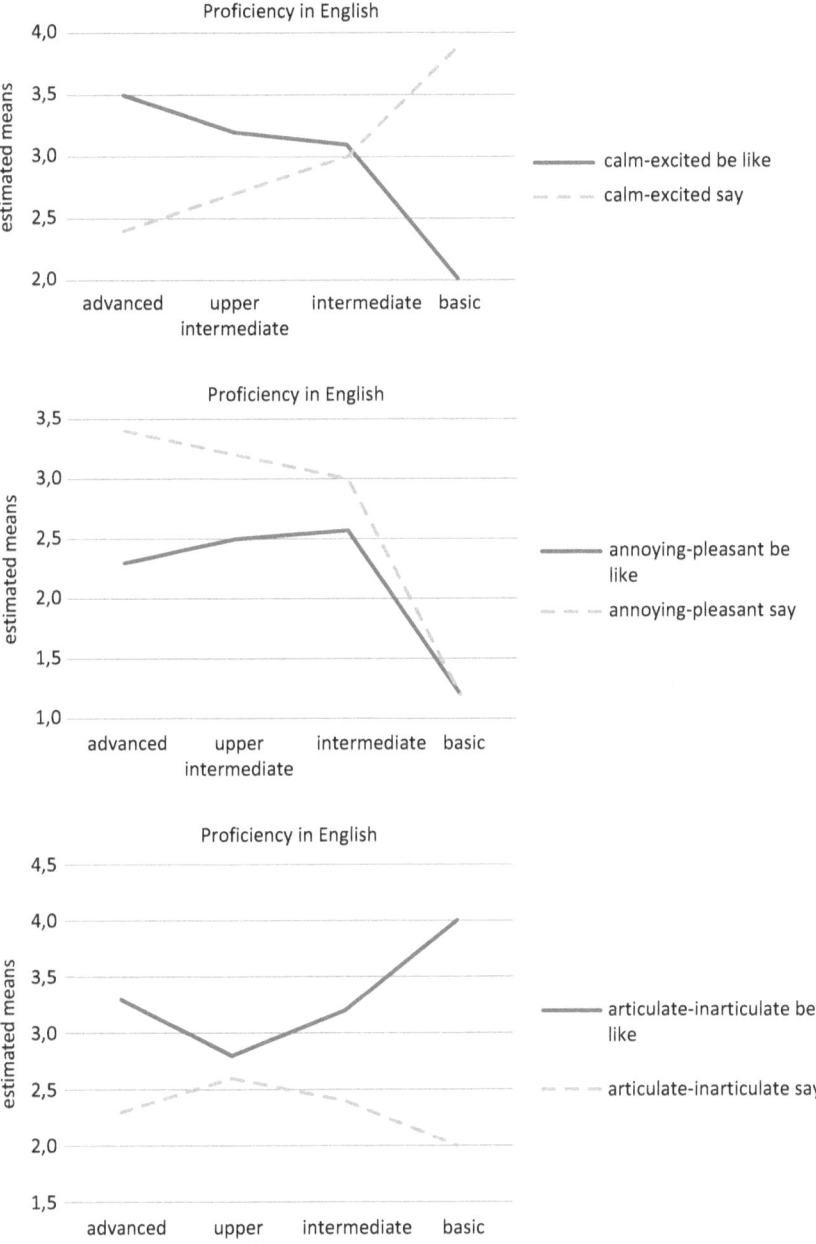

**Figure 11:** Co-variation between mean evaluations provided by German students of features "calm/excited", "annoying/pleasant", "articulate/inarticulate" and self-reported proficiency (from Davydova, Tytus, and Schleef 2017: 14).

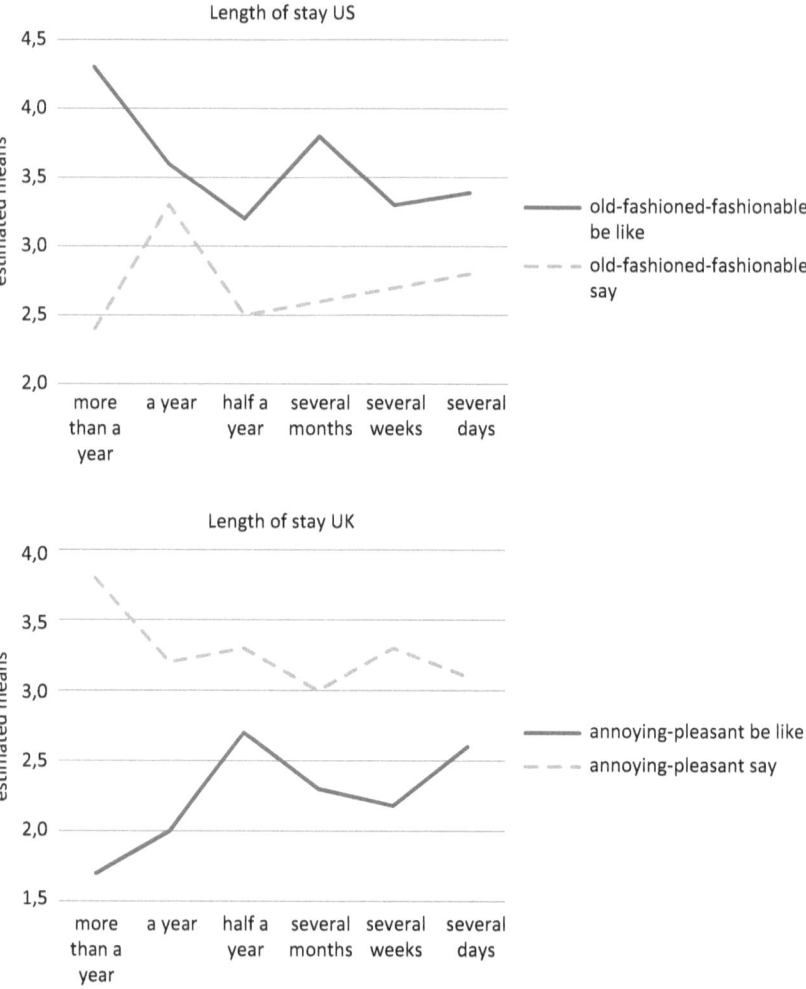

**Figure 12:** Co-variation between mean evaluations provided by German students features "old-fashioned/fashionable", "annoying/pleasant" and the length of stay-abroad exposure (from Davydova, Tytus, and Schleef 2017: 15).

ecology, communicative competence in English is constructed through stay-abroad experiences, which, ostensibly, are positively correlated with perceived proficiency in the target language.

Significantly, in Indian English, students' general communicative competence appears to be enhanced through speakers' emotional attachments to an English-speaking country. A growing body of the most recent empirical research into second- and foreign- language attainment (Dewaele 2015; Dewaele and Salomidou 2017; Dewaele et al. 2017; Ross and Stracke 2016) indicates that learners' positive emotions are vital to language learning. These studies reveal that an emotionally safe intimate learning environment, inherently enjoyable state-of-flow experiences (Czimmermann and Piniel 2016), a cultivated sense of learner's autonomy and an instilled sense of pride all support and promote performance in the target language.

The results reported here contribute to the growing bulk of evidence on the role of positive experiences in second- and foreign-language learning. In so doing, they point out that socio-psychological variables such as personally meaningful associations with a parent variety may be particularly important in those L2 settings where physical access to native speakers is generally not available. It is in these kinds of settings that emotional attachments harboured by L2 individuals towards a reference culture come to the fore and begin to guide their interlanguage towards higher levels of ultimate attainment. The findings reported in Figures 8 through 12 facilitate the formulation of the following hypotheses. These could be subjected to further empirical testing and, therefore, might be beneficial to second-language research. In the absence of sustained face-to-face contact with L1 speakers, positive emotional attachments to the target culture will support and guide learners' interlanguage towards the higher levels of sociolinguistic competence (as formulated in Chapter 2). Conversely, in situations where prolonged contact to L1 is assured, the levels of communicative and sociolinguistic competence will be a function of naturalistic exposure to the target language (see also Davydova and Buchstaller 2015).

Having taken a brief, but hopefully informative, explanatory detour, let us now return our attention to quotative *be like* and consider how ESL/EFL speakers perceive the *like*- and non-*like*-guise in terms of various social characteristics. Table 79 reveals that JNU students believe Speaker A (the *like*-guise) exercises a non-academic profession (31%) in contrast to Speaker X (the non-*like*-guise), whom they believe to be an academic (28%). Furthermore, my ESL informants unanimously assert that Speaker A comes from the US (31%), whereas Speaker X could have a variety of regional backgrounds (16% vs. 15% vs. 16%). Neither sex, nor social class or ethnicity triggers any further significant associations in this data set.

A slightly different picture emerges once the German data set is taken into account. My UM students seem to have developed an entire range of tacit associations regarding speaker sex, social class, ethnicity, occupation, and provenance of *be like*. These are reported in Table 80. UM students map the use of *be like* onto female speech (36%), a finding that is broadly consistent with those reported for the UK (Buchstaller 2006, 2014) and the US (-Dailey O'Cain 2000; Buchstaller 2006, 2014). They also feel strongly that the speaker not using *like* must belong to

**Table 79:** Associations of *be like* and *say* with speaker sex, social class, ethnicity, professional occupation, and origin provided by Indian students (responses = 294).

| Social category | | Speaker A (*be like*) N (%) | Speaker X (*say*) N (%) | $\chi^2$ test |
|---|---|---|---|---|
| Sex | male | 57 (19%) | 49 (17%) | $\chi^2(2) = 0.976$, |
| | female | 82 (28%) | 90 (30%) | $p < 0.614$ |
| | no data | 8 (3%) | 8 (3%) | |
| Social class | working | 59 (20%) | 58 (20%) | $\chi^2(2) = 0.014$, |
| | middle | 84 (29%) | 85 (29%) | $p < 0.993$ |
| | no data | 4 (1%) | 4 (1%) | |
| Ethnicity | White | 81 (28%) | 65 (22%) | $\chi^2(5) = 7.779$, |
| | Latino | 12 (4%) | 9 (3%) | $p < 0.169$ |
| | Asian | 29 (10%) | 39 (13%) | |
| | Black | 3 (1%) | 9 (3%) | |
| | Other | 11 (4%) | 16 (5%) | |
| | no data | 11 (4%) | 9 (3%) | |
| Occupation | academic | 52 (18%) | 81 (28%) | $\chi^2(2) = 11.820$, |
| | non-academic | 91 (31%) | 62 (21%) | $p < 0.003$ |
| | no data | 4 (1%) | 4 (1%) | |
| Origin | UK | 19 (6%) | 46 (16%) | $\chi^2(3) = 31.820$, |
| | US | 90 (31%) | 44 (15%) | $p < 0.000$ |
| | Other | 28 (9%) | 47 (16%) | |
| | no data | 10 (3%) | 10 (3%) | |

Note: The statistical analyses employed here and in Table 80 are the chi-square tests of independence.

the middle class (41%), although they are far less certain regards his/her ethnicity, assigning fairly equal values to both *like*- and non-*like*-guise. Similarly to JNU students, my UM informants link the use of *be like* to the non-academic occupation (38%) and its non-use to an employment in academia (35%). In Buchstaller's (2014: 228–230) study, L1 speakers from the UK and the US assigned the *like*-guise to a less educated persona with a tendency towards the working-class background. Finally, a conspicuous proportion of German learners related the *like*-guise to the US (37%) and the *say*-guise to the UK (28%). Both Indian and German informants, thus, assign the use of *be like* to the US in contrast to their L1 peers, who perceive *be like* as an inherent feature of their own dialect (Buchstaller 2014: 222–225).

Furthermore, respondents from both groups estimate the *like*-user to be younger than the speaker quoting with *say*. My Indian informants estimated Speaker A (*be like*) to be 27 years on average and Speaker X (*say*) was assessed to be of age 32. The test of within-subjects effects indicates that this difference

**Table 80:** Associations of *be like* and *say* with speaker sex, social class, ethnicity, professional occupation, and origin provided by German students (responses = 392), from Davydova, Tytus, and Schleef (2017: 19).

| Social category | | Speaker A (*be like*) N (%) | Speaker X (*say*) N (%) | $\chi^2$ test |
|---|---|---|---|---|
| Sex | male | 56 (14%) | 94 (24%) | $\chi^2(1) = 15.594$, |
|  | female | **140 (36%)** | 102 (26%) | $p < 0.000$ |
| Social class | working | 97 (25%) | 37 (0.09%) | $\chi^2(1) = 40.819$, |
|  | middle | 99 (25%) | **159 (41%)** | $p < 0.000$ |
| Ethnicity | White | 146 (37%) | 157 (40%) | $\chi^2(4) = 17.211$, |
|  | Latino | 16 (4%) | 3 (0.7%) | $p < 0.010$ |
|  | Asian | 4 (0.1%) | 14 (4%) | |
|  | Black | 11 (3%) | 5 (1%) | |
|  | Other | 19 (5%) | 17 (4%) | |
| Occupation | academic | 46 (12%) | **143 (35%)** | $\chi^2(1) = 96.133$, |
|  | non-academic | **150 (38%)** | 53 (14%) | $p < 0.000$ |
| Origin | UK | 27 (7%) | **110 (28%)** | $\chi^2(2) = 101.803$, |
|  | US | **146 (37%)** | 49 (13%) | $p < 0.000$ |
|  | Other | 23 (6%) | 37 (9%) | |

is, indeed, statistically significant ($F$ (1, 134) = 19.136, $p$ = 0.000). Similarly, German students reported the *like*-guise to be 22 years old, while estimating the *say*-guise to be aged 33 on average. Here again, the difference in the mean evaluations of age is statistically significant ($F$ (1, 193) = 106.568, $p$ = 0.000). The ESL/EFL learners' perceptions regarding age of persona using *be like* are very much in line with those of native speakers. Buchstaller (2014: 227, 229) documents the mean age ratings ranging between 26.8 and 23.24 for the *like*-guise and those ranging between 35.2 and 32.82 for the *say*-guise in her American and British data sets.

Summing up, the results reported in Table 79 and 80 indicate that both ESL and EFL learners have largely appropriated the meanings that native speakers attach to quotative *be like* without reversing these patterns of evaluations. In comparison to Indian informants, German learners are a bit more adept at replicating the patterns of social evaluations of the newcomer variant. Coupled with the results for personality traits, these observations are informative in that they suggest that the fundamental differences characterising ESL/EFL attitudinal mindsets reported in Chapter 4 might be ultimately responsible for the slightly different ways in which these learners appropriate the ideological baggage of the innovative variant under study. Deeply attuned to the external norms of the L1

English world, German learners strive (and actually manage) to replicate a vast majority of implicit associations attached to quotative *be like*. While exhibiting an essentially endonormative orientation, Indian speakers evaluate *be like* along similar lines but, in all appearance, do not care if they replicate all of the ideological and social assessments of *be like* in minute detail and, in so doing, develop new meanings grounded in standard language ideologies (see Table 77).

## 8.2 Overt attitudes' task

This section explores whether the same perceptual links between *be like* and various social categories can still be attested once learners' attention is purposefully steered towards the variant. In the second part of the survey, the students were presented with two short excerpts highlighting the uses of *like* – *like* as a DisPrt and *like* as a quotative marker (recall Figure 7). Initially, students from both communities demonstrated a fairly high level of metalinguistic awareness with respect to the feature under analysis. When presented with the two conversation snippets and asked whether or not they could differentiate between the two uses of *like*, the majority of ESL and EFL respondents claimed that they, in fact, could do so (99 (67%) out of 147 for JNU, and 114 (58%) out of 196 for UM).

Those respondents from India who could differentiate between the two uses of *like* were also able to assign both uses to the speech of younger speakers. The distribution of the two uses across all the other social categories, i.e. sex, education, social class, and origin, does not reach the level of statistical significance in this data set.

Table 81: Associations of *like* as a DisPrt and *be like* with age, sex, education, social class, ethnicity, and origin provided by Indian students (responses = 198).

| Social category | | Use 1 (*like* as a DisPrt) N (%) | Use 2 (*be like*) N (%) | $\chi^2$ test |
|---|---|---|---|---|
| Age | younger | 68 (34%) | 49 (25%) | $\chi^2(2) = 8.846$, |
| | older | 22 (11%) | 29 (15%) | $p < 0.012$ |
| | don't know | 9 (4%) | 21 (11%) | |
| Sex | male | 25 (13%) | 17 (8%) | $\chi^2(2) = 2.027$, |
| | female | 47 (24%) | 54 (27%) | $p < 0.363$ |
| | don't know | 27 (14%) | 28 (14%) | |
| Education | educated | 43 (22%) | 52 (26%) | $\chi^2(2) = 2.312$, |
| | little education | 40 (20%) | 30 (15%) | $p < 0.315$ |
| | don't know | 16 (8%) | 17 (9%) | |

**Table 81** (continued)

| Social category | | Use 1 (*like* as a DisPrt) N (%) | Use 2 (*be like*) N (%) | $\chi^2$ test |
|---|---|---|---|---|
| Social class | middle class | 43 (22%) | 39 (20%) | $\chi^2(2) = 0.528$, |
| | working class | 34 (17%) | 34 (17%) | $p < 0.768$ |
| | don't know | 22 (11%) | 26 (13%) | |
| Ethnicity | white | 39 (20%) | 36 (18%) | $\chi^2(2) = 1.158$, |
| | ethnic minority | 18 (9%) | 14 (7%) | $p < 0.560$ |
| | don't know | 42 (21%) | 49 (25%) | |
| Origin | US English | 44 (22%) | 42 (21%) | $\chi^2(2) = 0.233$, |
| | English spoken elsewhere | 30 (15%) | 29 (15%) | $p < 0.890$ |
| | don't know | 25 (13%) | 28 (14%) | |

**Note:** The statistical analyses employed here and in Table 83 are the chi-square tests of independence.

JNU students exhibiting lower levels of metalinguistic awareness support the opinion expressed by their better-informed peers by linking the general use of *like* to younger speakers. In addition, they also associate *like* with female middle-class speech. Whereas they are quite unsure about the ethnicity of speakers using *like*, they contend unanimously that these speakers must hail from the US.

**Table 82:** Associations of general expressions with *like* with age, sex, education, social class, ethnicity, and origin provided by Indian students (responses = 48).

| Social category | | *Like* generally N (%) | $\chi^2$ test |
|---|---|---|---|
| Age | younger | **41 (85%)** | $\chi^2(2) = 58.875$, |
| | older | 2 (5%) | $p < 0.000$ |
| | don't know | 5 (10%) | |
| Sex | male | 2 (4%) | $\chi^2(2) = 26.375$, |
| | female | **31 (65%)** | $p < 0.000$ |
| | don't know | 15 (31%) | |
| Education | educated | 22 (46%) | $\chi^2(2) = 3.875$, |
| | little education | 15 (31%) | $p < 0.144$ |
| | don't know | 11 (23%) | |
| Social class | middle class | **25 (52%)** | $\chi^2(2) = 7.875$, |
| | working class | 10 (21%) | $p < 0.019$ |
| | don't know | 13 (27%) | |

(continued)

**Table 82** (continued)

| Social category | | *Like* generally N (%) | $\chi^2$ test |
|---|---|---|---|
| Ethnicity | white | 17 (36%) | $\chi^2(2) = 19.625$, |
| | ethnic minority | 3 (6%) | $p < 0.000$ |
| | don't know | **28 (58%)** | |
| Origin | US English | **23 (48%)** | $\chi^2(2) = 6.125$, |
| | English spoken elsewhere | 9 (19%) | $p < 0.047$ |
| | don't know | 16 (33%) | |

Note: The statistical analyses employed here and in Table 84 are the chi-square goodness-of-fit tests.

The German respondents appear to attach similar social stereotypes to *like*, as outlined in Table 83 and Table 84. Those students who could distinguish between *like* in its DisPrt and quotative function assign both uses to younger female speech with little education, although an admittedly conspicuous number of respondents remained unsure about users' sex or education, as revealed through the category 'I don't know' (see Table 83).

**Table 83:** Associations of *like* as a DisPrt and *be like* with age, sex, education, social class, ethnicity, and origin provided by German students (responses = 288), adopted from Davydova, Tytus, and Schleef (2017: 20).

| Social category | | Use 1 (*like* as a DisPrt) N (%) | Use 2 (*be like*) N (%) | $\chi^2$ test |
|---|---|---|---|---|
| Age | younger | 106 (37%) | 118 (41%) | $\chi^2(2) = 7.754$, |
| | older | 21 (7%) | 7 (2%) | $p < 0.050$ |
| | don't know | 17 (6%) | 19 (7%) | |
| Sex | male | 23 (8%) | 8 (3%) | $\chi^2(2) = 8.224$, |
| | female | **60 (21%)** | **70 (24%)** | $p < 0.050$ |
| | don't know | 61 (21%) | 66 (23%) | |
| Education | educated | 35 (12%) | 25 (9%) | $\chi^2(2) = 6.053$, |
| | little education | **62 (22%)** | **52 (18%)** | $p < 0.050$ |
| | don't know | 47 (16%) | 67 (23%) | |
| Social class | middle class | 41 (14%) | 34 (12%) | $\chi^2(2) = 1.129$, |
| | working class | 55 (19%) | 55 (19%) | $p < 0.569$ |
| | don't know | 48 (17%) | 55 (19%) | |

Table 83 (continued)

| Social category | | Use 1 (*like* as a DisPrt) N (%) | Use 2 (*be like*) N (%) | χ² test |
|---|---|---|---|---|
| Ethnicity | white | 46 (16%) | 53 (18%) | χ²(2) = 0.755, p < 0.685 |
| | ethnic minority | 12 (4%) | 11 (4%) | |
| | don't know | 86 (30%) | 80 (28%) | |
| Origin | US English | 87 (30%) | 92 (32%) | χ²(2) = 2.121, p < 0.346 |
| | English spoken elsewhere | 28 (10%) | 19 (7%) | |
| | don't know | 29 (10%) | 33 (11%) | |

Table 84: Associations of general expressions with *like* with age, sex, education, social class, ethnicity, and origin provided by German students (responses = 52), from Davydova, Tytus, and Schleef (2017: 21).

| Social category | | *Like* generally N (%) | χ² test |
|---|---|---|---|
| Age | younger | **49 (94%)** | χ²(2) = 86.808, p < 0.000 |
| | older | 1 (2%) | |
| | don't know | 2 (4%) | |
| Sex | male | 2 (4%) | χ²(2) = 20.808, p < 0.000 |
| | female | **27 (52%)** | |
| | don't know | 23 (44%) | |
| Education | educated | 5 (9%) | χ²(2) = 19.654, p < 0.000 |
| | little education | **31 (60%)** | |
| | don't know | 16 (31%) | |
| Social class | middle class | 12 (23%) | χ²(2) = 14.000, p < 0.01 |
| | working class | **30 (58%)** | |
| | don't know | 10 (19%) | |
| Ethnicity | white | 14 (27%) | χ²(2) = 20.462, p < 0.000 |
| | ethnic minority | 6 (11%) | |
| | don't know | 32 (62%) | |
| Origin | US English | **38 (73%)** | χ²(2) = 38.000, p < 0.000 |
| | English spoken elsewhere | 4 (8%) | |
| | don't know | 10 (19%) | |

The metalinguistically less informed cohort paints a more detailed social portrait of vernacular *like*, reported in Table 84. Despite admitting they could not tell the difference between its two uses, they still manage to forge a link between *like* and the categories 'younger', 'female', 'little education', 'working class', and 'US English', while remaining unsure about users' ethnicity.

In the next survey task students from both communities were presented with a list featuring different professions. They were then instructed to assess on a scale from 1 to 10 how likely the use of *like* was for each profession type. Mean ratings of various professions listed in Figure 13 and Figure 14 are presented in ascending order for each group. Figure 13 informs us that JNU students believe that representatives of creative professions such as DJs, comedians, filmmakers and so on are more likely to use vernacular *like* in their speech. In contrast, professions associated with the educational, financial, and marketing sectors (lawyers, managers, teachers, and such) exhibit a weaker link to the vernacular feature. This is exactly how native speakers predict the use of *like* across different professions. Within-subjects comparisons for profession mean ratings by JNU students indicate that these differences are statistically significant ($F\ (7,\ 857)\ =\ 10.815$, $p\ =\ 0.000$). UM students assess the use of *like* for this dimension along very similar lines as illustrated in Figure 14. Consequently, they display more confidence than their peers in India as revealed by the effect size of within-subject comparisons ($F\ (6,\ 1101)\ =\ 120.747,\ p\ =\ 0.000$). Similar to ESL speakers, my German respondents assign significantly lower ratings regarding the use of *like* for educational, financial, and marketing jobs and significantly higher ratings for creative occupations, yet their overall evaluations are more volatile than those attested for Indian students.

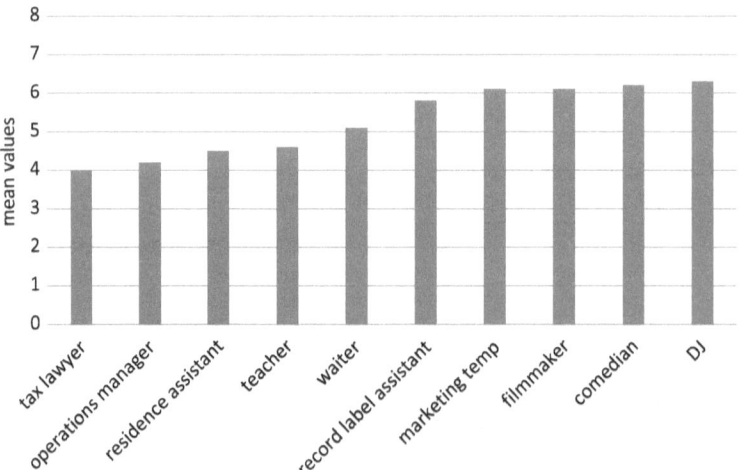

**Figure 13:** Mean rates for an association between *like* and different professions by Indian students.

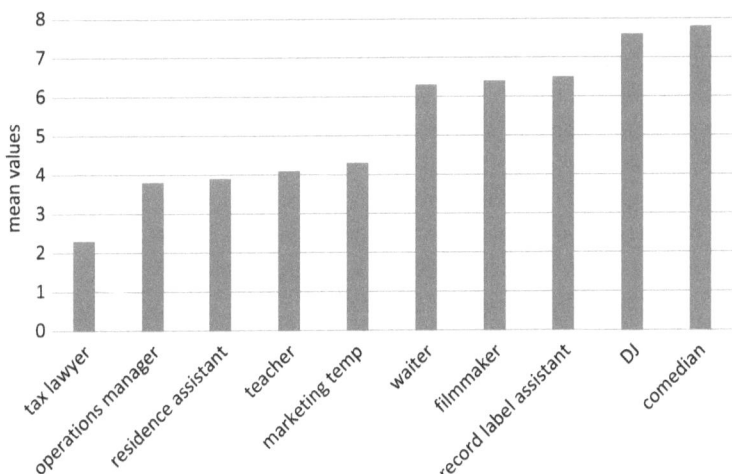

**Figure 14:** Mean rates for an association between *like* and different professions by German students, from Davydova, Tytus, and Schleef (2017: 22).

In summary, results of the overt attitudes' task confirm the findings reported for the VGT. Whereas both ESL and EFL speakers manage to have developed patterns of social evaluations largely consistent with those harboured by native speakers, German learners seem to do a slightly better job of reconstructing evaluative patterns of (quotative) *like*, a finding which can be arguably traced back to the fundamental differences characterising ESL/EFL attitudinal mindsets described in Chapter 4. The finding is informative in that it suggests that the general predisposition to emulate an L1 target seem to play a fostering role in acquisition of social evaluations of specific variants. The generalisation that can be drawn here is that the exonormatively oriented mind of an EFL learner is likely to result in a more wholesale replication of social assessments of a specific variant. With this said, the exonormative orientation appears to be less of a good predictor for the acquisition of variable patterns of use (recall from Chapter 7 that both ESL and EFL learners accurately replicate language-internal constraints governing the use of *be like* as well as their specific ordering), thereby suggesting that other factors must be at work, guiding acquisition of the variable grammar by L2 learners. I will address this issue in Chapter 9.

Finally, students from both communities were asked if they thought they used *like* in their speech and how often. This assignment is an indirect measure designed to ascertain the degree to which learners attach positive (as opposed to negative) evaluations to *like*. The fundamental notion is that the more often students report the use of *like* in their speech, the more likely it is that they have embraced this feature as part of their informal linguistic repertoire (Gumperz 1972: 230). As in previous tasks, the distinction was drawn between students who believed they could differentiate between the two uses of *like* and those who could not.

Let us now peruse the patterns of self-reported uses of *like* produced by JNU students. Table 85 indicates that a large majority of students have embraced *like* as part of their vernacular irrespective of their ability to differentiate between the two uses. More than 80% of respondents admit to using *like* either sometimes or often. The finding nicely dovetails with another observation. When asked for their general opinion of *like*, 72% of students (N 106/147) professed either positive or neutral evaluations of the vernacular feature.

**Table 85:** Self-reported uses of *like* provided by Indian students (responses: 198 for Use 1 and Use 2 and 48 for *like* generally).

|  | often | sometimes | never | don't know | $\chi^2$test |
|---|---|---|---|---|---|
| Use 1 (DisPrt *like*) | **34 (34%)** | **47 (48%)** | 17 (17%) | 1 (1%) | $\chi^2(3) = 48.677, p < 0.000$ |
| Use 2 (*be like*) | **32 (32%)** | **48 (49%)** | 16 (16%) | 3 (3%) | $\chi^2(3) = 46.172, p < 0.000$ |
| *Like* generally | 8 (17%) | **35 (73%)** | 5 (10%) | 0 (0%) | $\chi^2(3) = 34.125, p < 0.000$ |

**Note:** Here and in Table 86, results for '*like* generally' were culled from students would could not differentiate between the two uses of *like*.

A slightly different picture emerges after considering the UM data, presented in Table 86. Approximately 80% of all German students admit to using quotative *be like* irrespective of their ability to differentiate between the two uses. When asked their overall view of *like*, 76% (N 149/196) responded that their general attitude towards the linguistic item was either positive or neutral. This is a clear indication that, similar to their L1 and Indian peers, German learners have welcomed *like* into their vocabularies as a 'youthful' feature of colloquial speech. Simultaneously, as much as 46% of metalinguistically informed learners are reluctant to accept the discourse use of *like*, reporting that they never use *like* in this function.

**Table 86:** Self-reported uses of *like* provided by German students (responses: 144 for Use 1 and Use 2 and 52 for *like* generally) from Davydova, Tytus, and Schleef (2017: 22).

|  | often | sometimes | never | don't know | $\chi^2$test |
|---|---|---|---|---|---|
| Use 1 (DisPrt *like*) | 11 (7%) | 63 (44%) | **66 (46%)** | 4 (3%) | $\chi^2(3) = 91.056, p < 0.000$ |
| Use 2 (*be like*) | **35 (25%)** | **87 (60%)** | 20 (14%) | 2 (1%) | $\chi^2(3) = 111.50, p < 0.000$ |
| *Like* generally | 3 (6%) | **38 (73%)** | 9 (17%) | 2 (4%) | $\chi^2(3) = 66.308, p < 0.000$ |

The findings presented in Table 85 and Table 86, therefore, report a range of generally positive attitudes harboured by ESL/EFL learners towards *like*. However, these results also indicate that EFL learners seem to be more attuned to the ideological message promoted through the English language purists dismissing *like* as a "meaningless" feature associated with "sloppy, lazy, ignorant, or vulgar speech" (D'Arcy 2007: 387). Their exonormative orientation, it appears, does not merely guide EFL learners' acquisition of social evaluations of specific variants. It also makes them somewhat more vulnerable to prescriptivist pressures promoted by L1 pundits and the influence of conservative attitudes towards linguistic changes in progress and vernacular items more generally (see Buchstaller 2014: 198–207).

Having explored in close detail the social meanings that ESL/EFL speakers attach to vernacular (*be*) *like*, I would like to return to the question formulated at the outset of this chapter, 'How can one explain the fact that L2 learners replicate so closely the variable grammar of *be like* and yet, do not adopt this variant with a noticeably higher frequency in their speech?' This chapter has revealed that both ESL and EFL learners have developed a differentiated set of attitudes towards quotative *be like*, comprising positive but also, importantly, quite a few negative associations. Furthermore, evidence presented here has pinpointed a remarkably high level of metalinguistic awareness about vernacular *like* and its different functions demonstrated by both groups of respondents. Both JNU and UM students seem to realise, both consciously and unconsciously, that *be like* is a trendy vernacular feature to which a person should take an occasional recourse if they want to sound hip and socially attractive. These fairly positive feelings about *be like* surely contribute to successful acquisition of the constraint system detailed in Chapter 7 for both ESL and EFL English.

At the same time, both speaker groups realise that this informal variant comes with a price and that using *be like* in their speech necessarily entails putting themselves at risk of sounding less cultivated. Being acutely aware of the stigmatised connotations that quotative *be like* prompts, young adults from both India and Germany have adopted this informal feature only to a moderate degree in their speech. With this said, the modest rate at which the vernacular variant is adopted in young adults' speech is a very skilful, if only semi-conscious, psychological strategy pursued by ESL/EFL speakers. The strategy aims at managing linguistic resources in a way that helps my students reconcile the contradictory ideological baggage attached to the newcomer *be like* and, consequently, retain it in their speech.

Another factor might be evoked by way of accounting for the modest degree of adoption of *be like* in speech of Indian students. Chapter 4 has revealed that endonormatively oriented, speakers of Indian English draw on a variety of linguistic resources (languages and their varieties) and each code evokes a distinctive meaning. While drawing on their multiple linguistic resources, speakers of Indian

English employ the American variety in order to sound "causal", "colloquial", "simple", and "funny". American English is also a form of language that helps my Indian informants to signal modernity: being up-to-date, young, and hip. Crucially, American English (and the feature (*be*) *like* that comes along with it) is just one (out of many) linguistic bases that an endonormatively oriented multilingual mind is striving to process and integrate on a day-to-day basis. Given this multiplicity of available sources, it is perhaps not entirely surprising that L2 speakers adopt a linguistic variant associated with a specific linguistic code in a modest fashion so that other linguistic variants, potentially associated with other linguistic resources and meanings, could thrive as well. Chapter 5 revealed that JNU students use a plethora of substrate- and superstrate-based variants while introducing quotation in their speech. Particularly notable features are represented by local innovations containing the discourse marker *okay* (*fine*) promoted by bilingual speakers with a balanced control of both Hindi and English. Quotative constructions containing *okay* (*fine*) are truly innovative community-specific means of constructing dialogue that have been on the rise ever since 2007 (Davydova 2015b, 2016a). An interesting issue that could be explored in the future is whether or not JNU speakers are aware of this incipient variant in their speech and what kind of meanings they attach to it. Do they identify this feature as distinctively Indian English usage? Pursuing this strand of research has a potential to contribute to our understanding of the socio-cognitive processes that govern the linking of sociolinguistic information of various kinds (linguistic varieties, gender, social background, etc.) to specific linguistic variants (cf. Campbell-Kibler 2011: 437). In a related vein, further inquiry might help us understand the indexical field for the global and local innovative quotative markers in indigenised English. While studying how speakers of indigenised English incorporate sociolinguistic information into newly emerged linguistic structures, we can make further, more detailed generalisations about the relationship existing between socio-ideological evaluations of specific variants and their subsequent distributions in speech communities. These types of analyses are important as they have wider implications for the study of language change.

Summing up, this chapter has demonstrated that both ESL and EFL speakers have developed a mixed baggage of attitudes comprising both positive and negative evaluations of (*be*) *like*. These attitudes are largely consistent with those reported for L1 speakers of English; neither Indian nor German students demonstrate reversed patterns of assessment for quotative *be like*. The mixed feelings harboured towards the innovative feature offer an explanation for the highlighted fact that L2 speakers from distinctive sociolinguistic ecologies have adopted the newcomer at a comparable, but considerably low rate in their speech. Given non-native speakers' overall evaluations of *be like* as described in this chapter as well as specifics of their respective sociolinguistic ecologies, it is not very likely that this vernacular feature will expand in indigenised and Learner grammar beyond its current rate of use any time soon. That is unless for some unforeseeable reason, the socio-ideological tapestry of meanings mapped on *be like* will undergo a sudden transformation in L1 English and speakers of indigenised and Learner English will pick up on the trend or develop overwhelmingly positive associations with the variant.

# 9 Putting it all together

This book has been concerned with two overarching questions:

> RQ1: How do non-native speakers, i.e. second- and foreign-language learners, appropriate patterns of sociolinguistic variation attested in L1 vernaculars? And more importantly, how and to what extent do they adopt global linguistic innovations attested in native-speaker varieties?

> RQ2: Which system-internal, socio-psychological (attitudinal), and psycholinguistic mechanisms underpin the evolution of the newly emerging forms of English, while shaping its linguistic outcomes?

While exploring the ways in which speakers of indigenised and Learner English cope with patterns of language variation within their local sociolinguistic ecologies, I relied on the construct of sociolinguistic competence, which has provided me with a list of clearly defined parameters that I used as a methodologically rigorous metric in my comparisons of both norm developing and norm dependent English-speaking communities. Introduced in Chapter 2 and listed for convenience here, these parameters include (Clark and Schleef 2010: 299; Meyerhoff and Schleef 2012: 409):
(a)  the relevant variants and their relative frequencies;
(b)  the language-internal and sociolinguistic predictors of variation;
(c)  the ordering of specific constraints;
(d)  similar social evaluations of specific variants.

Having described the variable grammar constraining the use of quotative *be like* grounded in the grammaticalisation theory (Ferrara and Bell 1995) in Chapter 3, I proceeded with an observation in Chapter 4 that in order to be able to understand how non-native speakers go about appropriating variable linguistic features, including globally spreading linguistic innovations, we need to understand the general attitudes, both tacit and explicit, that these speakers harbour towards mainstream donor varieties, notably American English. Relying on converging evidence stemming from a method mix, Chapter 4 concluded with two hypotheses. Firstly, I hypothesised that the endonormatively oriented mindset of an ESL-speaker community licences daily code-switching practices between Hindi (dialects) and English, and these, in turn, can be expected to foster bilingual mode of psycholinguistic activity in the sense of Grosjean (1998, 2001), which ultimately enhances cross-linguistic diversity at the microsociolinguistic level in a newly emerging variety. In contrast, the exonormative attitudinal orientation characterising EFL English imposes a cultural expectation of monolingual language practices, and these largely result in a monolingual state of psycholinguistic activity, which, in turn, affects the way in which language is structured at the micro-level. More specifically, I hypothesised that the predominantly monolingual mode of sociolinguistic practices (in which code-switching practices are non-existent or reduced to a minimum) would inhibit linguistic creativity and ensuing variability in a given domain of language. Presented and discussed in Chapter 5 and 6, detailed analyses of sociolinguistic variation brought forth evidence largely substantiating this hypothesis. The system of quotative marking as it is attested in the Learner variety of German English is perhaps best described as a balanced constellation of traditional and innovative variants reported for L1 vernaculars. German learners seem to be closely following the range of options set out by the speakers of the donor varieties, which is even more surprising given the fact that quotatives are essentially discourse-pragmatic phenomena (albeit morphosyntactically embedded) and, by this token, largely open to lexical and, at least to some degree constructional, enrichment. In other words, German learners do not innovate.

This contrasts with how speakers of Indian English, who by and large follow an endonormative practice allowing for code-switching, construct dialogue throughout narration. Chapter 5 revealed that ESL speakers exhibit a heterogeneous system of quotative marking comprising traditional and innovative variants. Furthermore, the system of Indian English quotation exhibits an elevated token number of linguistic variants including quote types that have not been attested in either L1 English or EFL English. These include substrate-induced quotative constructions featuring 'verb + *that*' as well as local contact-induced innovations featuring discourse marker *okay* (*fine*). Crucially, the study has brought forth evidence demonstrating that speakers who were educated through a mix of English and Hindi in high school and who used both languages extensively throughout their daily interactions acted as agents promoting contact-induced innovative variants stemming from the local ecology. I argued that their extensive bilingual upbringing, coupled with a newly emerging socio-cultural norm licencing the practice and simultaneous use of two or more languages in a conversation, has led to the creation of new linguistic items drawing on the interaction of two linguistic resources – English and Hindi.

Overall, the results reported here yield the following generalisation: An exonormatively oriented monolingual state of mind inhibits contact-induced linguistic innovations, whereas an endonormatively oriented bilingual mode of linguistic communication seems to promote those. Stemming from deeply entrenched beliefs about language, socio-cultural norms and practices adopted by a social group will serve as a trigger determining the mode of psycholinguistic reality (monolingual versus bilingual state) in which this group will live. Subsequently, these will determine the level of linguistic diversity encountered in situations of language and dialect contact. This claim has been schematised in Figure 15 for convenience.

Secondly, relying on evidence demonstrating the attitudinal differences characterising ESL and EFL English (endonormative versus exonormative orientation), I hypothesised in Chapter 4 that given their overall commitment to the target-vernacular norms, German learners will adopt *be like* at a higher rate and they will be more adept at replicating the constraints governing the variable use of the innovative variant. Presented in Chapter 5 through 7, analyses of sociolinguistic variation have, however, ascertained that, generally speaking, both norm developing (ESL) and norm dependent (EFL) learners appropriated *be like* at a very modest rate in their speech hovering around 20%, and Chapter 8 presented evidence arguing that a generally low rate of adoption of this global innovation can be attributed to the fact that speakers of both indigenised and Learner English have developed a mixed baggage of ideological associations which they attach to *be like*. The associations comprise both positive and negative values grounded in standard language ideologies, and these have, in turn, prevented both speaker groups from an appropriation of the globetrotter *be like* with a more robust frequency.

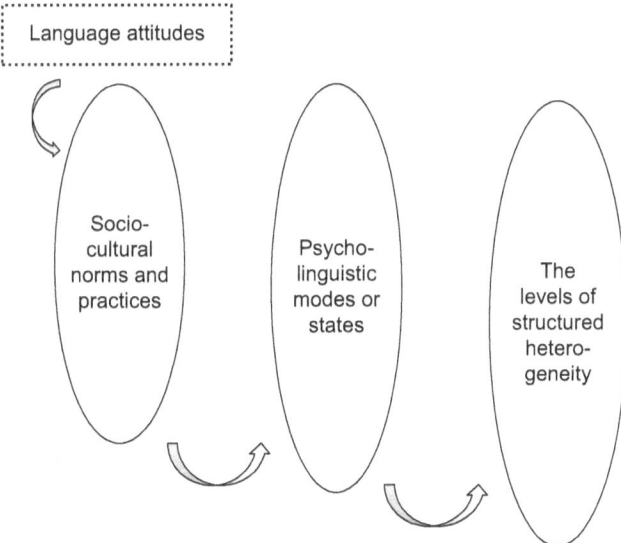

**Figure 15:** Socio-cultural reconstruction of psycholinguistic reality: A language-contact model.

However, it is significant that both young speakers from ESL and EFL speech communities have managed to reconstruct the variable grammar underlying the use of quotative *be like* without a major re-organisation of the language-internal constraint system. Chapter 7 has demonstrated unambiguous parallels in the structural conditioning underlying the variable use of quotative *be like* in both indigenised and Learner English. Chapter 8 has furthermore reported that young adults from both ESL and EFL ecologies exhibit largely consistent social evaluations of quotative *be like*, echoing those documented for L1 English. Coupled together, results documented in these two chapters pinpoint a case of a fairly successful, largely wholesale acquisition of sociolinguistic competence, at least in terms of the parameters listed in (b) through (d).

This finding is remarkable and necessitates an explanation as it runs counter to what we know about the acquisition of sociolinguistic variation by adult language learners. In Chapter 7, I have provided ample evidence illustrating that complete acquisition of variable patterns of use by second language learners is not a given. Indeed, as Schleef, Meyerhoff, and Clark (2011: 225) caution, "variation is an extraordinarily complex and challenging thing to acquire and [...] a range of outcomes are possible". Furthermore, Meyerhoff and Schleef (2012: 409) argue that acquiring independent linguistic and non-linguistic predictors of variation and the ordering of specific constraints within those factors are cognitively complex tasks to the extent that transformation of the constraint system is almost inevitable. In a similar vein, Labov (2007: 383) claims that "adults who are the borrowing agents do not faithfully reproduce the structural patterns of the system they are borrowing from".

With this said, how could one explain the high level of accuracy with which ESL and EFL learners reconstruct the variable patterns of use attested for *be like* on the one hand and its socio-ideological evaluations on the other? In other words, which phenomena play a fostering role in the development of adult speakers' sociolinguistic competence? In the remainder of this book, I will elaborate on the notions of frequency and salience by way of exploring their contribution to successful acquisition of sociolinguistic competence in adult learners. I will also comment on other factors which might be at work here. In so doing, I will outline possible directions of future research for studies investigating how patterns of structured variation and their social evaluations are acquired in a second language.

## 9.1 Frequency

One of the basic tenets underpinning much of modern linguistic theorising is a strict separation of linguistic forms used in communication from their mental representations. Earlier accounts (de Saussure 1966[1915]: 25, 30) postulated a distinction between *langue* (knowledge about language) and *parole* (language use). Having gone down in history as the Generative Grammar approach, this idea is also enshrined in Chomsky's (1965: 4) primary distinction between competence (implicit knowledge about the major properties of language believed to be innate) and performance (actual language use). This view of language has, however, been challenged by a more recently developed exemplar theory and a usage-based theory, regarding grammatical structures as dynamic phenomena that emerge (Hopper 1987) gradually from language processing (see *inter alia* Bybee 2002; Johnson 1997; Kruschke 1992; MacWhinney 2001) and language use (see *inter alia* Croft 2001a, 2001b; Goldberg 1995, 2003, 2006; Tomasello 1999, 2003). Originally introduced in cognitive psychology as a model accounting for the processes of categorisation in perception, the exemplar theory has been largely inspired by the connectionist approach (e.g. Elman 2005; Elman et al. 1996; Kersten and Earles 2001), "a school of thought in cognitive science which attempts to explain mental and/or behavioural phenomena as emergent processes of a network of mutually connected units" (Hinskens 2011: 439).[1]

The usage-based theory is, in turn, grounded in the constructionist approach, also known as Construction Grammar, a school of linguistic thought that views linguistic structures (called 'constructions') as learned form-meaning pairings, accepted by the social convention and established as fully-fledged linguistic knowledge in the speaker's mind (Ellis 2013: 365). Importantly, this linguistic knowledge, so constructionists, is not completely fixed even in adulthood and "linguistic ability is sensitive to exposure to language use in the surrounding community" (Croft 2001b: 58). Constructions are hypothesised to come into existence following two main stages: (i) building an inventory of frequently used, lexically anchored items containing detailed exemplar-based sociolinguistic information (Pierrehumbert 2001: 140–143) that is retrieved by individuals every time they experience language, and (ii) categorising or generalising through the process of analogy in order to build more abstract, and oftentimes structurally more complex, representations from those lexically based frames (Rowland 2007: 110–111; Tomasello 2003: 145–195).

Both usage-based and connectionist approaches emphasise that frequency of occurrence of a given linguistic construction in discourse is an important determinant of language use and diachronic change (see Diessel 2007 for an overview). Moreover, a growing bulk of research on socio-cognitive aspects of language

---

**1** See Harrington (2001: 100–101) for a discussion of traditional and connectionist approaches to language processing.

acquisition indicates that usage-based models are particularly useful in explaining how patterns of structured variation and their underlying constraint systems are mastered by adult learners (Chevrot and Foulkes 2013; Nardy, Chevrot, and Barbu 2013). Davydova and Buchstaller (2015: 462) argue:

> [t]his is because knowledge about language structures – variable as well as categorical ones – is built up from speakers' actual linguistic experiences in their linguistic and social context (see Foulkes, Docherty, and Watt 1999; Kemmer and Barlow 2000; Tomasello 2003, 262–81; 2006). Over time, language learners [...] accumulate context-rich exemplars and extract information out of the regularity of occurrence between certain linguistic features (sound sequences, morphosyntactic patterns, lexical material, and so on) with other types of factors (the linguistic context as well as situational, interactional or social factors). Language acquisition is thus "a gradual process based on links made between a stock of memorised traces leading to the formation of schemas and constructions (Nardy, Chevrot, and Barbu 2013, 278) [...] In other words, language learning involves the accretion of a "structured inventory of meaningful linguistic constructions", including their constraining factors (Tomasello 2006, 259)".

Crucially, usage-oriented theories of second-language acquisition maintain that input frequency is also fundamental to the development of learner interlanguage (Ellis and Collins 2009). Frequent linguistic units are argued to have a stronger representation than less frequent units (Bybee 2002: 216). Furthermore, frequency of exposure to linguistic items is vital to language learners because it is ultimately responsible for automated production and processing in language requiring the minimum of effort on their part. In other words, frequency fosters the development of procedural L2 knowledge through memorisation of linguistic material required for actual language use. A broad cognitive mechanism, automatisation is a key to successful performance not only in language but in other skills as well, which include, for example, playing a musical instrument or various sport games (Bybee 2008: 233). In what follows, I present a selection of case studies illustrating how input frequency supports and guides L2 learners' mastering of a new linguistic system.

Fuchs, Götz, and Werner (2016) study the acquisition of the English present perfect by intermediate and advanced German learners and find out that the present perfect is largely underused in both writing and speech by this learner cohort, a finding that echoes that reported in Davydova (2011: 277). The authors conclude that "[...] the low frequency of the [category] in the input that learners receive is likely to contribute to explaining the late emergence of the [present perfect]" (Fuchs, Götz, and Werner 2016: 327). In a similar vein, Wulff et al. (2009) explore the emergence of the tense and aspect categories by L2 learners from a wide variety of L1 backgrounds and come to the conclusion that individuals are sensitive to the frequency of occurrence of individual verbs, thereby determining why progressives are acquired prior to the simple past tense. "The input for the progressive tends to be less noisy", Wulff et al. (2009: 365) explain "in the sense that the verbs most strongly associated with the progressive also tend to be the most frequent, whereas the verbs most closely related to past tense may occupy relatively lower frequency bands".

Several studies investigating frequency as a contributing factor in second-language acquisition also strive to disentangle the effects produced by type and token frequency. In a nutshell, token frequency is a count of occurrence of a particular linguistic item in the input. Linguistic items with a high token frequency are believed to be independently represented in the mind (see, for instance, Croft 2001b: 149). Type frequency, in contrast, refers to "the number of distinct lexical items that can be substituted in a given slot in a construction, whether it is a word-level construction for inflection or a syntactic construction specifying the relation among words" (Ellis and Collins 2009: 330). In other words, type frequency is a number of distinctive items that can fit in a given linguistic pattern. High token frequencies assist speakers in establishing a single word form in their mental representation, a process called entrenchment, whereas high type frequencies foster analogical thinking (Burridge and Bergs 2017: 129–130) and, by this token, assist learners in establishing patterns in speech that they are exposed to. Furthermore, high type frequency, i.e. the ability of a construction to pattern with various linguistic items, facilitates the parsing of a construction and renders it more available for use with new linguistic items (Bybee 2008: 221). Thus, high type frequency ensures the productivity of a given linguistic construction and strengthens its representational schema (Bybee and Thompson 2000: 384).

McDonough and Kim (2009) investigated the relationship between input and production of *wh*-questions. The authors elicit interrogative forms in students' speech by manipulating the type and token frequency of *wh*-questions in the input provided by the instructor. Following McDonough and Mackey (2008), McDonough and Kim (2009) conclude that that low type/high token frequency of syntactic priming help learners with the immediate production of the target structures. In other words, upon hearing a syntactic prime and being presented with a lexical verb and a *wh*-question word identical to the ones contained in the prime, learners were able to produce another target-like structure closely modelled on the pattern contained in the prime, a phenomenon called 'lexical boost' (Pickering and Ferreira 2008). Yet high type frequency fostered successful and productive use of interrogative constructions. McDonough and Kim (2009: 387) report that "learners who produced *wh*-questions with lexical verbs and *wh*-question words that had not occurred in the preceding primes were more likely to advance to a higher stage of question development than learners who [simply] repeated the lexical verbs and *wh*-questions modelled in the primes".

The implication of this finding is that greater lexical diversity activates learners' category-building abilities via analogical thinking (Tomasello 2003: 145), and boosts the learning of linguistic patterns. In other words, inherently linked to lexical diversity, high type frequency determines learners' ability to spot the productivity of a given construction and start using it actively in their speech (see also Bybee 2008: 221).

Similarly, exploring L2 acquisition of verb-argument constructions (i.e. verb locative, verb object locative, and ditransitive) in English, German, Dutch, French, and Swedish by speakers of Punjabi, Italian, Turkish, Arabic, Spanish, and Finnish, Ellis and Ferreira-Junior (2009) managed to obtain evidence demonstrating that whereas type frequency spurs the productive use of a construction, it is highly frequent items that help learners detect the existing pattern in the first place. In combination, these studies suggest that token frequency initiates and type frequency ultimately drives acquisition of more abstract representations extracted from linguistic material available in the input.

Finally, Casenhiser and Goldberg (2005) demonstrate that both type and token frequency are important to productive construction learning. The study was carried out with children but nevertheless offers an important insight that could be applied to adult second language learning as well. More specifically, the study is a vivid illustration demonstrating how type frequency and token frequency conspire in order to produce an additive impact ensuring successful acquisition of a construction. In that study, English-speaking children, aged five to seven, had to learn nonce verbs (representing token frequency) in a construction with an unusual syntactic pattern (representing type frequency). All the subjects were presented with sentences containing a subject, a verb, and an object. In each case, the verb was placed in a sentence-final position, what is ungrammatical in English and thus novel to children. The children were divided into two groups. The first group was treated with sentences in which three nonce verbs were presented twice and two other verbs just once. This condition emphasised the high type frequency. In the second group, the children heard sentences in which one nonce verb was presented as many as four times, whereas all the other verbs surfaced only once. This condition then highlighted the high token frequency of a nonce verb. It was the latter condition that prompted the better learning of the construction. The implications of this finding can be summed up along the following lines. Each and every category consists of members varying in their frequency of use. Category members exhibiting higher levels of frequency will also be registered as more central or prototypical members of that category. These members are more accessible to learners in their immediate experience of language and it is through them that the productive acquisition of a construction will begin. This observation entails that while maintaining linguistic diversity within a construction may generally support the internalisation of a given construction, be it a morphosyntactic structure or a more abstract word-order pattern, holding an item constant within a construction over an extended number of repetitions is crucial as it makes the learner become familiar with the relations existing between construction members and, therefore, facilitates the learning of this construction as such (see also Bybee 2008: 223). It follows then that both type and token frequency play a key role in construction learning, and within a productive pattern, it is a highly frequent member (for instance, a verb or a noun) that will guide acquisition of a construction as a whole.

Let us now scrutinise the variable under study with respect to the parameter 'frequency', while maintaining the distinction between type frequency and token frequency. First and foremost, as an overall construction type, quotative marking shows elevated rates of occurrence in spontaneous vernacular speech. Adapted from Tagliamonte and D'Arcy (2007), Table 87 cross-tabulates the frequency of English quotatives with native speakers' numbers documented for various geographic locales. It informs us that adult speakers of English are capable of producing up to 228.8 instances of quotation per hour in a naturally flowing conversation.

**Table 87:** Number of quotatives per speaker in L1 English (based on Tagliamonte and D'Arcy 2007: 200).

| N (speakers) | N (quotes) | Ratio quotes/speaker | Age | Community | Source |
|---|---|---|---|---|---|
| 115 | 485 | 4.2 | 18–40 (or above) | Texas | Ferrara and Bell (1995) |
| 14 | 3203 | 228.8 | 14–89 | Springville | Cukor-Avila (2002) |
| 136 | 1371 | 10.1 | 45 (below or above) | all areas of the US | Buchstaller (2004) |
| 64 | 2064 | 32.25 | 45 (below or above) | Derby, Newcastle | Buchstaller (2004) |
| 44 | 665 | 15.1 | 18–28 | York | Tagliamonte and Hudson (1999) |
| 23 | 612 | 26.6 | 18–28 | Ottawa | Tagliamonte and Hudson (1999) |
| 44 | 2058 | 46.8 | 10–19 | Toronto | Tagliamonte and D'Arcy (2004) |
| 16 | 184 | 11.5 | 8–16 | St. John's | D'Arcy (2004) |

As reported in Table 88, the data from the Toronto English Corpus reveals that quotative markers are particularly robust in speech of individuals aged 15 to 39. Informants in the older age bracket (40 to 60 and above) tend to produce fewer quotative markers within an hour of conversation.

**Table 88:** The number of quotatives per speaker in the Toronto English Corpus (adapted from Tagliamonte and D'Arcy 2007: 203).

| N (speakers) | N (quotes) | Ratio quotes/speaker | Age |
|---|---|---|---|
| 14 | 396 | 28.3 | 9–12 |
| 7 | 204 | 29.1 | 13–14 |
| 12 | 505 | **42.1** | 15–16 |
| 54 | 1992 | **36.9** | 17–19 |
| 38 | 1138 | **29.9** | 20–29 |
| 13 | 524 | **40.3** | 30–39 |
| 25 | 550 | 22.0 | 40–49 |
| 16 | 503 | 31.4 | 50–59 |
| 20 | 552 | 27.6 | >60 |
| 199 | 6364 | 31.9 | Total |

Moreover, Rathje (2011: 75) reports 7.89 quotations per 1000 words as encountered in speech of young adults in Denmark, which contrasts with production rates of quotative markers by middle-aged and older population groups; 3.9 variants on average per 1000 words. Taken together, both studies yield evidence that as a discourse-pragmatic device, quotation is robustly present in naturalistic L1 speech. Moreover, existing evidence suggests that as a construction type, quotative marking has been on the rise in L1 vernaculars spoken worldwide.

Secondly, the quotative template NOUN PHRASE + COPULA VERB/VERBUM DICENDI + (DISCOURSE MARKER) + QUOTE underpin highly conventionalised surface structures used by L1 speakers as "a routinised sequence of words" (Buchstaller 2014: 15) in order to express a particular meaning (i.e. reporting of speech and thought). Crucially, the quotative template is a productive construction type in L1 English, continuously expanding its remit via analogical extension, as discussed in Chapter 3, and attracting new lexical material into the DISCOURSE MARKER slot. This is evidenced by the following quotative items attested in different varieties of English: *be like, say like, be git, say git, be kinda, say kinda, be sorta, think sorta, be totally, think totally,* etc. (Buchstaller 2014: 16–18). The claim that innovative quotatives represent a productive construction type in English is further supported by cross-linguistic evidence. Following Buchstaller and Van Alpen (2012: xiv), Buchstaller (2014: 20–23) reports novel quotative constructions for a variety of typologically related and unrelated languages (see also discussion in Chapter 5). Crucially, she argues that innovative quotative constructions have evolved in these languages along similar semantic pathways. To begin with, speakers tend to insert lexical material denoting similarity and approximation into the quotative template (e.g. Afrikaans *soos* 'so + as', Buang (*na*) *be* 'like', English *like*, Finnish *niinku* (*niin kuin*) 'as if', Greek *tipou* 'type', Russian *tipa* 'type', Spanish *como* 'like, as', Thai *bœ:p* 'like', etc.). The lexical material with comparative/simulative semantics is, indeed, wide-spread in quotative constructions because of the hedging effect it triggers. The latter is very useful in that it mitigates the inaccurate rendition of opinions and attitudes (Romaine and Lange 1991: 241). The second important source of the quotative construction productivity stems from lexical items with demonstrative and deictic functions (e.g. Dutch *zo* 'so', Finnish *siihen et(tä)* 'to–that', Russian *takoj* 'such', Spanish *asi* 'so', etc.). The recruitment of such material for quotative function seems to be motivated by the fact that demonstrative and deictic elements help speakers to re-enact a story in the here and now, thereby adding to its vividness. Furthermore, quantifiers provide a valuable cross-linguistic source for quotative markers (e.g. Dutch *helemaal* 'all', English *all*, Estonian *täiega* 'totally', Finnish *vaa(n)*, Swedish *ba (ra)* 'just, only'). Choosing boosting and maximising elements such as *all* or *totally* help speakers to express their commitment to the accuracy of the material reproduced in a quote. In contrast, the use of downtoners such as *just*, *kinda*, *sorta*, etc. help them to highlight the fact that they are anything but committed to the quoted utterance. Overall, it appears that speakers of both related and distantly related languages draw on universally available semantic resources, thereby enhancing the productivity of the existing quotative template.

An important observation from the perspective of second-language acquisition is that as a discourse-pragmatic device, quotation schema is experienced with various items in speech and thus exhibits a fairly high type frequency. The lexical diversity inherent in the quotative template, in turn, facilitates the parsing of quotative constructions and provides the necessary cognitive prerequisites instigating the active learning of patterns. This is compounded by fairly high token frequencies of quotation in the discourse, reported in Table 87 and Table 88, which inevitably contributes to a successful acquisition of the quotative construction as a whole.

Moreover, as Buchstaller (2014: 16) notes, "it appears that the subconstruction type NOUN PHRASE + *be* + *like* + QUOTE has, since its earliest attestation in the 1980s, provided a fertile template for the creation of new forms". Being attested at elevated rates in North American English, the epicentre of global innovation, *be like* is a high-frequency and, therefore, a prototypical member of the category in the major donor variety. We can recall that whereas type frequency is important for the acquisition of a new category, it is repeated exposure to a specific token (a construction schema) that ultimately ensures successful acquisition of a linguistic pattern (Casenhiser and Goldberg 2005).

Effectively, this means that young ESL/EFL learners have enhanced chances of encountering the productive construction type NOUN PHRASE + COPULA VERB/VERBUM DICENDI + (DISCOURSE MARKER) + QUOTE and its most central member, quotative *be like*, in the input. In other words, coupled with a relatively high type frequency of the quotative template, the distributional frequencies of quotative *be like* provide L2 learners with ideal circumstances for a cognitively challenging task – the acquisition of a constraint system. This may be a compelling explanation aligned with the major thrust of the most recent SLA research (see, for instance, Ellis 2013). However, quotative marking is not the only sociolinguistic variable demonstrating high levels of type and token frequency. Let us consider briefly the variable (ing). Similar to other functional elements, suffix *–ing* has been described as a frequently occurring bound morpheme with an independent status since it combines with word stems in predictable ways (Mintz 2013: 1). The high token frequency of this suffix is accompanied a high type frequency of a construction of the type WORD STEM + ING. Similar to the quotative template, the construction is highly productive in English, particularly with verbs and verb-like structures (e.g. participles, gerunds). At the same time, not a single word could be pinpointed as a prototypical example of the category WORD STEM + ING, even though some lexical items could be shown to be more closely linked to *–ing* than others in naturally occurring data. To illustrate this point, in his study exploring lexical frequency effects on the occurrence of the velar variant as attested in speech of 11 respondents from a middle-class community in Philadelphia, Abramowicz (2007: 32) reports as many as 15 lexical items combining with (ing) most frequently and accounting for 46% of the tokens in the data. This is clearly in contrast with the overall composition of lexical items in the quotative template, where, at least in North American English, the element 'be + like' reigns at the rate ranging from 68% to 72% in the overall construction type NOUN PHRASE + COPULA VERB/VERBUM DICENDI + (DISCOURSE MARKER) + QUOTE (Buchstaller 2014: 119; Tagliamonte and D'Arcy 2004: 501). It is this lack of a prototypical or central element in the construction of the type WORD STEM + ING which may be contributing to the re-organisation of language-internal predictors and thus less successful acquisition of the constraint system underlying variable realisation of the velar [ɪŋ] reported in Schleef, Meyerhoff, and Clark (2011).

Overall, while stemming from variationist research, the analysis presented above lends weight to the hypothesis that both the range of different construction types and the repeated type are instrumental to successful acquisition of a hierarchically organised system of patterns. The former helps to parse a construction and, in so doing, secures its mental representation on a more abstract (non-item-based) level, whereas the latter familiarises the learners with the relations existing within the construction (Bybee 2008: 225). These may include not only syntagmatic relations but also, quite possibly, the relations existing between a variable item and language-internal determinants underlying its use.

In summary, the foregoing discussion has demonstrated that frequency may play a facilitative role in the acquisition of the linguistic construction consisting of copula *be* and discourse marker *like* as well as the underlying constraint system. However, as Ellis and Ferreira-Junior (2009: 382) notice, distinguishing it as "the root cause of category acquisition is problematic and probably naïve". Instead, one should strive for a more holistic explanation of factors leading to successful outcomes in second-language learning. With this said, what other factors may assist learners in the process of acquiring the rules of weighted probabilities underlying the variable occurrence of *be like*? It has been noticed in the previous literature (Davydova and Buchstaller 2015: 463; Levon and Buchstaller 2015: 326) that the quotative frame including schematic construction *be like* exhibits a high level of socio-cognitive salience. Here, I propose that it is this particular property that may lie at the core of the mechanism ensuring successful appropriation of this variable feature, its system-internal conditioning and social assessment. The relevant question here is, 'What is it exactly that renders innovative *be like* a salient feature of speech from a socio-cognitive perspective?' The prefinal section of this book will address this issue.

## 9.2 Salience

Over the past decades, the construct of 'salience' has become increasingly popular among physiologists, cognitive scientists, and social psychologists as a theoretical building block modelling the functioning of the human brain and the human mind more generally (see *inter alia* Itti, Koch and Niebur 2002; Rosch 1973; Taylor and Fiske 1978; Treisman and Gelade 1980). In linguistics, the concept has come to the attention of dialectologists, sociolinguists, and specialists in first- and second-language acquisition (Bardovi-Harlig 1987; Buchstaller 2016; Cintrón-Valentín and Ellis 2016; Ellis 2016; Kerswill 1985; Kerswill and Williams 2002; Levon and Buchstaller 2015; Levon and Fox 2014; Mufwene 1991; Rácz 2013; Slobin 1985; Trudgill 1986).

The idea of salience seems to be intuitively straightforward and this is perhaps one of the reasons why for a considerably long time, the notion was employed by different linguists as a general cover term and applied to phenomena as diverse as phonetic prominence, morphological naturalness, and socio-cognitive representations. The notion of salience has a reasonably long history in the study of language going back to the work of Schirmunski (1930, cited in Kerswill and Williams 2002: 82), which introduced the concept of *Auffälligkeit* discussing the difference between dialect features susceptible to change and loss. Later on, the notion found recognition in the works of Paul Kerswill (Kerswill 1985), Anthony J.

Naro (Naro 1981), Peter Trudgill (Trudgill 1986), and Salikoko Mufwene (Mufwene 1991), all of whom explored the contribution of linguistic prominence as an explanatory variable in situations of language and dialect contact.

In their account, Kerswill and Williams (2002: 105) argue that as an explanatory concept, salience often involves the presence of linguistic items that are transferred from language variety to another through diffusion (see also Naro 1981: 97). In other words, they are suggesting that "salience is only relevant in the case of dynamic linguistic phenomena (those involved in acquisition and change)" (Kerswill and Williams 2002: 81). The implicit assumption underlying their argument is that the adoption or non-adoption of linguistic forms from one linguistic variety into another is determined by the structural properties of language features on the one hand and social psychological factors on the other. Importantly, these authors introduce the idea that the definition of salience must include both structure-specific and extralinguistic parameters.

Drawing on this fundamental distinction, more recent sociolinguistic studies (Buchstaller 2016; Levon and Buchstaller 2015; Levon and Fox 2014; and notably Rácz 2013) have sought to develop conceptually rigorous definitions of salience. Perhaps the most insightful finding that can be deduced from these discussions is that there are generally two major ways in which salience can be constructed as a linguistically viable concept. On the one hand, salience can be understood as a general and, at least to some degree objective, property of the linguistic system (see also Naro 1981: 97). Following Rácz (2013: 23), I refer to this type of salience as *cognitive salience*. Conversely, salience can be construed as a subjective property of the speaker's mind, ensuring substantial awareness about a given linguistic feature and thereby allowing for its social indexation. I term this type of salience *sociolinguistic salience*.

Before embarking upon a discussion of cognitive and sociolinguistic salience, I would like to clarify my position concerning the relationship between salience and frequency in the conceptual apparatus. In contrast to studies that use frequency to define or describe salience or salient features (Bardovi-Harlig 1987), I maintain that both phenomena should be kept conceptually distinct as they are highly relevant to our descriptions of dialect and language contact, including situations of second language (dialect) acquisition. Using the concept of frequency in order to define salience will only lead to the circularity of the argument ("This feature is salient because it occurs with frequency X; and because it occurs with frequency X, it must be salient"). Such an approach does not inform our understanding of the processes at work in adaptation and propagation of linguistic features from speaker community to speaker community.

For instance, a hypothesis that only low frequency features (Rácz 2013 8–11) are salient because they have a high surprisal value for a speaker of a different dialect, as determined by transition probabilities, seems intuitively plausible.[2] The claim seems to be working well on the phonological level and can also be applied to levels extending beyond phonology. For instance, the Irish *after*-perfect (*I am after meeting* her meaning 'I have just met her') is a low-frequency morphosyntactic feature (Davydova 2013: 208) exhibiting substantial levels of sociocognitive prominence (it's an analytical, chunk-like structure with fairly high levels of noticeability).

However, the claim is not always borne out by empirical evidence and we can find counter examples to the formula 'low frequency → high surprisal value = high salience'. The hypothesis does not stand once one takes a closer look at the domain of variable quotative marking and the use of quotative *be like*, which happens to be both frequent and, as will be argued below, socio-cognitively salient. With this said, our theory building should aim at describing how frequency and salience interact with each other in situations of language contact including scenarios of second-language acquisition, whereas our hypothesis building should seek to describe the results that such interactions might produce.

## 9.2.1 Cognitive salience

This section discusses cognitive salience. The definition of cognitive salience is grounded in one fundamental observation. The human brain cannot process the incoming input, either visual or auditory, in its entirety and is forced to integrate the incoming information on a selective basis. How does that happen? Computational modelling of rapid scene analysis suggests that the items are selected from the environment on the basis of feature contrast (Itti, Koch and Niebur 2002; see also Treisman and Gelade 1980: 132). For instance, a red dot surrounded by black dots is salient by virtue of it being red against a perceptually contrastive (black) background. A cognitively salient object or phenomenon is the one that "bulges out of its surroundings" (Rácz 2013: 31) on the visual, auditory or tactile basis, and, therefore, has increased chances of becoming the focus of our attention. In other words, "[t]he physical world, our embodiment, and our sensory systems come together to cause certain sensations to be more intense (louder, brighter, heavier, etc.) than others" (Cintrón-Valentín and Ellis 2016: 1). In sum, cognitive salience is "the ability of a stimulus to stand out from the rest" (Ellis 2016: 342; see also Fiske and Morling 1996: 489).

---

[2] Transition probability is a statistical construct that calculates the probability that given element A, the following segment in the linguistic structure is element B (see Rácz 2013: 37–38).

Defining salience in language along those lines is not an entirely straightforward task for a linguistic because language is an inherently dual system comprising both form and meaning. Whereas the surface properties of language are amenable to an analysis in terms of feature contrast, its semantic and discourse-pragmatic aspects cannot be as easily captured with the help of this notion. Nevertheless, my goal is to define salience with respect to all levels of linguistic structure. Ultimately, I will rely on the long-standing tradition of linguistic research into salience, while simultaneously following, as far as possible, the definition of salience adopted in the cognitive science. In so doing, I seek to contribute to the development of convergent knowledge grounded in interdisciplinary perspectives. As a starting point, I will adopt a relatively benign view shared by most linguists whereby salience can be regarded as a general property of speech difference (Rácz 2013: 2). With this preliminary definition in mind, let us address the following question, 'Which phonetic, suprasegmental, morphosyntactic, semantic, and discourse-pragmatic characteristics render linguistic features cognitively salient?'

At the phonetic level, salience has been described in terms of phonetic (auditory) discreteness (Kerswill 1985: 1) or phonetic distance (Trudgill 1986: 11). Any speech segment that may have two (or in some cases more) differing realisations in an otherwise identical sequence of sounds can in principle be construed as phonetically salient. Consider, for instance, the standard realisation of the word *milk* [mɪɫk] featuring the non-vocalised velarised realisation of the syllable-coda *l* and now contrast it with a more colloquial variant [mɪʊk] featuring the *l*-vocalisation, characteristic of south-eastern English varieties. Here, segments [ɫ] and [ʊ] can be analysed as phonetically distinct because they stand out as prominent elements against an otherwise identical linguistic background. This conceptualisation of phonetic salience is thus consistent with the definition that emphasises feature contrast as the fundamental property of cognitive salience. Importantly, "a phonetic feature which is salient in its environment will remain so irrespective of its frequency in a given chunk of speech" (Rácz 2013: 29; see also Kerswill and Williams 2002: 83–84).

At the suprasegmental level, linguistic material occurring in prosodically prominent positions can be understood as salient if it is set off from the neighbouring linguistic surroundings by a different intonation contour, pitch variations (Kerswill and Williams 2002: 87). Stress-bearing elements can also be construed as more salient than unstressed ones (Mufwene 1991: 139). Here, salience arises from our sensory experience of the contrast existing between emphasised and non-emphasised speech elements. The first stressed syllable of the word *janitor*/ˈdʒænətə/is thus more salient than the second and the third syllable, both of which are also phonetically reduced. In a similar vein, prepositional phrases and temporal adverbs are stressed in English and, by this token, more salient than verbal inflections and other grammatical function words, which are typically not stressed (Cintrón-Valentín and Ellis 2016: 3). To this end, Slobin (1985) reports that children have difficulty with unstressed morphemes, while Henrichsen (1984) presents similar evidence for L2 learners.

At the morphosyntactic level, analytical constructions are arguably more salient than synthetic forms by virtue of the fact that the former can be individuated or discerned from the surrounding linguistic environment more easily and thus become available for processing by the human brain. For instance, the English present perfect (a construction consisting of auxiliary *have* and a past participle of the main verb), the Irish *after*-perfect mentioned earlier, the progressive forms (comprising auxiliary *be* and a present participle of the main verb) are more salient than verbal inflections (*–ed*, *–s*, *–ing*). Other function words (for instance, articles, prepositions, conjunctions, etc.) fall somewhere in between. On the one hand, they are fairly independent language units which, simultaneously, cannot be used on their own, as a rule, and thus have the potential to develop into more dependent items such as clitics and inflectional affixes (Hopper and Traugott 2003: 7). That function words exhibit a higher degree of salience than inflectional marking is supported by the empirical finding that in situations of language contact, "[f]ree-standing grammatical forms (such as conjunctions and prepositions) are borrowed more easily than bound forms (such as a past tense or plural suffix)" (Burridge and Bergs 2017: 191; see also Mufwene 1991: 127–128). In a similar vein, nouns, adjectives and adverbs are more individuated in a speech stream and, by this token, more salient than derivational morphemes involved in their formation (*–s*, *–al*, *–ly*, etc.). In contrast to bound morphemes, an autonomous linguistic item stands out in speech material to a greater degree and is thus more conspicuous. Finally, word order patterns are least subject to individuation through the incoming speech signal. Relying on a cross-linguistic review provided in Slobin (1982), Tomasello (2003: 133) observes that small children acquire agent-patient distinctions faster if they learn how to speak languages with overt morphological case agreement. In contrast, languages in which agent-patient relations are regulated through word order present children with more difficulties. Tomasello (2003) argues this is because noun phrases have concrete phonology, whereas word order does not. "[W]ord order", he says "has no phonological content per se, and so it may be an extremely ephemeral cue for young children, whereas morphological markers give them some concrete phonology on which to base a semantic-syntactic distinction" (Tomasello 2003: 133). I take this observation to imply that linguistic units consisting of speech segments are arguably more salient than highly abstract linguistic structures such as word-order patterns which do not have any concrete linguistic substance. The previous content words/analytical constructions → function words → inflectional and derivational morphology → word order

**Figure 16:** The morphosyntactic cline of cognitive salience.

discussion makes clear that morphosyntactic salience is a gradual phenomenon and different features of morphosyntax can be postulated to exhibit varying degrees of cognitive salience, as illustrated in Figure 16.

The feature contrast emerges here as the immediacy with which a linguistic stimulus can be discerned distinctively from a speech signal and herewith become available to our sensory apparatus for further processing. Following this definition, content words and analytical constructions score higher than function words and bound morphemes with respect to their capacity of becoming available to cognitive processing, whereas word order patterns are fundamentally substance-*less* and, by this token, the least salient.

Semantically, salient forms have been defined as those associated with a "specific meaning" (Mufwene 1991: 139) or "particular semantics" (Buchstaller 2014: 15) mapped on a linguistic construction. This definition is consistent with Talmy's (2008: 32) observation that "a more specific referent tends to attract greater attention than a more general referent". For instance, the verb *hop*, as in *He hopped into the bathroom*, has more specific semantics than the verb *walk*, as in *He walked into the bathroom*, and, by this token, more salient. The former refers to a special type of movement, namely moving by jumping on one foot, whereas the latter designates movement generally and is, therefore, more inclusive as a term.

Furthermore, the idea of semantic salience presupposes a high level of correspondence between a linguistic form and its function. Therefore, processes in derivational and inflectional morphology have been assumed to be salient if there is "transparency in the form-meaning relationship" (Kerswill and Williams 2002: 87). Consistent with the general semiotic principle of 'one form, one meaning' Mayerthaler (1981: 34–35), such transparency in the form-meaning relationship has been argued to ensure productivity of analogical extension in the process of linguistic change (Chapman 1994, 1995). From a psycholinguistic perspective, linguistic material demonstrating a straightforward correspondence between a linguistic form and its function is easier to attend to. As a result, such linguistic items arguably become available to our senses more readily for further processing (Ellis 2016: 344–345). Where a language item is connected to multiple meanings, the associative strength between a surface form and its function is weakened and, by this token, less salient.

At the discourse-pragmatic level, cognitively prominent features play an important role in spontaneous oral communication (Kerswill and Williams 2002: 87) and, as a result, are highlighted through occurrence in "interactionally prominent positions" (Cheshire 1996: 6). These, in turn, are often associated with a "conceptual contrast" (Talmy 2008: 30). For instance, by foregrounding the temporal adjunct *right now* in *Right now I can't bring myself to read this article* the speaker suggests a pragmatic contrast between the moment of utterance and some future reference point, thereby implying that reading the article at a different time would actually be all right. Moreover, interactionally prominent positions have been argued to introduce "emotionally-heightened material" (Buchstaller 2003: 9) and, in so doing, to perform an "important textual structural function" (Buchstaller 2014: 14). They may also be of some informative value in so far as they may reveal speakers' communicative intentions or their attitudes towards communicated content. Thus defined, elements surfacing in interactionally prominent positions are capable of bringing the listener's attention into a specific focus, relevant to communicated content, and this is how they contrast with other (communicatively non-focused) elements of the discourse structure. To illustrate this point, one of the reasons why speakers are attracted to discourse markers and question tags and become easily aware of those during conversation (even though their referential scope is admittedly low) is because these 'small' bits of language engage in establishing a social rapport and creating an atmosphere of trust among discourse participants. Both are fundamentally important to human beings as these skills appear to be a result of our "biologically inherited social-cognitive ability […] to create and use social conventions and symbols" (Tomasello 1999: 216).

### 9.2.2 Sociolinguistic salience

Much of current sociolinguistic theorising rests on the assumption that some linguistic features are more readily available to speakers for social evaluation than others (Labov 1972b, 2001). This kind of awareness and ensuing assessment of linguistic material, in turn, determines the developmental trajectory of an incoming variant (Trudgill 1986). Taking this idea one step further, it is not unreasonable to surmise that such awareness also helps non-native speakers, however indirectly, to deal with the complexities of the variable input that they encounter in L1 discourse and, in so doing, reconstruct variable grammars of sociolinguistically salient features and their socio-ideological evaluations with more detail and precision. This is arguably because linguistic items that are more readily noticed by language learners are also more likely to "enter into subsequent cognitive processing and learning" (Cintrón-Valentín and Ellis 2016: 1).

Against this backdrop, sociolinguistic salience can be defined as a degree to which speakers are aware of an existing variant (and can therefore subject it to further social evaluation, Levon and Fox 2014: 185). Such an operationalisation of salience is rooted in a sociolinguistic premise that the level of social awareness is "a major property of linguistic change" (Weinreich, Labov, and Herzog 1968: 186). For instance, sociolinguistically salient features of speech are less likely to be omitted even if they were structurally reduced (Mufwene 1991: 139; Naro 1981: 73–75). Furthermore, the notion of sociolinguistic salience is largely aligned with the theories of second-language acquisition highlighting the role of attention and/or awareness as a precondition to learning (Cintrón-Valentín and Ellis 2016; Ellis 2015; Schmidt 1990, 2001). These theories predict that people learn about things they pay attention to, however indirectly, and do not learn much about things beyond the scope of their attention.

The notion of 'indirect attention' is significant and worthy of elaboration. It subsumes the concept of 'noticing' (Schmidt 1990) on the one hand and 'implicit learning' (Ellis 2002) on the other. Noticing presupposes conscious awareness about a linguistic item on the part of the learner (Schmidt 1990: 129). In contrast, implicit learning is an "automatic abstraction of the structural nature of the material arrived at from experience of instances" (Ellis 2015: 4) and, thus, largely unconscious.[3] This dichotomy seems to be largely compatible with Tomlin and Villa's (1994) distinction between conscious perception and nonconscious registration. Drawing on Schmidt (1990), I propose that both noticing and implicit learning are relevant to the process underlying L2 acquisition of linguistic variables. Whereas internalisation of vernacular grammars is, by and large, an indirect, unconscious process, it is also guided by the learner's various degrees of attention to ambient language (see also Talmy 2008: 27). Therefore, noticing is a gradient, rather than a categorical, phenomenon. The implication of this observation is that variable linguistic features with higher levels of noticeability are

---

3 The orthodox position maintained in cognitive psychology is that attention is a prerequisite to learning. The claim that unattended learning is still possible has been a subject of extensive debates in cognitive science (see Schmidt 2001: 28–32). Nevertheless, some experimental evidence (DeSchepper & Treisman 1996) appears to substantiate the view that learning can happen on the basis of unattended processing. While making a review of an experiment reported in DeSchepper & Treisman (1996), Schmidt (2001: 27) concludes that "there can be representation and storage in memory of unattended novel stimuli, something frequently claimed but not convincingly demonstrated in the past".

also more amenable to successful acquisition through implicit/naturalistic learning than less noticeable variants.

The relevance of both noticing and implicit learning to the emergence of L2 variable grammar can also be summed up along the following lines. While being exposed to ambient language, non-native speakers attend to it holistically, noticing some features and ignoring others given limited cognitive resources. However, noticing differs from explicit learning, equated typically with focused L2 instruction (Ellis 2015: 19). Indeed, nobody would expect that upon noticing a vernacular feature in their input, language learners would begin actively searching for patterns underlying its use. Firstly, the acquisition of such features occurs during spontaneous interactions offering only very little (if any) time for explicit metalinguistic analyses of the incoming speech material; and secondly, language learners are not focused on conscious learning tasks in such settings. Appropriating vernacular features as part of one's speech repertoire is not goal-directed and, to this extent, implicit.

And yet it is this general noticing of a linguistic item in ambient language, I argue, that is a necessary precondition for turning input, i.e. surrounding linguistic material, into intake, i.e. internalised linguistic material available for further use (see also Schmidt 1990: 149). To this effect, Schmidt and Frota (1986) present evidence indicating that there is a close connection between noticing of linguistic forms in the input and their emergence in production. It is this noticing that enables the human brain to register a variant and start building associative patterns of weighted probabilities mapping those on a linguistic variant. The relative plasticity of synaptic connections ensures the proper functioning of this mechanism (Ellis 2002: 146), which essentially consists of exemplar-based learning, i.e. the strength of synaptic connections underlying the representation of a construction and its language-internal conditioning is a function of previously experienced tokens (Ellis 2015: 5).

Situating linguistic variables at different levels of perceptual awareness (Buchstaller 2016: 202), sociolinguistic salience comes to play a role in successful appropriation of variably organised linguistic material. More "latent" (Ellis 2015: 16) and, therefore, less noticeable linguistic structures will be acquired by language learners, albeit to a limited extent. Exposure to utterances will set respective neuro-cognitive processes in motion (Ellis 2015: 6) resulting in a re-organised variable grammar. Studies reported in Chapter 7 provide ample evidence to that end. Yet, if a linguistic feature were to be acquired with a high degree of accuracy, it must be impressed in some special way upon the cognitive system of adult speakers. With this said, it is reasonable to assume that a relatively high level of awareness about a linguistic item must, at least to some extent, assist learners into successful acquisition of variable patterns underlying its use (see also

Schmidt 1990, 2001). This is because "[i]n acquiring associations, [...] learners are more likely to learn about the part of the environment which they selectively attend" (Ellis 2001: 63).

The previous discussion brings us to the next question, 'Under which conditions is a linguistic feature likely to come to the fore of the learner's attention and thus become noticed?' In accordance with Rácz (2013: 31), I argue that a cognitively salient feature may with time become sociolinguistically salient since it is generally noticeable (see also Kerswill and Williams 2002; Trudgill 1986). The assumption is logical: Features that stand out from the rest of linguistic material because of their formal and functional properties are also more likely to captivate listeners' attention throughout narrative discourse structures and with time, begin to be used for social indexation. It has, however, also been argued that sociolinguistic factors can override structural linguistic factors in influencing the levels of noticeability of a given language item (Kerswill and Williams 2002: 85). To be sure, an objective property of a language item, cognitive salience increases the chances of a linguistic feature becoming more noticeable to discourse participants. And yet it is just one (in addition to several other) contributing factors. With this said, there appears to be a set of extralinguistic variables mediating the process whereby a given feature of language comes to the fore of (non-native) speakers' attention. These include (i) overt commentary in the public discourse, including interactions in a classroom, and (ii) novelty.

Current research on sociolinguistic salience (Buchstaller 2016; Levon and Buchstaller 2015; Levon and Fox 2014) asserts that linguistic forms are salient if they are featured in "explicit meta-discourse" (Levon and Fox 2014: 187). The latter includes overt commentaries in newspaper articles and published letters to the editor; opinion pieces in the blogs and online sites; discussions and interviews with educationalists and "self-appointed language pundits" (Buchstaller 2014: 200) on the radio shows and television programmes. Associated with the so-called "complaint tradition" (Milroy and Milroy 2003: 26), prescriptive comments usually signal a high level of social awareness about a linguistic feature in the public sphere (Buchstaller 2016: 206). Importantly, these can attract non-native speakers' attention. In a classroom setting, teachers' explicit observations about language can become an additional source of metalinguistic awareness about an existing variant. Teachers' comments about language are particularly pertinent in the context of second-language acquisition and language learning because classroom interactions are instrumental in the development of an additional language.

Novelty is another factor increasing the chances that a given feature will come to the forefront of the learner's attention. This is because novel features are of high 'surprisal' value (Ellis 2016: 344) to speakers and are thus easily noticeable. In the cognitive sciences, surprise is taken to be a principal component governing human perception (Rácz 2013: 9). Cintrón-Valentín and Ellis (2016: 2) explain this position as follows:

> The evolutionary role of cognition is to predict what is going to happen next, given that anticipation affords survival value. [...] The brain is a prediction machine (Clark, 2013). One consequence of it is that it is surprisal – when prediction goes wrong – that maximally drives learning from a single trial.

Against this backdrop, features perceived as novel by speakers can also be assumed to be salient as these can be discerned in a conversation more easily. Such features are likely candidates for (further) social indexation (Rácz 2013: 26) and, in some cases, perhaps even re-analysis (Hopper and Traugott 2003: 50–70). From the perspective of second-language acquisition and language learning, linguistic variants that learners perceive as new are also the ones to which they are likely to pay more attention and the latter affords learning.

### 9.2.3 Socio-cognitive salience

This section outlines the major properties of socio-cognitive salience. These properties are the criteria allowing us to describe the degree to which a given linguistic feature can be understood as socio-cognitively salient. Here, I propose that a linguistic variant involved in situations of language/dialect contact (including second-language acquisition scenarios) can be assessed with respect to the following parameters:

(i) *Phonetic/phonological level*: whether it expresses phonetically different (discrete) contrasts (Kerswill 1985: 7; Trudgill 1986: 11); and whether it is involved in the maintenance of phonological contrasts (see Trudgill 1986 for a full discussion);

(ii) *Suprasegmental level*: whether a feature is used as suprasegmentally emphasised material (Mufwene 1991: 139);

(iii) *Morphosyntactic level*: the extent to which a feature can be individuated on the morphosyntactic level of organisation of linguistic structure (see Figure 16);

(iv) *Semantic level*: whether a feature can be described as possessing a "specific meaning" (Mufwene 1991: 139) or "particular semantics" (Buchstaller 2014: 14) clearly mapped on a linguistic construction; in other words, whether it is transparent in terms of form-meaning correspondences (Chapman 1995: 2; Kerswill and Williams 2002: 87);

(v) *Discourse-pragmatic level*: whether a feature is an "interactionally prominent" element (Cheshire 1996: 6) introducing (a) a "conceptual contrast"

(Talmy 2008: 30) and/or (b) "emotionally-heightened material" (Buchstaller 2003: 9);
(vi) *"Explicit meta-discourse"*: whether a feature is a subject of overt commentaries in the public discourse, including interactions in a classroom (Levon and Fox 2014: 187);
(vii) *Novelty*: whether a feature is perceived as novel by ordinary speakers of a given language or dialect since novel information fosters awareness (Schmidt 1990: 138).

Against this backdrop, socio-cognitive salience is a gradual (rather than an absolute) phenomenon resulting from a confluence of multiple factors (Buchstaller 2016: 201). Instead of conceiving of a linguistic feature as being either socio-cognitively salient or not, we should strive to describe the degree to which a given feature possesses this property. This view ties in with Talmy's (2008: 27) contention that "various [...] aspects of the expression, content, and context have differing degrees of salience". Classifying variable features into socio-cognitively salient, less salient or least salient, therefore, allows us to make more fine-tuned predictions regarding the extent to which these features, their conditioning systems, and socio-ideological assessments can be acquired by non-native speakers and, in so doing, promoted from one linguistic variety into another (see also Rácz 2013: 132). In the next section, I will describe the quotative frame with respect to the seven criteria listed above. In so doing, I will make a special reference to quotative *be like* to ascertain the degree to which this innovative feature of the English vernacular can be analysed in terms of socio-cognitive salience.

### 9.2.4 *Be like* as a socio-cognitively salient feature

Given the encroachment of quotative *be like* in various types of English, the variant clearly belongs to the group of "dynamic linguistic phenomena" (Kerswill and Williams 2002: 81–82), for which salience seems to be particularly suitable as a potential explanatory factor (Trudgill 1986). Relying on the metric developed in Section 9.2.3., let us now explore the extent to which innovative *be like* – as well as the quotative frame underlying it – conform to the requirements defining socio-cognitive salience.

Given that the linguistic variable investigated in this monograph rises above the level of phonetics and phonology, the criteria listed in (i) do not apply here. At the suprasegmental level, quoted material is oftentimes contrasted with surrounding speech by altered pitch variations, and intonation contours (see also Section 3.4.). "The particular intonation pattern and vocal tones" associated with quotation are in sharp contrast with a neutral delivery of linguistic material (Talmy 2008: 31). In other words, speakers tend to produce a quote in a different 'voice' (Bakhtin 1986[1979]). This is because quotation is used for demonstration of an event or a speech act and, therefore, for depicting rather than describing something (Clark and Gerrig 1990: 765–766). As a rule, quotation has clear suprasegmental boundaries – a beginning as well as an end – so that the listener can discern an enacted thought or utterance from the rest of the incoming speech signal. Importantly, *be like* is associated with mimetic, i.e. suprasegmentally marked, effects more than any other quotative marker. This is well evidenced by research into L1 English quotation (Buchstaller 2014; Buchstaller and D'Arcy 2009; Romaine and Lange 1991; Tagliamonte and Hudson 1999). It is this close link existing between quotative *be like* and prosodically highlighted content that renders the feature salient at the suprasegmental level.

In relation to its morphosyntactic composition, the quotative template has been argued to be a highly schematic construction (Davydova and Buchstaller 2015: 463), consisting of four relatively autonomous elements, i.e. NOUN PHRASE + COPULA VERB/VERBUM DICENDI + (DISCOURSE MARKER) + QUOTE (see also Section 3.1.). The template is reminiscent of, and comparable with, analytical constructions (e.g. present progressive or future tense marking in English) comprising two or more free-standing words. Notice that except for pronouns and following copula verbs, the structural elements constituting the quotative frame are not fused either with each other or with any other elements in a clause. This contrasts with low schematicity elements, such as *in/ing*-variation, or verbal (s) deletion (Tagliamonte 2012: 177–228), all of which are inherent in the lexical item they represent. With this said, linguistic items constituting the quotative template can be individuated in a speech stream far more easily than, for instance, variants of the aforementioned bound morphemes. In this sense, the quotative frame can be regarded as morphosyntactically salient.

Similar to other introducers of quoted material, *be like* exhibits a substantial level of morphosyntactic salience, which is enhanced by its propensity to occur with neuter pronoun *it*. Innovative *be like* is perhaps the only quotative variant that regularly surfaces with *it* as a grammatical subject. Indeed, IT IS LIKE, 'QUOTE' is a quotative schema that has gained wide currency in L1 vernaculars (Buchstaller 2014: 130). This analytical (chunk-like) structure featuring inanimate *it* contrasts with animate pronouns and noun phrases typically filling the slot of grammatical subject in quotative constructions. In fact, an animate grammatical subject is expected by default in a situation in which one reports one's own or someone else's speech or thought since reporting presupposes an active agent. Failing to fulfil such an expectation creates a feature contrast (grammatical subject: – animacy in place of expected + animacy) within a quotative schema.

And this contrast between listeners' sematic expectations and a surface realisation might, in turn, lead to greater noticeability of quotative *be like*. In other words, whenever one expects a specific semantic value with a corresponding surface form and is offered a different one instead, one is likely to end up making a note of this mismatch. It is in this way, that IT IS LIKE, 'QUOTE' contributes to the cognitive salience of the quotative construction featuring copula *be* and discourse marker *like*.

At the semantic level, Wierzbicka (1974) compared narratives containing quotations with "a piece of theatre". Buchstaller (2003), in turn, likened narrative passages containing quotes to a "radio play". These metaphors are suggestive in that they entail that the major function performed by the quotative template is that of re-enactment of speech and thought (see also Section 3.1., and Section 3.2.). Both speakers and listeners seem to be intuitively aware of this semantic meaning attached to quotative constructions. Thus, speakers know that while introducing quoted material they are expected to make a performance; not merely retell but *show* the narrated content (Clark and Gerrig 1990: 802). Likewise, listeners are aware that by introducing direct quotation in a story, a speaker is performing someone else's part (Buchstaller 2003: 3). The relationship obtaining between the quotative template and its 'performance' function is, indeed, transparent and, by this token, salient. In Section 9.2.3., I have also argued (relying on previous research) that a linguistic feature can be regarded as salient if it has a specific, i.e. more narrowly defined, meaning (Buchstaller 2014; Mufwene 1991; Talmy 2008). From this vantage point, quotative *be like* is employed – at least at the initial stages of its development – for re-enactment of inner states, both of which are reported thought in disguise (Romaine and Lange 1991: 237). Furthermore, speakers frequently accompany re-enactment of attitudes and feelings with facial and bodily expressions, in addition to gestures (Buchstaller 2003: 6; Tagliamonte and Hudson 1999: 152). Arguably, such paralinguistic behaviour enhances the noticeability of the semantic relationship obtaining between quotative *be like* and reported thought. It is this particularised meaning linked to a vivid depiction of inner monologues rather than general reporting speech and thought that renders quotative *be like* semantically salient, at least at the initial stages of grammaticalisation.

As a discourse-pragmatic device, the quotation frame is an "interactionally prominent" element (Cheshire 1996: 6). This is because a quotative marker serves as a pivot introducing a change in a vantage point from the narrator to the characters. This adds to the "vividness of the narrative" (Buchstaller 2014: 14), while allowing the speaker to "highlight a particularly dramatic peak in the performing of a story" (Fox 2012: 231) or "heighten the audience's sensation of closeness to the action at particularly dramatic points" (Moor 2011: 137). Against this backdrop, quotative markers arguably perform an important text-organising function: "[B]y demarcating key narrative events from non-focal narrative sequences (such as orientation elements [...]), quotation can be used as a guide to the listener, drawing their attention to the crucial events in the narrative" (Buchstaller 2014: 14). Being stylistically marked, innovative quotatives, including *be like*, furthermore allow speakers to introduce and emphasise emotionally prominent material (Buchstaller 2003: 9). It is this dramatising effect (Buchstaller 2014; Ferrara and Bell 1995; Golato 2000; Romaine and Lange 1991; Wolfson 1978) that introduces a "conceptual contrast" (Talmy 2008: 30) between communicatively focused/emotional, and non-focused/emotionally neutral sequences of narrated events, thereby rendering salient both quotative frame and quotative *be like*.

Overall, exhibiting a high level of suprasegmental prominence and morpho-syntactic schematicity combined with a transparent form-function relationship (performing a "piece of theatre", Wierbizcka 1974) and a vital textual function (steering listeners' attention towards dramatically emphasised and, therefore, communicatively pinpointed material, Buchstaller 2014), the quotative template is a sufficiently salient linguistic construction that provides the incoming variants (schemas) – of which quotative *be like* is one historically interesting example – with excellent opportunities to come to the fore of the listener's attention during spontaneous interactions. Crucially, it is this high level of cognitive salience exhibited by the quotative template that arguably fosters ESL and EFL learners' 'noticing' (Schmidt 1990) of quotative *be like* and, in so doing, guides them into a successful appropriation of its variable grammar.

As far as the meta-discourse level is concerned, the spread of *(be) like* has been accompanied by a highly volatile mix of comments in the public discourse, as discussed briefly at the outset of Chapter 8. On the one hand, *(be) like* has been subject to "vitriolic attacks from members of the prescriptivist camp" perhaps like no other vernacular feature (Buchstaller 2014: 200; see also D'Arcy 2007). Indeed, as pointed out in Bierma (2005, cited in Buchstaller 2016: 206), "any tirade about the state of the language is sure to say something about *like* as a plague on the language". The war pursued by language purists against *(be) like* reached its apogee during the public campaign launched by the 'Academy of Linguistic Awareness' at the University of California in 2006 (cited in Buchstaller 2014: 200–202). The institution issued two posters portraying two young people with apparent problems. Cathy (aged 20) from Santa Barbara complains she cannot achieve academic success because, reportedly, her teachers and friends do not find her convincing. Similarly, Paul (aged 23) from Los Angeles claims he lived a very happy, successful life (also skilfully revealed by the language he uses in the ad) until one day he confessed to his girlfriend, 'I, like, love you'. The sentence produced a disastrous effect on the addressee. The girlfriend left Paul, who now cries himself to sleep every night. Both ads end in a very eloquent fashion, 'Don't sound stupid, stop saying *like*'.

Simultaneously, (*be*) *like* has been discussed at some length in the blogs of writers who – instead of branding it as the major bane of the English language – pursued the goal of familiarising people with this linguistic innovation, its putative origin, its history as well as its major functions (Bierma 2005; Zwicky 2006). To illustrate this point, in his article celebrating *Clueless*, a film that supposedly popularised vernacular (*be*) *like* all over the US and beyond, Nathan Bierma from *Chicago Tribune* comments on the subtle functional difference existing between quotative *say* and *be like*. ""Said" precedes an exact quotation," he explains "… and "like" can also set up an approximate quotation in the tone of the original speaker" (Bierma 2005). This is an exact metalinguistic account of quotative *be like* reported with the help of Carmen Fought, an US sociolinguist actively engaged in promoting dialect diversity. In a similar vein, Arnold Zwicky, a trained linguist, explicitly explains the difference between the two vernacular functions of *like*, *like* as a discourse marker and *like* as a quotative marker, in a Language Log post (Zwicky 2006). Note that Zwicky has been writing regular contributions about quotatives in his blog ever since 2003.[4] Clearly, both Bierma (2005) and Zwicky (2006) exercise a completely different approach promoting a 'friendly' image of vernacular (*be*) *like*, sparkling curiosity and fostering awareness about linguistic heterogeneity and its main functions.

In a similar vein, quotative *be like* has been more recently discussed in blogs (Carey 2013; Rundell 2013) and an article published in an online version of the mainstream journal *The Boston Globe* (Peterson 2015a). These have been promoted further through the social media platform *Facebook*.[5] Furthermore, quotative *be like* has been a subject of overt discussions with a language columnist Britt Peterson on the US radio show *Here & Now* (Peterson 2015b). The audio file of the interview has been made publicly available and can be accessed online.[6] *Be like* has been furthermore portrayed in amateur videos made by the enthusiasts of the English language and posted on *YouTube*. In these videos, native speakers seek to teach ESL/EFL speakers around the globe how to speak English more naturally by staging conversation snippets featuring *be like*, being aware that these aspects of the English grammar are not the focus of explicit instruction in a classroom

---

[4] Source: https://arnoldzwicky.org/linguistics-notes/quotatives/, accessed June 26, 2017.
[5] Source: https://www.facebook.com/search/str/Quotative+be+like/keywords_search, accessed June 29, 2017.
[6] Source: http://www.wbur.org/hereandnow/2015/02/12/be-like-quotative-language, accessed June 29, 2017.

**Figure 17:** Quotative *be like* on a Webcomic of Romance, Sarcasm, Math, and Language.
**Note:** Source: https://xkcd.com/1483/, accessed June 30, 2017.

setting (Canguro English 2015; Schellenberg 2015). Last but certainly not least, quotative *be like* has been featured in comics, as illustrated in Figure 17.

The cases cited above are by no means exhaustive, yet they clarify the polarising nature of the treatment of *(be) like* in the media. Such a portrayal is diagnostic of L1 attitudes indicating that the variant has become a genuine linguistic 'stereotype' (Buchstaller 2016: 206), a socially meaningful linguistic item which has an extra high level of awareness attached to it. It is for this reason that some scholars have referred to such features as "maximally salient" (Buchstaller 2016: 208) or "ultra-salient" (Jensen 2013: 34) in their descriptions of native Englishes.

Given that quotative *be like* has been an object of extensive discussions in native-speaker circles and beyond for at least a decade, it is not unreasonable to surmise that speakers of indigenised and Learner English may have been paying attention to explicit meta-discourse accompanying the spread of *be like*, thereby 'taking a notice' of this feature (Schmidt 1990). Evidence reported in Chapter 8 can be brought forth to support this argument. Let us recall once again that students from both academic communities largely replicate both positive and negative evaluations of *be like*, while exhibiting a sufficiently high level of metalinguistic awareness about this feature of English vernacular. Crucially, these perceptions mirror the way in which L1 speakers of English treat this feature, embracing it for the social solidarity it affords in informal interactions, while simultaneously degrading the variant for its inarticulacy and lack of status. In this context, it is essential to realise that ESL/EFL speakers could not have acquired such fine-tuned knowledge about the indexical load attached quotative *be like* by native speakers had this feature not been a subject of extensive debates and overt discussions in the globally available public discourse.

Moreover, anecdotal evidence suggests that *be like* is subject to explicit comments in ESL/EFL educational contexts. Informal discussions with students from JNU and UM communities revealed that *be like* is sometimes featured in comments provided by English teachers. Reportedly, their remarks range from highly negative and hostile to neutral and, in individual cases, even friendly. Some teachers thus explicitly require that students refrain from using *be like* in their speech. Others signal a more amicable attitude by sparingly using it in their speech. (Note that in either case does the overt commentary entail that teachers engage in the discussion of the major functions of the quotative marker. Under no circumstances does it become an object of explicit instruction in an educational context (Norbert Schlüter personal communication March 18, 2015, cited in Davydova and Buchstaller 2015: 444). In other words, teachers appear to be only instrumental in disseminating attitudes towards *be like*.) By and large, the ESL/EFL educational settings echo the mixed messages accompanying the advancement of *be like* around the globe.

Let us now consider novelty as a major property of sociolinguistic salience and its role in the acquisition of *be like*. In contrast to explicit meta-discourse, which considers the representation of a given feature within a larger public context, the parameter 'novelty' appeals to the speaker's internal perspective on the incoming variation. The main assumption is that speakers are sensitive to language features which they perceive as new (since novelty fosters surprise) and become more attuned to them during the communicative act, as a result. Against this backdrop, *be like* is a feature of colloquial style that has been around for more than three decades, which, in turn, may have given English speakers (including those from ESL/EFL settings) enough time to get used to it. Unfortunately, there are to date no studies that explicitly address the question of whether speakers of English perceive *be like* as new relative to other vernacular features. Indeed, this issue presents one potential venue for future research. Exploring the extent to which quotative *be like* (still) affords surprisal value in conversation relative to other non-standard features, might help us gain a better understanding of novelty as a contributing factor in language variation and change across different forms of English.

Summing up the previous discussion of quotative *be like* within the framework of socio-cognitive salience, I hope to have demonstrated that various aspects of socio-cognitive salience discussed so far have been at work guiding non-native speakers' acquisition of probabilistic patterns underlying the use of *be like* – supported by a high level of type and token frequency. In turn, explicit meta-discourse must have played a key role in steering learners' attention in the acquisition of the perceptual load attached to the innovative feature and, in so doing, exerted an impact on the extent to which the variant has been adopted in the recipient varieties (see also Chapter 8).

## 9.3 Other factors

I conclude this book with an observation that factors other than frequency and salience might underpin successful outcomes in learning how to use structured variation and to evaluate it. From a variationist perspective, two are particularly pertinent as they lend themselves to a methodologically rigorous investigation. These include the concepts of complexity and L1 influence. To begin with, complexity has been proposed to be an important factor constraining acquisition of variation (Ender 2017; Hudson Kam and Newport 2009; Meyerhoff and Schleef 2013; Schleef 2017). One of the ways to approach this issue is to operationalise complexity as the amount of cognitive load that a learner will need to handle while extracting and processing probabilistic constraints from the variable input. The more factors are implicated in the occurrence of a linguistic variable and the more numerous are the constraints constituting a given factor, the more demanding, one could argue, is the task for a second-language learner. In other words, the more constrained a given linguistic variant is and the more detailed are the constraining hierarchies, the more effort, time, and exposure an L2 learner will need in order to process the variable input and single out the relevant predictors as well as their weighted probabilities of occurrence. I will call this type of complexity 'constraint complexity'.

We will now explore variable quotative marking with respect to constraint complexity and contrast it with another extensively studied feature, variable (ing). As far as language-internal parameters are concerned, quotative marking is constrained by four language-internal parameters, i.e. (1). mimesis, (2). quote type, (3). grammatical subject, and (4). tense, whereas the variable realisation of (ing) may be contingent upon as many as six system-specific predictors, i.e. (1). preceding and (2). following phonological context, (3). grammatical category, (4). number of syllables in the word, (5). realisation of previous (ing) variable, and (6). presence (absence) of a preceding nasal sound in a word (Schleef, Meyerhoff, and Clark 2011: 212–215). In addition, variable (ing) exhibits constraint systems within individual predictors that are superior in their constraint complexity to those reported for quotative marking. To illustrate this point, a consistent predictor of (ing), the factor 'grammatical category' alone comprises eight individual values (proper noun e.g. *Flemming*, pronoun e.g. *I don't know anything about it*; simple noun e.g. *ceiling*; adjective e.g. *amazing*; gerund e.g. *we like going to hot places*; verb e.g. *he is running*; preposition e.g. *during*; and discourse marker e.g. *or something*, cited in Schleef, Meyerhoff, and Clark 2011: 214). In contrast, the number of individual constraints attested within the system of quotative marking ranges between two (mimesis) and four (tense). Overall, it is clear that when compared with the system underlying the variable use of *be like*, the variable realisation of the velar nasal sound in the English morpheme (ing) draws upon a set of more numerous language-internal distinctions. Therefore, the variable (ing) is more complex than the variable quotative marking if we regard complexity as constraint complexity. Indeed, as argued by Labov (2007: 371), patterns of complexity exhibited by phonological variables "cannot be learned as a second dialect [and language] even by children".

Certainly, such an approach to complexity appears to be somewhat straightforward in that it does not assess the relationship between the linguistic variable and the constraints involved. Following a proposal in Sorace (2005: 143), Meyerhoff and Schleef (2013: 120) suggest that linguistic variables that require so-called 'interface knowledge' are also more demanding from the perspective of second-language acquisition. Essentially, interface knowledge is the knowledge about how a linguistic item is correlated with different levels of linguistic structure, i.e. phonological, morphosyntactic, and semantic-pragmatic. Following this logic, a linguistic variable that is connected to more than one aspect of linguistic structure via language-internal conditioning, would also require elaborate interface knowledge and will thus be much more difficult to acquire in a native-like fashion. I will call this type of complexity 'interface complexity'. When considered from this perspective, quotative *be like* is an admittedly complex variable, as argued by Meyerhoff and Schleef (2013), since the variable realisation of this variant is inextricably linked to phonological (mimesis), morphosyntactic (grammatical subject, tense), and semantic-pragmatic (quote type) aspects of linguistic structure. By comparison, the variable realisation of the velar nasal variant is primarily phonologically conditioned although it also requires some fine-grained knowledge about the grammatical categories as well. With this said, future research should explore the relationship between constraint complexity (relating to the cognitive load on an L2 learner exerted via language processing) and interface complexity (relating to the learner's overall knowledge about patterned variation at different levels of linguistic structure) to estimate their relative contribution to successful acquisition of vernacular variability.

Another factor that surely merits further investigation concerns the influence of learners' L1 knowledge exerted on the development of sociolinguistic competence. From a variationist perspective the task would require collecting sociolinguistic data on ESL/EFL speakers' L1, in this case Hindi and German, and explore the system-internal and sociolinguistic conditioning of the features exhibiting functional equivalence in the varieties involved in cross-linguistic contact (see also Meyerhoff 2009: 313). Systematic comparisons of the underlying predictors of variation attested in L1 and L2 systems will help to ascertain the degree to which speakers' native languages support the acquisition of L2 variability.

## 9.4 Concluding remarks

The study has presented a sociolinguistic account of variable quotative marking in two newly emerging linguistic varieties of indigenised and Learner English. I hope to have demonstrated that World Englishes is a vibrant, fast-growing field providing the analyst with a unique opportunity to bring the sociolinguistic and psycholinguistic endeavours together. Method-wise, the study has argued that the exploration of language attitudes is essential to the study of language variation and change as these are an important determinant in the evolution of a globally available language exerting an impact on sociolinguistic practices of an L2 community and, ultimately, shaping their psycholinguistic reality, which is, in turn, manifested at the micro-level of linguistic structure. My second methodological point concerns the ways in which we should dissect the enormous heterogeneity inherent in modern English. It is through meticulous exploration of diverse sociolinguistic contexts underlying L2 acquisition and use of English that we master our understanding of its linguistic outcomes in a local setting.

While investigating diverse sociolinguistic ecologies, the study has demonstrated that the degree to which a global trend catches on in a local group of L2 speakers depends on face-to-face interactions with L1 speakers of the donor variety. The finding tallies nicely with the traditional variationist hypothesis postulating the primary role of the interpersonal contact played in the spread of vernacular features. At the same time, the study has been able to present empirical evidence substantiating the claim that "globally travelling features" (Buchstaller 2006: 375) and variable grammars underlying them float not only through space but also through "mediated forms of communication" (Buchstaller and D'Arcy 2009: 322), notably English-speaking films and television.

Yet, perhaps the most outstanding result of this variationist enterprise is the fact that both ESL and EFL speakers of English are, indeed, quite capable of an accurate reconstruction of probabilistic constraints underlying the use of a variable linguistic feature, an outcome not documented previously. While acknowledging that a host of different factors may account for this remarkable result,

I have argued here that frequency and socio-cognitive salience are important explicatory tools for the presented results. Our future endeavours should aim at developing a unified theory predicting the ways in which both interact with each other and with other phenomena (complexity, L1 influence, etc.) as these might help us to make detailed predictions concerning the outcomes of variable microlinguistic structure.

# References

Abramowicz, Łukas. 2007. Sociolinguistics meets exemplar theory: Frequency and recency effects in (ing). *University of Pennsylvania Working Papers in Linguistics* 13(2). 27–37.

Adamson, Hugh D. & Vera Regan. 1991. The acquisition of community speech norms by Asian immigrants learning English as a second language. *Studies in Second Language Acquisition* 13(1). 1–22.

Adolphs, Svenja. 2005. I don't think I should learn all this – a longitudinal view of attitudes towards "native speaker" English. In Claus Gnutzmann & Frauke Intemann (eds.), *The globalisation of English and the English language classroom*, 115–127. Tübingen: Gunter Narr Verlag.

Alford, Daniel Moonhawk. 1982–83. A new English language quotative. Not Just Words: *The Newsletter of Transpersonal Linguistics* 2. 6.

Allan, Stuart & Barbie Zelizer. 2004. *Reporting war: Journalism in wartime*. London & New York: Routledge.

Allison, Desmond. 1999. *Language testing and evaluation. An introductory course*. Singapore [etc.]: Singapore University Press/World Scientific.

Androutsopoulos, Jannis (ed.). 2014a. *Mediatization and sociolinguistic change*. Berlin: Mouton de Gruyter.

Androutsopoulos, Jannis. 2014b. Mediatization and sociolinguistic change. Key concepts, research traditions, open issues. In Jannis Androutsopoulos (ed.), *Mediatization and sociolinguistic change*, 3–48. Berlin: Mouton de Gruyter.

Auer, Peter & Frans Hinskens. 2005. The role of interpersonal accommodation in a theory of language change. In Peter Auer, Frans Hinskens & Paul Kerswill (eds.), *Dialect change. convergence and divergence in European languages*, 335–357. Cambridge: Cambridge University Press.

Baird, Sarah. 2001. How 'to be like' a Kiwi: Verbs of quotation in New Zealand English. *New Zealand English Journal* 15(1). 6–19.

Ball, Peter. 1983. Stereotypes of Anglo-Saxon and non-Anglo-Saxon accents: some exploratory Australian studies with the matched-guise technique. *Language Sciences* 5(2). 163–184.

Baker, Colin. 1992. *Attitudes and language*. Clevedon, Philadelphia & Adelaide: Multilingual Matters.

Bakhtin, Mikhail M. 1986 [1979]. *Speech genres and other late essays* [М. М. Бахтин. Эстетика словесного творчества, Moscow: Искусство]. Austin, Texas: University of Texas Press.

Bardovi-Harlig, Kathleen. 1987. Markedness and salience in second-language acquisition. *Language Learning* 37(3). 385–407.

Bayard, Donn, Ann Weatherall, Cynthia Gallois & Jeffery F. Pittam. 2001. Pax Americana? Accent attitudinal evaluations in New Zealand, Australia and America. *Journal of Sociolinguistics* 5(1). 22–49.

Bayley, Robert. 1994. Interlanguage variation and the quantitative paradigm: Past-tense marking in Chinese English. In Elaine E. Tarone, Susan M. Gass & Andrew Cohen (eds.), *Research methodology in second language acquisition*, 97–120. Amsterdam & Philadelphia: John Benjamins.

Bell, Alan & Devyani Sharma (eds.). 2014. Debate: Media and language change. [Special issue]. *Journal of Sociolinguistics* 18(2). 213–286.

Bernaisch, Tobias. 2012. Attitudes towards Englishes in Sri Lanka. *World Englishes* 31(3). 279–291.

Bernaisch, Tobias & Christopher Koch. 2016. Attitudes towards Englishes in India. *World Englishes* 35(1). 118–132.

Bierma, Nathan. 2005. It's been, like, 10 whole years since 'Clueless' helped spread Valley slang. *Chicago Tribune* July 20.http://articles.chicagotribune.com/2005-07-20/features/0507190293_1_clueless-slang-amy-heckerling (accessed 26 June 2017).

Blondeau, Hélène & Naomi Nagy. 1998. Double marquage du sujet das le français parlé par les jeunes anglo-montréalais [Subject doubling in the spoken French of young Montreal Anglophones]. In John T. Jensen & Gerard Van Herk (eds.), *Actes du congrès annuel de l'association canadienne de Linguistique*, 59–70. Ottawa, Canada: Cahiers Linguistiques d'Ottawa.

Blondeau, Hélène & Naomi Nagy. 2008. Subordinate clause marking in Montreal Anglophone French and English. In Miriam Meyerhoff & Naomi Nagy (eds.), *Social lives in language – Sociolinguistics and multilingual speech communities*: Celebrating the work of Gillian Sankoff, 273–313. Amsterdam & Philadelphia: John Benjamins.

Blyth, Carl Jr., Sigrid Recktenwald & Jenny Wang. 1990. *I'm like, 'Say what?!*': A new quotative in American oral narrative. *American Speech* 65(3). 215–227.

Britain, David. 2002. Diffusion, levelling, simplification and re-allocation in past tense BE in the English Fens. *Journal of Sociolinguistics* 6 (1).16–43.

Buchstaller, Isabelle. 2003. The co-occurrence of quotatives with mimetic performances. *Edinburgh Working Papers in Applied Linguistics* 12. 1–10.

Buchstaller, Isabelle. 2004. *The sociolinguistic constraints on the quotative system: British English and US English compared*. Edinburgh: University of Edinburgh dissertation.

Buchstaller, Isabelle. 2006. Social stereotypes, personality traits and regional perception displaced: Attitudes towards the "new" quotatives in the UK. *Journal of Sociolinguistics* 10(3). 362–381.

Buchstaller, Isabelle. 2008. The localization of global linguistic variants. *English World-Wide* 29(1). 15–44.

Buchstaller, Isabelle. 2011. Quotations across generations: A multivariate analysis of speech and thought introducers across 5 decades of Tyneside speech. *Corpus Linguistics and Linguistic Theory* 7(1). 59–92.

Buchstaller, Isabelle. 2014. *Quotatives. New trends and sociolinguistic implications*. (Language in Society 41). Malden [etc.]: Wiley Blackwell.

Buchstaller, Isabelle. 2015. Exploring linguistic malleability across the life span: Age-specific patterns in quotative use. *Language in Society* 44(4). 457–496.

Buchstaller, Isabelle. 2016. Investigating the effect of socio-cognitive salience and speaker-based factors in morpho-syntactic life-span change. *Journal of English Linguistics* 44(3). 199–229.

Buchstaller, Isabelle & Alexandra D'Arcy. 2009. Localised globalisation: A multi-local, multivariate investigation of quotative *be like*. *Journal of Sociolinguistics* 13(3). 291–331.

Buchstaller, Isabelle & Ingrid Van Alpen (eds.). 2012. *Quotatives: Cross-linguistic and cross-disciplinary perspectives*. Amsterdam & Philadelphia: John Benjamins.

Butters, Ronald R. 1982. Editor's note [on *be like* "think"]. *American Speech* 57(2). 149.

Burridge, Kate & Alexander Bergs. 2017. *Understanding language change*. London & New York: Routledge.

Bybee, Joan. 2002. Phonological evidence for exemplar storage of multiword sequences. *Studies in Second Language Acquisition* 24(2). 215–222.

Bybee, Joan. 2008. Usage-based grammar and second language acquisition. In Peter Robinson & Nick C. Ellis (eds.), *Handbook of cognitive linguistics and second language acquisition*, 216–236. New York & London: Routledge.

Bybee, Joan & Sandy Thompson. 2000. Three frequency effects in syntax. *Berkeley Linguistic Society* 23. 65–85.

Campbell-Kibler, Kathryn. 2010. Sociolinguistics and perception. *Language and Linguistics Compass* 4(6). 377–389.

Campbell-Kibler, Kathryn. 2011. The sociolinguistic variant as a carrier of social meaning. *Language Variation and Change* 22(3). 423–441.

Canale, Michael 1983. From communicative competence to communicative language pedagogy. In Jack C. Richards & Richard W. Schmidt (eds.), *Language and communication*, 2–27. London: Longman.

Canale, Michael & Merrill Swain. 1980. Theoretical basis of communicative approaches to second language teaching and testing. *Applied Linguistics* 1(1). 1–47.

Canguro English. 2015. Direct speech with "be like" and "go". Learn English. Canguro English. *YouTube*, June 18. https://www.youtube.com/watch?v=FxDlxnreH9I (accessed 30 June 2017).

Carey, Stan. 2013. And I'm like, Quotative 'like' isn't just for quoting. *Sentence first. An Irishman's blog about the English language* (online blog), August 1.https://stancarey.wordpress.com/2013/08/01/and-im-like-quotative-like-isnt-just-for-quoting/#more-16096 (accessed 29 June 2017).

Cargile, Aaron Castelan, Jiro Takai & José I. Rodríguez. 2006. Attitudes toward African-American Vernacular English: A US export to Japan? *Journal of Multilingual and Multicultural Development* 27(6). 443–456.

Carvalho, Ana Maria. 2004. I speak like the guys on TV: Palatalization and the urbanization of Uruguayan Portuguese. *Language Variation and Change* 16(2). 127–151.

Casenhiser, Devin M. & Adele E. Goldberg. 2005. Fast mapping of a phrasal form and meaning. *Developmental Science* 8(6). 500–508.

Chambers, Jack K. 1992. Linguistic correlates of gender and sex. *English World-Wide* 13(2). 173–218.

Chambers, Jack K. 1998. TV makes people sound the same. In Laurie Bauer & Peter Trudgill (eds.), *Language myths*, 123–131. London: Penguin.

Chapman, Carol. 1994. A diachronic argument against the Split Morphology Hypothesis – the case of analogical umlaut in German dialects. *Transactions of the Philological Society* 92. 25–39.

Chapman, Carol. 1995. Perceptual salience and analogical change: Evidence from vowel lengthening in modern Swiss German dialects. *Journal of Linguistics* 31(1). 1–13.

Cheshire, Jenny. 1996. Syntactic variation and the concept of prominence. In Juhani Klemola, Merja Kytö & Matti Rissanen (eds.), *Speech past and present: Studies in English dialectology in memory of Ossi Ihalainen*, 1–17. Frankfurt: Peter Lang.

Cheshire, Jenny, Paul Kerswill, Sue Fox & Eivind Torgersen. 2011. Contact, the feature pool and the speech community: The emergence of Multicultural London English. *Journal of Sociolinguistics* 15(2). 151–196.

Chevrot, Jean-Pierre & Paul Foulkes. 2013. Introduction: Language acquisition and sociolinguistic variation. *Linguistics* 51(2). 251–254.

Chomsky, Noam. 1965. *Aspects of the theory of syntax*. Cambridge, MA: MIT Press.

Cintrón-Valentín, Myrna C. & Nick C. Ellis. 2016. Salience in second language acquisition: Physical form, learner attention, and instructional focus. *Frontiers in Psychology* 7(1284): 1–21. https://doi.org/10.3389/fpsyg.2016.01284 (accessed 17 May 2017).

Clark, Andy. 2013. Whatever next? Predictive brains, situated agents, and the future of cognitive science. *Behavioral and Brain Sciences* 36. 1–73.

Clark, Herbert H. & Richard J. Gerrig. 1990. Quotations as demonstrations. *Language* 66(4). 764–805.

Clark, Lynn & Schleef, Erik. 2010. The acquisition of sociolinguistic evaluation among Polish-born adolescents learning English: evidence from perception. *Language Awareness* 19(4). 299–322.

Clift, Rebecca. 2006. Indexing stance: Reported speech as an interactional evidential. *Journal of Sociolinguistics* 10(5). 569–595.

Collentine, Joseph. 2004. The effects of learning contexts on morphosyntactic and lexical development. *Studies in Second Language Acquisition* 26(2). 227–248.

Collins, Beverley & Inger M. Mees. 2003. *Practical phonetics and phonology. A resource book for students.* London & New York: Routledge.

Collins, Peter (ed.). 2015. *Grammatical change in English world-wide* (Studies in Corpus Linguistics Series 67). Amsterdam & Philadelphia: John Benjamins.

Coppieters, René. 1987. Competence difference between native and near-native speakers. *Language* 63(3). 544–573.

Croft, William. 2001a. *Radical construction grammar: Syntactic theory in typological perspective.* Oxford: Oxford University Press.

Croft, William. 2001b. *Explaining language change. An evolutionary approach.* Harlow [etc.]: Longman, Pearson Education.

Coupland, Nikolas, Angie Williams & Peter Garrett. 1999. 'Welshness' and 'Englishness' as attitudinal dimensions of English language varieties in Wales. In Dennis R. Preston (ed.), *Handbook of perceptual dialectology*, Volume 1, 333–343. Amsterdam: John Benjamins.

Cukor-Avila, Patricia. 2002. She say, She go, She be like: Verbs of quotation over time in African American Vernacular English. *American Speech* 77(1). 3–31.

Czimmermann, Éva & Piniel Katalin. 2016. Advanced language learners' experiences of flow in the Hungarian EFL classroom. In Peter D. MacIntyre, Tammy Gregersen & Sarah Mercer (eds.), *Positive psychology in SLA*, 193–214. Bristol: Multilingual Matters.

Dailey-O'Cain, Jennifer. 2000. The sociolinguistic distribution and attitudes towards focuser *like* and quotative *like*. *Journal of Sociolinguistics* 4(1). 60–80.

D'Arcy, Alexandra. 2004. Contextualizing St. John's youth English within the Canadian quotative system. *Journal of English Linguistics* 32(4). 323–345.

D'Arcy, Alexandra. 2005. The development of linguistic constraints: Phonological innovations in St. John's. *Language Variation and Change* 17(3). 327–355.

D'Arcy, Alexandra. 2007. "Like" and language ideology: Disentangling fact from fiction. *American Speech* 82(4). 386–419.

D'Arcy, Alexandra. 2012. The diachrony of quotation: Evidence from New Zealand English. *Language Variation and Change* 24(3). 343–371.

D'Arcy, Alexandra. 2013. Variation and change. In Robert Bayley, Richard Cameron & Cecil Lucas (eds.), *The Oxford handbook of sociolinguistics*, 484–502. Oxford: Oxford University Press.

Davydova, Julia. 2011. *The present perfect in non-native Englishes. A corpus-based study of variation* (Topics in English Linguistics 77). Berlin & Boston: Mouton de Gruyter.

Davydova, Julia. 2012. Englishes in the Outer and Expanding Circles: A comparative study. *World Englishes* 31(3). 366–385.

Davydova, Julia. 2013. Detecting historical continuity in a linguistically diverse urban area. In Joana Duarte & Ingrid Gogolin (eds.), *Linguistic superdiversity in urban areas. Research approaches* (Hamburg Studies on Linguistic Diversity 2), 193–225. Amsterdam & Philadelphia: John Benjamins.

Davydova, Julia. 2014. Morphosyntactic analysis in sociolinguistics. In Janet Holmes & Kirk Hazen (eds.), *Research methods in sociolinguistics. A practical guide*, 149–163. Malden [etc.]: Wiley Blackwell.

Davydova, Julia. 2015a. A study in the perception of native and non-native Englishes by German learners. *Journal of Linguistics and Language Teaching* 6(1).https://sites.google.com/site/linguisticsandlanguageteaching/home-1/volume-6-2015-issue-1—article-davydova (accessed 1 May 2017).

Davydova, Julia. 2015b. Linguistic change in a multilingual setting: A case study of quotatives in Indian English. In Peter Collins (ed.), *Grammatical change in English world-wide*. (The Studies in Corpus Linguistics Series 67), 297–334. Amsterdam & Philadelphia: John Benjamins.

Davydova, Julia. 2016a. Indian English quotatives in a real-time perspective. In Elena Seoane & Cristina Suárez-Gómez (eds.), *World Englishe: New theoretical and methodological considerationss* (Varieties of English around the World 57), 173–204. Amsterdam & Philadelphia: John Benjamins.

Davydova, Julia. 2016b. The present perfect in New Englishes: Common patterns in situations of language contact. In Valentin Werner, Elena Seoane & Cristina Suárez-Gómez (eds.), *Re-assessing the present perfect in English: Corpus studies and beyond* (Topics in English Linguistics 91), 169–194. Berlin & Boston: Mouton de Gruyter.

Davydova, Julia. 2016c. *Quotatives. New trends and sociolinguistic implications* by Isabelle Buchstaller. Wiley Blackwell. Reviewed in *Folia Linguistica* 50(1). 329–334.

Davydova, Julia, Agniezska Ewa Tytus & Erik Schleef. 2017. Acquisition of sociolinguistic awareness by German learners of English: A study in perceptions of quotative *be like*. *Linguistics. An Interdisciplinary Journal of the Language Sciences* 55(4): 1–30.

Davydova, Julia & Isabelle Buchstaller. 2015. Expanding the circle to Learner English: Investigating quotative marking in a German student community. *American Speech* 90(4). 441–478.

Deaton, Angus & Jean Dreze. 2002. Poverty and inequality in India: A re-examination. *Economic and Political Weekly* 37(36). 3729–3748.

De Saussure, Ferdinand. 1966 [1915]. *Course in general linguistics*, 2nd edition. New York: McGraw-Hill.

DeSchepper, Brett & Anne Treisman. 1996. Visual memory for novel shapes: Implicit coding without attention. *Journal of Experimental Psychology: Learning, Memory and Cognition* 22(1). 27–47.

Dewaele, Jean-Marc. 2004. Retention and omission of the *ne* in advanced French interlanguage: The variable effect of extralinguistic factors. *Journal of Sociolinguistics* 8(3). 433–450.

Dewaele, Jean-Marc. 2015. On emotions in foreign language learning and use. *The Language Teacher* 39(3). 13–15.

Dewaele, Jean-Marc, John Witney, Kazuya Saito & Livia Dewaele. 2017. Foreign language enjoyment and anxiety: The effect of teacher and learner variables. *Language Teaching Research*. 1–22.http://journals.sagepub.com/doi/pdf/10.1177/1362168817692161 (accessed 15 March 2017).

Dewaele, Jean-Marc & Lora Salomidou. 2017. Loving a partner in a foreign language. *Journal of Pragmatics* 108. 116–130.

Dimova, Slobodanka, Anna Kristina Hultgren & Christian Jensen (eds.). 2016. *English-medium instruction in European higher education* (Language and Social Life 4). Berlin & Boston: Mouton de Gruyter.

Diessel, Holger. 2007. Frequency effects in language acquisition, language use, and diachronic change. *New Ideas in Psychology* 25(2). 108–127.
Dörnyei, Zoltán. 2003. Questionnaires in second language research: Construction, administration and processing. Mahwah, NJ: Lawrence Erlbaum.
Durham, Mercedes, Bill Haddican, Eytan Zweig, Daniel Ezra Johnson, Zipporah Baker, David Cockeram, Esther Danks & Louise Tyler. 2011. Constant linguistic effects in the diffusion of be like. *Journal of English Linguistics* 40(4). 316–337.
Eckert, Penelope. 2003. Dialogue – sociolinguistics and authenticity: an elephant in the room. *Journal of Sociolinguistics* 7(3). 392–431.
Edwards, Alison. 2014. The EFL-ESL continuum and the case of the Netherlands: A comparative analysis of the progressive aspect. *World Englishes* 33(2). 173–194.
Edwards, Alison & Samantha Laporte. 2015. Outer and expanding circle Englishes: The competing roles of norm orientation and proficiency levels. *English World-Wide* 36(2). 135–169.
Ellis, Nick C. 2001. Memory for language. In Peter Robinson (ed.), *Cognition and second language instruction* (The Cambridge Applied Linguistics Series), 33–68. Cambridge: Cambridge University Press.
Ellis, Nick C. 2002. Frequency effects in language processing: A review with implications for theories of implicit and explicit language acquisition. *Studies in Second Language Acquisition* 24(2). 143–188.
Ellis, Nick C. 2013. Second language acquisition. In Thomas Hoffmann & Graeme Trousdale (eds.), *Oxford handbook of construction grammar*, 365–378. Oxford: Oxford University Press.
Ellis, Nick C. 2015. Implicit AND explicit learning: Their dynamic interface and complexity. In Patrick Rebuschat (ed.), *Implicit and explicit learning of languages*, 3–23. Amsterdam: John Benjamins.
Ellis, Nick C. 2016. Salience, cognition, language complexity, and complex adaptive systems. *Studies in Second Language Acquisition* 38(2). 341–351.
Ellis, Nick C. & Fernando Ferreira-Junior. 2009. Construction learning as a function of frequency, frequency distribution and function. *The Modern Language Journal* 93(3). 370–385.
Ellis, Nick C. & Laura Collins. 2009. Input and second language acquisition: The roles of frequency, form and function. Introduction to the special issue. *The Modern Language Journal* 93(3). 329–336.
Elman, Jeffrey L. 2005. Connectionist models of cognitive development: Where next? *Trends in Cognitive Sciences* 9(3). 111–117.
Elman, Jeffrey L., Elisabeth A. Bates, Mark H. Johnson, Annette Karmiloff-Smith, Domenico Parisi & Kim Plunkett. 1996. *Rethinking innateness. A connectionist perspective on development*. Cambridge, MA: MIT Press.
Ender, Andrea. 2017. What is the target variety? The diverse effects of standard–dialect variation in second language acquisition. In Gunther De Vogelaer & Matthias Katerbow (eds.), *The acquisition of sociolinguistic variation*, 155–185. Amsterdam & Philadelphia: John Benjamins.
Ferrara, Kathleen & Barbara Bell. 1995. Sociolinguistic variation and discourse function of constructed dialogue introducers: The case of be + like. *American Speech* 70(3). 265–290.
Fillmore, Charles J. 1988. The mechanisms of construction grammar. *Berkeley Linguistics Society* 14. 35–55.
Fiske, Susan T. & Beth A. Morling. 1996. Salience. In Antony S. R. Manstead & Miles Hewstone (eds.), *The Blackwell encyclopedia of social psychology*, 489. Oxford & Cambridge, MA: Blackwell.

Foulkes, Paul, Gerry Docherty & Dominic Watt. 1999. Tracking the emergence of structured variation: Realisation of (t) by Newcastle children. *Leeds Working Papers in Linguistics and Phonetics* 7: 1–25.

Foulkes, Paul & Gerard Docherty. 1999. Urban voices: Overview. In Paul Foulkes & Gerard Docherty (eds.), *Urban voices: Accent studies in the British Isles*, 1–24. London: Arnold.

Fox, Sue. 2012. Performed narrative: The pragmatic function of this is + speaker and other quotatives in London adolescent speech. In Isabelle Buchstaller & Ingrid van Alpen (eds.), *Quotatives: Cross-linguistic and cross-disciplinary perspectives*, 231–258. Amsterdam & Philadelphia: John Benjamins.

Fuchs, Robert, Sandra Götz & Valentin Werner. 2016. The present perfect in learner Englishes: A corpus-based case-study on L1 German intermediate and advanced speech and writing. In Valentin Werner, Elena Seoane & Cristina Suárez-Gómez (eds.), *Re-assessing the present perfect in English: Corpus studies and beyond* (Topics in English Linguistics 91), 297–337. Berlin & Boston: Mouton de Gruyter.

Galloway, Nicola & Heath Rose. 2015. *Introducing Global Englishes*. London & New York: Routledge.

Gardner, Matt, Derek Denis, Marisa Brook & Sali A. Tagliamonte. 2013. The new global flow of linguistic influence: *Be like* at the saturation point. Paper presented at New Ways of Analysing Variation (NWAV) 42, University of Pittsburgh and Carnegie Mellon University, 17–20 October.

Garrett, Peter. 2010. *Attitudes to language* (Key Topics in Sociolinguistics). Cambridge: Cambridge University Press.

Geeslin, Kimberly L., Lorenzo J. García-Amaya, Maria Hasler, Nicholas C. Henriksen & Jason Killam. 2012. Variability in the L2 acquisition of perfective past time reference in Spanish in an abroad immersion setting. In Kimberly L. Geeslin & Manuel Díaz-Campos (eds.), *Selected proceedings of the 14th Hispanic linguistics symposium*, 197–213. Somerville, MA: Cascadilla Proceedings Project.

Gigli, Susan. 2004. Children, youth and media around the world: An overview of trends & issues. *Report by InterMedia Survey Institute for UNICEF*. http://www.unicef.org/videoaudio/intermedia_revised.pdf (accessed 11 May 2016).

Gnutzmann, Claus, Jenny Jakisch & Frank Rabe. 2015. Communicating across Europe. What German students think about multilingualism, language norms and English as a lingua franca. In Andrew Linn, Neil Bermel & Gibson Ferguson (eds.), *Attitudes towards English in Europe* (Language and Social Life 2), 165–191. Berlin & Boston: Mouton de Gruyter.

Golato, Andrea. 2000. An innovative German quotative for reporting on embodied actions. *Und ich so/und er so* "and I'm like/and he's like". *Journal of Pragmatics* 32(1). 29–54.

Goldberg, Adele E. 1995. *Constructions: A construction grammar approach to argument structure*. Chicago: University of Chicago Stress.

Goldberg, Adele E. 2003. Constructions: A new theoretical approach to language. *Trends in Cognitive Sciences* 7(5). 219–224.

Goldberg, Adele E. 2006. *Constructions at work: The nature of generalisation in language*. Oxford: Oxford University Press.

González, Adriana. 2010. English and English teaching in Colombia: tensions and possibilities in the expanding circle. In Andy Kirkpatrick (ed.), *The Routledge handbook of World Englishes*, 332–351. London & New York: Routledge.

Grosjean, François. 1998. Studying bilinguals: methodological and conceptual issues. *Bilingualism: Language and Cognition* 1(2). 131–149.

Grosjean, François. 2001. The bilinguals' language modes. In Janet Nicol (ed.), *One mind, two languages*, 1–22. Malden, MA: Wiley-Blackwell.

Grosjean, François. 2004. Studying bilinguals: methodological and conceptual issues. In Tej K. Bhatia & William Ritchie (eds.), *The handbook of bilingualism*, 32–63. Malden, MA [etc.]: Blackwell.

Gumperz, John. 1972. The speech community. In Pier Paolo Giglioli (ed.), *Language and social context*, 219–231. Harmondsworth: Penguin.

Harrington, Michael. 2001. Sentence processing. In Peter Robinson (ed.), *Cognition and second language instruction* (The Cambridge Applied Linguistics Series), 91–124. Cambridge: Cambridge University Press.

Henrichsen, Lynn. 1984. Sandhi-variation: a filter of input learners of ESL. *Language Learning* 34(3). 103–126.

Hinskens, Frans. 2011. Lexicon, phonology and phonetics. Or: rule-based and usage-based approaches to phonological variation. In Peter Siemund (ed.), *Linguistic universals and language variation* (Trends in Linguistics Studies and Monographs 231), 425–466. Berlin & New York: Mouton de Gruyter.

Hnatkovska, Viktoria & Amartya Lahiri. 2012. The rural-urban divide in India. *International Growth Centre (IGC)*.http://www.theigc.org/wp-content/uploads/2014/09/Hnatkovska-Lahiri-2012-Working-Paper-March.pdf (accessed10 March 2017).

Hohenthal, Annika. 2003. English in India: Loyalty and attitudes. *Language in India* 3 (5). http://www.languageinindia.com/may2003/annika.html#chapter5 (accessed 28 October 2016).

Hopper, Paul J. 1987. Emergent grammar. In Jon Aske, Natasha Berry, Laura Michaelis & Hana Filip (eds.), *Berkely Linguistics Society 13*: *General session and parasession on grammar and cognition*, 139–157. Berkeley: Berkeley Linguistics Society.

Hopper, Paul J. & Elisabeth Closs Traugott. 2003. *Grammaticalization* (Cambridge Textbooks in Linguistics). Cambridge: Cambridge University Press.

Howard, Martin, Isabelle Lemée & Vera Regan. 2006. The L2 acquisition of a phonological variable: The case of/l/deletion in French. *French Language Studies* 16(1). 1–24.

Hudson Kam, Carla L. & Elissa L. Newport. 2009. Getting it right by getting it wrong: when learners change languages. *Cognitive Psychology* 59(1). 30–66.

Hundt, Marianne & Ulrike Gut (eds.). 2012. *Mapping unity and diversity world-wide*. Amsterdam & Philadelphia: John Benjamins.

Hundt, Marianne & Joybrato Mukherjee. 2011. Introduction. Bridging a paradigm gap. In Joybrato Mukherjee & Marianne Hundt (eds.), *Exploring second-language varieties of English and Learner Englishes – Bridging a paradigm gap*, 1–5. Amsterdam & Philadelphia: John Benjamins.

Huygens, Ingrid & Graham Vaughan. 1983. Language attitudes, ethnicity and social class in New Zealand. *Journal of Multilingual Development* 27(2). 413–429.

Hymes, Dell. 1966. Two types of linguistic relativity: Some examples from American Indian ethnography. In William Bright (ed.), *Sociolinguistics: Proceedings of the UCLA Sociolinguistic Conference, 1964*, 114–165. The Hague: Mouton.

Hymes, Dell. 1972. On communicative competence. In John B. Pride & Janet Holmes (eds.), *Sociolinguistics*, 269–293. Baltimore: Penguin Education.

Itti, Laurent, Christof Koch & Ernst Niebur. 2002. A model of saliency-based visual attention for rapid scene analysis. *Pattern Analysis and Machine Intelligence* 20(11). 1254–1259.

Jenkins, Jennifer. 2007. *English as a lingua franca: Attitude and identity*. Oxford: Oxford University Press.

Jenkins, Jennifer. 2015. *Global Englishes. A resource book for students*, 3rd edition. London & New York: Routledge.

Jensen, Marie. 2013. *Salience in language change: A socio-cognitive study of Tyneside English*. Newcastle, England: University of Northumbria dissertation.
Johnson, Daniel Ezra. 2009. Getting off the GoldVarb Standard: Introducing Rbrul for mixed-effects variable rule analysis. *Language and Linguistics Compass* 3(1). 359–383.
Johnson, Keith 1997. Speech perception without speaker normalization: An exemplar model. In Keith Johnson & John W. Mullennix (eds.), *Talker variability in speech processing*, 145–165. San Diego: Academic Press.
Kachru, Braj B. 1985. Standards, codification and sociolinguistic realism: The English language in the outer circle. In Randolph Quirk & Henry G. Widdowson (eds.), *English in the world: Teaching and learning the language and literatures*, 11–30. Cambridge: Cambridge University Press and the British Council.
Kachru, Braj B. 1994. English in South Asia. In Robert Burchfield (ed.), *The Cambridge history of the English language*. Vol. V. *English in Britain and overseas: Origins and development*, 497–553. Cambridge: Cambridge University Press.
Katz, Elihu. 1999. Theorizing diffusion: Tarde and Sorokin revisited. *Annals of the American Academy of Political and Social Science* 566(1). 144–155.
Kemmer, Suzanne & Michael Barlow. 2000. Introduction. A usage-based conception of language. In Michael Barlow & Suzanne Kemmer (eds.), *Usage-Based Models of Language*, vii–xxviii. Stanford, CA: CSLI Publications.
Kersten, Alan W. & Julie L. Earles. 2001. Less really is more for adults learning a miniature artificial language. *Journal of Memory and Language* 44(2). 250–273.
Kerswill, Paul. 1985. A sociophonetic study of connected speech processes in Cambridge English: An outline and some results. *Cambridge Papers in Phonetics and Experimental Linguistics* 4. 1–39.
Kerswill, Paul & Ann Williams. 2002. "Salience" as an explanatory factor in language change: evidence from dialect levelling in urban England. In Mari Jones & Edith Esch (eds.), *Language change: The interplay of internal, external and extra-linguistic factors*, 81–110. Berlin: Mouton de Gruyter.
Kirkpatrick, Andy. 2010. *The Routledge handbook of World Englishes*. London & New York: Routledge.
Kirkpatrick, Andy & Zhichang Xu, 2002. Chinese pragmatic norms and "China English". *World Englishes* 21(2). 269–279.
Knaus, Valerie & Terry Nadasdi. 2001. Être ou ne pas être in immersion French. *The Canadian Modern Language Review* 58(2). 287–306.
Kortmann, Bernd, Edgar W. Schneider, Kate Burridge, Rajend Mesthrie & Clive Upton (eds.), 2004. *A handbook of varieties of English*. Berlin & New York: Mouton de Gruyter (two volumes).
Koul, Omkar N. 2008. *Modern Hindi grammar*. Springfield VA: Dunwoody Press.
Kruschke, John K. 1992. ALCOVE: An exemplar-based connectionist model of category learning. *Psychological Review* 99(1). 22–44.
Labov, William. 2010 [1972a]. The social motivation of a sound change. In Miriam Meyerhoff & Erik Schleef (eds.), *The Routledge sociolinguistics reader*, 292–322. London & New York: Routledge.
Labov, William. 1972b. *Sociolinguistic patterns*. Philadelphia: University of Pennsylvania Press.
Labov, William. 1990. The intersection of sex and social class in the course of linguistic change. *Language Variation and Change* 2(2). 205–254.
Labov, William. 2001. *Principles of linguistic change*, Vol. 2. *Social Factors*. Malden [etc.]: Blackwell.
Labov, William. 2007. Transmission and diffusion. *Language* 83(2). 344–387.

Labov, William. 2013. Preface: The acquisition of sociolinguistic variation. *Linguistics* 51(2). 247–250.
Ladegaard, Hans J. 1998. National stereotypes and language attitudes: the perceptions of British, American and Australian language and culture in Denmark. *Language & Communication* 18(4). 251–274.
Ladegaard, Hans J. & Itesh Sachdev. 2006. "I like the Americans … but I certainly don't aim for an American accent": language attitudes, vitality and foreign language learning in Denmark". *Journal of Multilingual and Multicultural Development* 27(2). 91–108.
Laerd Statistics. 2013. The ultimate IBM® SPSS® guides. https://statistics.laerd.com/ (accessed 3 March2017 ).
Lakoff, George. 2013a. Cascade theory: Embodied cognition and language from a neural perspective. A public lecture at the Central European University (CEU), 16 October. https://www.youtube.com/watch?v=XWYaoAoijdQ (accessed 14 December 2016).
Lakoff, George. 2013b. What studying the brain tells us about arts education. Talk presented at *Big Ideas Fest 2012*, Half Moon Bay, California, 17 February. https://www.youtube.com/watch?v=fpIa16Bynzg (accessed 14 December 2016).
Lambert, Wallace E., Richard C. Hodgson, Robert Gardner & Samuel Fillenbaum. 1960. Evaluational reactions to spoken languages. *Journal of Abnormal and Social Psychology* 60 (1). 44–51.
Langacker, Ronald W. 1987. *Foundations of cognitive grammar*. Volume 1. Stanford: Stanford University Press.
Lange, Claudia. 2012. *The syntax of spoken Indian English*. Amsterdam: John Benjamins.
Le Page, Robert B. & André Tabouret-Keller. 1985. *Acts of identity*: Creole-based approaches to language and ethnicity. Cambridge: Cambridge University Press.
Levey, Stephen. 2003. "He's like: Do it now! And I'm like, 'No!'" *English Today* 0(1). 24–32.
Levon, Erez & Isabelle Buchstaller. 2015. Perception, recognition, and linguistic structure: The effect of linguistic modularity and cognitive style on sociolinguistic processing. *Language Variation and Change* 27(3). 319–348.
Levon, Erez & Sue Fox. 2014. Social salience and the sociolinguistic monitor: A case study of ING and TH-fronting in Britain. *Journal of English Linguistics* 42(3). 185–217.
Linn, Andrew. 2016. *Investigating English in Europe: Contexts and agendas* (Language and Social Life 10). Berlin & Boston: Mouton de Gruyter.
Lippi-Green, Rosina. 1997. English with an accent. Language, ideology, and discrimination in the United States. London & New York: Routledge.
Macaulay, Ronald. 2001. You're like 'why not?' The quotative expressions of Glasgow adolescents. *Journal of Sociolinguistics* 5(1). 3–21.
Macaulay, Ronald. 2006. Pure grammaticalisation: The development of a teenage intensifier. *Language Variation and Change* 18(3). 267–283.
MacWhinney, Brian. 2001. The competition model: the input, the context, and the brain. In Peter Robinson (ed.), *Cognition and second language instruction* (The Cambridge Applied Linguistics Series), 69–90. Cambridge: Cambridge University Press.
Mair, Christian. 2016. Beyond and between the "Three Circles". World Englishes research in the age of globalisation. In Elena Seoane & Cristina Suárez-Gómez (eds.), *World Englishes*: *New theoretical and methodological considerations* (Varieties of English around the World 57), 17–35. Amsterdam & Philadelphia: John Benjamins.
Matras, Yaron. 2009. *Language contact* (Cambridge Textbooks in Linguistics). Cambridge: Cambridge University Press.
Mayerthaler, Willi. 1981. *Morphologische Natürlichkeit*. Wiesbaden: Athenaion.
McArthur, Tom. 1998. *The English languages*. Cambridge: Cambridge University Press.

McCroskey, James C. & Thomas J. Young. 2006. The use and abuse of factor analysis in communication research. *Communication Research* 5(4). 375–382.
McGrew, Anthony G. 1992. Conceptualizing global politics. In Anthony G. McGrew & Paul G. Lewis (eds.), *Global Politics: Globalisation and the Nation State*, 1–28. Cambridge: Polity Press.
McDonough, Kim & Joujin Kim. 2009. Syntactic priming, type frequency and EFL learners' production of *wh*-questions. *The Modern Language Journal* 93(3). 386–398.
McDonough, Kim & Alison Mackey. 2008. Syntactic priming and ESL question development. *Studies in Second Language Acquisition* 30(1). 31–47.
McKenzie, Robert M. 2008a. Social factors and non-native attitudes towards varieties of spoken English: a Japanese case study. *International Journal of Applied Linguistics* 18(1). 63–88.
McKenzie, Robert M. 2008b. The role of variety recognition in Japanese university students' attitudes towards English speech varieties. *Journal of Multilingual and Multicultural Development* 29(2). 139–153.
Mesthrie, Rajend & Rakesh M. Bhatt. 2008. *World Englishes. The study of new linguistic varieties* (Key Topics in Sociolinguistics). Cambridge: Cambridge University Press.
Mesthrie, Rajend, Joan Swann, Andrea Deumert & William L. Leap. 2000. *Introducing Sociolinguistics*. Philadelphia: John Benjamins.
Meyer, Charles F. 2002. *English corpus linguistics. An introduction*. Cambridge: Cambridge University Press.
Meyerhoff, Miriam. 2003. Formal and cultural constraints on optional objects in Bislama. *Language Variation and Change* 14(3). 323–346.
Meyerhoff, Miriam. 2009. Replication, transfer, and calquing: Using variation as a tool in the study of language contact. *Language Variation and Change* 21(3). 297–317.
Meyerhoff, Miriam & Erik Schleef. 2012. Variation, contact and social indexicality in the acquisition of (ing) by teenage migrants. *Journal of Sociolinguistics* 16(3). 398–416.
Meyerhoff, Miriam & Erik Schleef. 2013. Hitting an Edinburg target: Immigrant adolescents' acquisition of variation in Edinburgh English. In Robert Lawson (ed.), *Sociolinguistic perspectives on Scotland*, 103–128. Basingstoke: Palgrave Macmillan.
Meyerhoff, Miriam & Nancy Niedzielski. 2003. The globalisation of vernacular variation. *Journal of Sociolinguistics* 7(4). 534–555.
Meriläinen, Lea & Heli Paulasto. 2014. Embedded inversion as an angloversal: Evidence from Inner, Outer and Expanding Circle Englishes. In Markku Filppula, Juhani Klemola & Devyani Sharma (eds.), *The Oxford handbook of World Englishes*. Oxford: Oxford University Press.
Milroy, James & Lesley Milroy. 1977. Speech and context in an urban setting. *Belfast Working Papers in Language and Linguistics* 2. 1–85.
Milroy, James & Lesley Milroy. 2003. *Authority in language. Investigating standard English*. London & New York: Routledge.
Mintz, Toben H. 2013. The segmentation of sub-lexical morphemes in English-learning 15-month-olds. *Frontiers in Psychology* 4(24). 1–12.
Moore, Colette. 2011. *Quoting speech in Early English*. Cambridge: Cambridge University Press.
Mougeon, Raymond, Katherine Rehner & Terry Nadasdi. 2004. The learning of spoken French variation by immersion students from Toronto, Canada. *Journal of Sociolinguistics* 8(3). 408–432.
Mufwene, Salikoko. 1991. Pidgins, creoles, typology and markedness. In Francis Byrne & Thom Huebner (eds.), *Development and structures of creole languages*, 123–143. Amsterdam & Philadelphia: John Benjamins.
Mufwene, Salikoko. 2001. *The ecology of language evolution*. Cambridge: Cambridge University Press.

Mukherjee, Joybrato. 2010. The development of the English language in India. In Andy Kirkpatrick (ed.), *The Routledge handbook of World Englishes*, 167–180. London & New York: Routledge.

Mukherjee, Joybrato & Marianne Hundt (eds.). 2011. *Exploring second-language varieties of English and Learner Englishes – Bridging a paradigm gap*. Amsterdam & Philadelphia: John Benjamins.

Nardy, Aurélie, Jean-Pierre Chevrot & Stéphanie Barbu. 2013. The acquisition of sociolinguistic variation: Looking back and thinking ahead. *Linguistics*: 51(2). 255–284.

Naro, Anthony J. 1981. The social and structural dimensions of a syntactic change. *Language* 57(1).63–98.

Nesselhauf, Nadja. 2009. Co-selection phenomena across New Englishes: Parallels and (differences) to foreign learner varieties. *English World-Wide* 30(1). 1–26.

Nevalainen, Terttu. 2002. Language and woman's place in earlier English. *Journal of English Linguistics* 30(2). 181–199.

Nihalani, Paroo, R. K. Tongue, Priya Hosali & Jonathan Crowther. 2004. *Indian and British English*: *A handbook of usage and pronunciation*, 2nd edn. Delhi: Oxford University Press.

Ota, Ichiro & Shoji Takano. 2014. The media influence on language change in Japanese sociolinguistic contexts. In Jannis Androutsopoulos (ed.), *Mediatization and sociolinguistic change*, 171–203. Berlin: Mouton de Gruyter.

Pal, Parthapratim & Jayati Gosh. 2007. Inequality in India: A survey of recent trends. *DESA Working Papers* 45 (online). http://nabamtuki.org/Arunachal%20Reports/Inequality%20in%20India%202007.pdf (accessed 10 March 2017).

Peterson, Britt. 2015a. Linguists are like, 'Get used to it!' Why a new way to quote has taken English by storm. *The Boston Globe* (online) January 25. http://www.bostonglobe.com/ideas/2015/01/25/linguists-are-like-get-used/ruUQoV0XUTLDjx72JojnBI/story.html (accessed 29 June 2017).

Peterson, Britt. 2015b. Interviewed on the *Here & Now* show, February 12. http://www.wbur.org/hereandnow/2015/02/12/be-like-quotative-language (accessed 29 June 2017).

Pickering, Martin J. & Victor S. Ferreira. 2008. Structural priming: A critical review. *Psychological Bulletin* 134(3). 427–459. https://www.ncbi.nlm.nih.gov/pmc/articles/PMC2657366/ (accessed 14 April 2017).

Pierrehumbert, Janet. 2001. Exemplar dynamics: word frequency, lenition, and contrast. In Joan Bybee & Paul Hopper (eds.), *Frequency effects and emergence of linguistic structure*, 137–157. Amsterdam & Philadelphia: John Benjamins.

Poplack, Shana. 1987. Contrasting patterns of code-switching in two local communities. In Erling Wande, Jan Anward, Bengt Nordberg, Lars Steensland & Mats Thelander (eds.), *Aspects of bilingualism*: *Proceedings from the fourth Nordic symposium on bilingualism, 1984*, 51–77. Sweden: University of Uppsala.

Rácz, Péter. 2013. *Salience in sociolinguistics. A quantitative approach* (Topics in English Linguistics 84). Berlin & Boston: Mouton de Gruyter.

Rathje, Marianne. 2011. Quotations and quotatives in the speech of three Danish generations. In Frans Gregersen, Jeffrey K. Parrott & Pia Quist (eds.), *Language variation – European perspectives* III: *Selected papers from the 5th international conference on language variation in Europe* (ICLaVE 5), 71–82. Amsterdam & Philadelphia: John Benjamins.

Raumolin-Brunberg, Helena & Arja Nurmi. 1997. Dummies on the move: prop-one and affirmative DO in the 17th century. In Terttu Nevalainen & Leena Kahlas-Tarkka (eds.), *To explain the present*: *Studies in the changing English language in honour of Matti*

*Rissanen* (Mémoires de la Société Linguistique 52), 395– 417. Helsinki: Modern Language Society.
Regan, Vera. 1995. The acquisition of sociolinguistic native speech norms. In Barbara F. Freed (ed.), *Second language acquisition in a study abroad context*, 245–267. Amsterdam & Philadelphia: John Benjamins.
Regan, Vera. 1996. Variation in French interlanguage: A longitudinal study of sociolinguistic competence. In: Richard Bayley & Denis Preston (eds.), *Second language acquisition and linguistic variation*, 177–201. Amsterdam & Philadelphia: John Benjamins.
Regan, Vera. 2004. The relationship between the group and the individual and the acquisition of native speaker variation patterns: A preliminary study. *IRAL, International Review of Applied Linguistics in Language Teaching* 42(4). 335–348.
Regan, Vera & Caitríona Ní Chasaide (eds.). 2010. Language practices and identity construction by multilingual speakers of French L2: The acquisition of sociolinguistic variation. Bern: Peter Lang.
Regan, Vera, Martin Howard, & Isabelle Lemée. 2009. *The acquisition of sociolinguistic competence in a study abroad context*. Bristol, UK: Multilingual Matters.
Rehner, Katherine & Raymond Mougeon. 1999. Variation in the spoken French of immersion students: To *ne* or not to *ne*, that is the sociolinguistic question. *The Canadian Modern Language Review* 56(1). 124–154.
Rehner, Katherine, Raymond Mougeon, & Terry Nadasdi. 2003. The learning of sociolinguistic variation by advanced FSL learners. The case of *nous* versus *on* in immersion French. *Studies in Second Language Acquisition* 25(1). 127–156.
Rodrígez Louro, Celeste. 2013. Quotatives down under: *Be like* in cross-generational Australian English speech. *English World-Wide* 34(1). 48–76.
Romaine, Suzanne & Deborah Lange. 1991. The use of like as a marker of reported speech and thought: A case of grammaticalisation in progress. *American Speech* 66(3). 227–279.
Rosch, Eleanor H. 1973. Natural categories. *Cognitive Psychology* 4(3). 328–350.
Ross, Andrew & Elke Stracke. 2016. Learner perceptions and experiences of pride in second language education. *Australian Review of Applied Linguistics* 39(3). 272–291.
Rowland, Caroline F. 2007. Explaining errors in children's questions. *Cognition* 104(1). 106–134.
Rundell, Michael. 2013. What's not to like about 'like'? *MacMillan Dictionary Blog*. http://www.macmillandictionaryblog.com/whats-not-to-like-about-like (accessed 29 June 2017).
Salgado-Robles, Francisco. 2011. The acquisition of sociolinguistic variation by learners of Spanish in a study abroad context. Gainesville: University of Florida dissertation.
Sanchez, Tara & Anne Charity. 1991. Use of *be like* and other verbs of quotation in a predominantly African-American community. Paper presented at the 28th annual conference on New Ways of Analyzing Variation (NWAV 28), University of Toronto, 14–17 October.
Sankoff, David. 1988. Sociolinguistics and syntactic variation. In Frederick J. Newmeyer (ed.), *Linguistics*: *The Cambridge survey*, 140–161. Cambridge: Cambridge University Press.
Sankoff, David, Sali A. Tagliamonte & Eric Smith. 2005. Goldvarb X. A multivariate analysis application. Department of Linguistics. University of Toronto and Department of Mathematics, University of Ottawa. http://individual.utoronto.ca/tagliamonte/Goldvarb/GV_index.htm (accessed10 October 2015).
Sankoff, Gillian, Pierrette Thibault, Naomi Nagy, Hélène Blondeau, Marie-Odile Fonollosa & Lucie Gagnon. 1997. Variation in the use of discourse markers in a language contact situation. *Language Variation and Change* 9(2). 191–217.

Sayers, Dave. 2014. The mediated innovation model: A framework for researching media influence in language change (Focus article). *Journal of Sociolinguistics* 18(2). 185–212.

Savignon, Sandra J. 1972. *Communicative competence: An experiment in foreign-language teaching*. Philadelphia: The Centre for Curriculum Development, Inc.

Schellenberg, Ian. 2015. Quotative *like*. Natural English grammar. *YouTube*, February 2. https://www.youtube.com/watch?v=tOCLP80BWXI (accessed 30 June 2017).

Schilling, Natalie. 2013. *Sociolinguistic fieldwork* (Key Topics in Sociolinguistics). Cambridge: Cambridge University Press.

Schleef, Erik. 2013. Migrant teenagers' acquisition of sociolinguistic variation: The variables (ing) and (t). In Peter Auer, Javier Caro & Göz Kaufmann (eds.), *Language variation – European perspectives IV*, 201–213. Amsterdam: John Benjamins.

Schleef, Erik. 2014. Written surveys and questionnaires in sociolinguistics. In Janet Holmes & Kirk Hazen (eds.), *Research methods in sociolinguistics. A practical guide*, 42–57. Malden [etc.]: Wiley Blackwell.

Schleef, Erik. 2017. Developmental sociolinguistics and the acquisition of T-glottalling by immigrant teenagers in London. In Gunther de Vogelaer & Matthias Katerbow (eds.), *Variation in language acquisition*, 311–347. Amsterdam: John Benjamins.

Schleef, Erik, Miriam Meyerhoff & Lynn Clark. 2011. Teenagers' acquisition of variation. A comparison of locally-born and migrant teens' realisation of English (ing) in Edinburgh and London. *English-World-Wide* 32(2). 206–236.

Schmidt, Richard W. 1990. The role of consciousness in second language learning. *Applied Linguistics* 11(2). 129–158.

Schmidt, Richard W. 2001. Attention. In Peter Robinson (ed.), *Cognition and second language instruction* (The Cambridge Applied Linguistics Series), 3–32. Cambridge: Cambridge University Press.

Schmidt, Richard W. & Sylvia Frota. 1986. Developing basic conversational ability in a second language: A case study of an adult learner of Portuguese. In Richard Day (ed.), *Talking to learn: Conversation in second language acquisition*, 237–324. Rowley, MA: Newbury House.

Schneider, Edgar W. 2000. Feature diffusion vs. contact effects in the evolution of New Englishes: A typological case study of negation patterns. *English World-Wide* 21(2). 201–230.

Schneider, Edgar W. 2003. The dynamics of New Englishes: From identity construction to dialect birth. *Language* 79(2). 233–281.

Schneider, Edgar W. 2007. *Postcolonial English. Varieties around the world*. Cambridge: Cambridge University Press.

Selinker, Larry. 1972. Interlanguage. IRAL, International Review of Applied Linguistics in Language Teaching 10(3). 219–231.

Sharma, Devyani. 2005. Dialect stabilization and speaker awareness in non-native varieties of English. *Journal of Sociolinguistics* 9(2). 194–224.

Sharma, Devyani. 2009. Typological diversity in New Englishes. *English World-Wide* 30(2). 170–195.

Sharma, Devyani & Lavanya Sankaran. 2011. Cognitive and social forces in dialect shift: Gradual change in London Asian speech. *Language Variation and Change* 23(3). 399–428.

Silverstein, Michael. 2003. Indexical order and the dialectics of sociolinguistic life. *Language & Communication* 23(3/4). 193–229.

Slobin, Dan I. 1982. Universal and particular in the acquisition of language. In Eric Wanner & Lila R. Gleitmann (eds.), *Language acquisition: The state of the art*, 128–170. Cambridge: Cambridge University Press.

Slobin, Dan I. 1985. Crosslinguistic evidence for the language-making capacity. In Dan I. Slobin (ed.), *The crosslinguistic study of language acquisition. Vol. 2. Theoretical Issues*, 1157–1249. Hillsdale, NJ: Lawrence Erlbaum.

Slobin, Dan I. 1993. Adult language acquisition: A view from child language study. In Clive Perdue (ed.), *Adult language acquisition: Cross-linguistic perspectives*, 239–249. Cambridge: Cambridge University Press.

Sorace, Antonella. 2005. Near-nativeness. In Catherine J. Doughty & Michael H. Long (eds.), *The handbook of second language acquisition*, 130–151. Oxford: Blackwell.

Siemund, Peter, Julia Davydova, Michaela Hilbert & Lukas Pietsch. 2011. Comparing varieties of English: problems and perspectives. In Peter Siemund (ed.), *Linguistic universals and language variation* (Trends in Linguistics), 291–324. Berlin & New York: Mouton de Gruyter.

Stein, Ellen. 1990. "I'm sitting there": Another new quotative? *American Speech* 65. 303.

Singler, John Victor. 2001. Why you can't do a varbrule study of quotatives and what such a study can show us. *University of Pennsylvania Working Papers in Linguistics* 7. 257–278.

Stewart, Mark, Ellen Bouchard Ryan & Howard Giles. 1985. Accent and social class effects on status and solidarity evaluations. *Personality and Social Psychology Bulletin* 11(1). 98–105.

Stuart-Smith, Jane. 2011. The view from the couch: changing perspectives on the role of the television in changing language ideologies and use. In Tore Kristiansen & Nikolas Coupland (eds.), *Standard languages and language standards in a changing Europe standard language ideology in contemporary Europe*, 223–239. Oslo: Novus.

Stuart-Smith, Jane. 2012. English and the media: Television. In Alexander Bergs & Laurel J. Brinton (eds.), *Historical linguistics of English. An international handbook*, 1075–1088. Berlin & New York: Mouton de Gruyter.

Stuart-Smith, Jane, Gwilym Pryce, John Benjamin, Claire Timmins & Barrie Gunter. 2013. Television is also a factor in language change: Evidence from an urban dialect. *Language* 89(3). 501–536.

Tagliamonte, Sali A. 2006. *Analysing sociolinguistic variation* (Key Topics in Sociolinguistics). Cambridge: Cambridge University Press.

Tagliamonte, Sali A. 2012. *Variationist sociolinguistics: Change, observation, interpretation*. Malden, MA [etc.]: Wiley-Blackwell.

Tagliamonte, Sali A. & Alexandra D'Arcy. 2004. He's like; She's like: The quotative system in Canadian youth. *Journal of Sociolinguistics* 8(4). 493–514.

Tagliamonte, Sali A. & Alexandra D'Arcy. 2007. Frequency and variation in the community grammar: Tracking a new change through the generations. *Language Variation and Change* 19(2). 199–217.

Tagliamonte, Sali A., Alexandra D'Arcy & Celeste Rodríguez Louro. 2016. Outliers, impact, and rationalization in linguistic change. *Language* 92(4). 824–849.

Tagliamonte, Sali A. & Chris Roberts. 2005. So weird; so cool; so innovative: The use of intensifiers in the television series *Friends*. *American Speech* 80(3). 280–300.

Tagliamonte, Sali A. & Derek Denis. 2010. The *stuff* of change: General extenders in Toronto, Canada. *Journal of English Linguistics* 38(4). 335–368.

Tagliamonte, Sali A. & Rachel Hudson. 1999. *Be like* et al. beyond America: The quotative system in British and Canadian youth. *Journal of Sociolinguistics* 3(2). 147–172.

Talmy, Leonard. 2008. Aspects of attention in language. In Peter Robinson & Nick C. Ellis (eds.), *Handbook of cognitive linguistics and second language acquisition*, 27–65. New York & London: Routledge.

Tan, Ying-Ying & Christina Castelli. 2013. Intelligibility and attitudes: How American English and Singapore English are perceived around the world. *English World-Wide* 34(2). 177–201.

Tannen, Deborah. 1986. Introducing constructed dialogue in Greek and American conversational and literary narrative. In Florian Coulmas (ed.), *Direct and indirect speech*, 311–332. Amsterdam: Mouton de Gruyter.
Taylor, Shelley E. & Susan T. Fiske. 1978. Salience, attention, and attribution: Top of the head phenomena. *Advances in Experimental Social Psychology* 11. 249–288.
Tomasello, Michael. 1999. *The cultural origins of human cognition*. Cambridge, MA: Harvard University Press.
Tomasello, Michael. 2003. *Constructing a language. A usage-based theory of language acquisition*. Cambridge, MA & London, England: H arvard University Press.
Tomasello, Michael. 2006. Acquiring linguistic constructions. In William Damon & Richard M. Lerner (eds.), *Handbook of Child Psychology, Vol. 2. Cognition, Perception, and Language*, 255–298. New York: Wiley.
Tomlin, Russell S. & Victor Villa. 1994. Attention in cognitive science and second language acquisition. *Studies in Second Language Acquisition* 16(2). 183–203.
Traugott, Elisabeth Closs & Graeme Trousdale. 2013. *Constructionalization and constructional changes*. Oxford: Oxford University Press.
Treisman, Anne M. & Garry Gelade. 1980. A feature-integration theory attention. *Cognitive Psychology* 12(1). 97–136.
Trudgill, Peter. 1986. *Dialects in contact*. Oxford: Blackwell.
Trudgill, Peter. 2002. *Sociolinguistic variation and change*. Edinburgh: Edinburgh University Press.
Trudgill, Peter. 2014. Diffusion, drift and the irrelevance of media influence. *Journal of Sociolinguistics* 18(2). 214–222.
Weinreich, Uriel, William Labov & Marvin Herzog. 1968. Empirical foundations for a theory of language change. In Winfred P. Lehmann & Yakov Malkiel (eds.), *Directions for historical linguistics*, 95–188. Austin: University of Texas Press.
Wierzbicka, Anna. 1974. The semantics of direct and indirect discourse. *Papers in Linguistics* 7(3/4). 267–307.
Williams, Jessica. 1987. Non-native varieties of English: A special case of language acquisition. *English World-Wide* 8(2). 161–199.
Williams, Angie, Peter Garrett & Nikolas Coupland. 1999. Dialect recognition. In Dennis R. Preston (ed.), *Handbook of perceptual dialectology. Volume 1*, 345–373. Amsterdam: John Benjamins.
Winford, Donald. 2003. *An introduction to contact linguistics*. Malden, MA [etc.]: Blackwell Publishing.
Winter, Joanne. 2002. Discourse quotatives in Australian English: Adolescents performing voices. Australian. *Journal of Linguistics* 22(1). 5–21.
Wolfram, Walt. 1985. Variability in tense marking: A case for the obvious. *Language Learning* 35(2). 229–253.
Wolfson, Nessa. 1978. A feature of performed narrative: The Conversational Historical Present. *Language in Society* 7(2). 215–237.
Wulff, Stefanie, Nick C. Ellis, Ute Römer, Kathleen Bardovi-Harlig & Chelsea J. Leblanc. 2009. The acquisition of tense-aspect: Converging evidence from corpora and telicity ratings. *The Modern Language Journal* 95(3). 354–369.
Young, Richard. 1991. *Variation in interlanguage morphology*. New York: Peter Lang.
Zwicky, Arnold. 2006. Like, a Christmas gift card. *Language Log*, December 28. http://itre.cis.upenn.edu/~myl/languagelog/archives/003978.html (accessed 26 June 2017).

# Appendix A: Interview Schedule

Authors: J. Davydova, S. Maurer

*Demographics*:

What is your name?

Where were you born?

And where did you grow up?

What is your mother tongue?

How long have you been learning English? How many years?

Where did you learn it?

Is English spoken in your family?

Have you ever been abroad in an English-speaking country for more than 4 weeks?

Where have you been and what was the purpose of your visit?

What variety of English do you associate yourself with?

0. *Conversation Module: English and attitudes to English*
   - Can you think of funny experiences with English or any other language in the past? What are these? Can you think of a funny story?
   - What role does English play in India (Germany)?
   - Do you think there is a difference in the way the Indians (the Germans) perceive British English and American English? If so, what is the difference? Why?
   - When you hear the term 'Indian English' ('German English'), what comes to your mind?
   - What are Indian (German) people's attitudes toward Indian English? What do you think?
   - What about the differences between younger and older people in the way they speak English? Have you ever noticed any?
   - When you hear the term 'European English' ('Indian English'), what comes to your mind?

- What are Indian (German) people's attitudes toward European (Indian) English, such as, for instance, English spoken in Germany?
- Do you think that non-native forms of English are perceived differently than native forms of English?
- What happens when people switch between English and Hindi (German) when they talk?

1. *Conversation Module: Family*

- Do you feel that your (grand) parents have influenced your life? In what ways? Do you have story to tell?
- Do you ever play tricks on your brother (sister, parents)? Tell me a story.
- Has your brother/sister ever made you laugh till you 'drop dead'?
- Do you have fun story to tell from one of the last family celebrations?

2. *Conversation Module: University*

- JNU (UM) is such a colourful community! How would you describe students who study at your university? Are there different social networks here?
- Have you ever been late for an exam/class? What was your teachers' reaction?
- Have you ever witnessed a student who reacted inadequately in class? What was your reaction to that behaviour? What was other students' reaction?
- Have you ever cheated in an exam? Do you know anyone who has?
- Have you ever had a funny episode here at the university that you can tell me?

3. *Conversation Module: Intercultural Encounters*

- Have you ever been abroad? What countries have you visited? Why did you choose to go there?
- Have you ever been to other states in India? Which ones?
- What was your (least) favourite stay? What happened?
- What did you like most about the country/state and its people? Any story to tell?
- In what ways do people you met in the foreign country/in that state differ from the people of your own country (community)? Can you give any specific examples?
- What was the most fascinating/awful trip abroad?
- Do you have a fun story to tell about an intercultural/interethnic encounter? Misunderstandings based on language and/or culture etc.?
- Tell a story about the best/worst intercultural/interethnic encounter you have had so far.

4. *Conversation Module*: *Experiences*
- What was the happiest (saddest) day in your life?
- Did you ever have to call the police? Why?
- Have you ever met a famous person (sports/cinema/TV/politics)? What happened?
- Tell me about the biggest sports event/musical festival ... you have ever been to. Is there an interesting story?

5. *Conversation Module*: *Hobbies/Free Time/Vacation*
- What is the funniest/coolest/worst thing that ever happened to you in your holiday?
- What was the funniest/coolest/worst thing that ever happened to you on a night out?
- Have you ever been locked in/out and didn't know what to do?

6. *Conversation Module*: *TV/Sports*
- What is your favourite TV series? Tell me about the funniest/saddest/most emotional episode.
- What is your favourite TV show? What was the funniest/saddest/most emotional moment?
- What is your favourite sports person/team? Can you tell me a funny story about your favourite sports team?

# Appendix B: Background Questionnaire (JNU)

DATE:  PLACE:  PARTICIPANT CODE (PC):
(to be filled in by the researcher)

**BIODATA**

**1. Name**  Family name  (PC)

**2. Are you:** ☐ male  ☐ female?

**3. When were you born?**

**4. Where did you grow up?**

**EDUCATION**

**5. What is the highest level of formal education you have completed?**
☐ Junior High or equivalent
☐ High school or equivalent
☐ Bachelor's Degree, Diploma of Higher/Further Education, or equivalent
☐ Master's Degree, Doctorate, or equivalent
☐ PhD or equivalent
☐ none of the above, specify

**6. What type of school did you get your Junior High education?**
☐ public school
☐ missionary school
☐ vernacular (government) school
☐ other  Please specify _____

**7. What type of school did you get your High School education?**
☐ public school
☐ missionary school
☐ vernacular (government) school
☐ other  Please specify _____

**LANGUAGE BACKGROUND**

**8. What language has been or what languages have been spoken in your family?**
_____

**9. What language has been spoken most often in your family?**
_____

**10. Through what languages were you predominantly taught at primary school?**
☐ English
☐ Hindi

☐ English and Hindi
☐ other                    Please specify _____

**11. Through what languages were you predominantly taught at secondary school?**
☐ English
☐ Hindi
☐ English and Hindi
☐ other                    Please specify _____

**12. Describe which languages (for example, English, Hindi, etc.) you use in your everyday life and how often you use them by filling out the following table.**

| Language | Every day | Occasionally | Hardly ever |
|---|---|---|---|
|  |  |  |  |
|  |  |  |  |
|  |  |  |  |
|  |  |  |  |

**13. Describe which languages (for example, English, Hindi, etc.) you use at school/university and how often you use them by filling out the following table.**

| Language | Every day | Occasionally | Hardly ever |
|---|---|---|---|
|  |  |  |  |
|  |  |  |  |
|  |  |  |  |
|  |  |  |  |

**14. Which language(s) do you typically use while talking to your friends?**
_____

**14.1. If you use English, how often do you use this language while talking to your friends?**
☐ every day
☐ two or three times a week
☐ once a week
☐ less than once a week
☐ never

**15. Which languages do you use, while doing the following things?**

|  | English | Hindi | other | other |
|---|---|---|---|---|
| a. e-mail and letter writing | ☐ | ☐ | ☐ | ☐ |
| b. blog writing in the Internet | ☐ | ☐ | ☐ | ☐ |
| c. chats, SMS writing | ☐ | ☐ | ☐ | ☐ |
| d. TV watching, videos | ☐ | ☐ | ☐ | ☐ |
| e. watching films | ☐ | ☐ | ☐ | ☐ |

## EXPOSURE TO ENGLISH

**16. Since when have you been able to speak English (fluently)?**
☐ since I was 2 years old or younger
☐ since I was 4 years old or younger
☐ since primary school
☐ since secondary school
☐ I learned English as an adult

**17. How often do you watch original TV shows or movies in English?**
☐ every day
☐ two or three times a week
☐ once a week
☐ less than once a week
☐ never

**18. How often do you read English literature that is not meant as a class assignment?**
☐ every day
☐ two or three times a week
☐ once a week
☐ less than once a week
☐ never

**19. How well do you feel you know English? Cross the appropriate box and please try to give as honest a response as possible.**

|  | advanced | upper-intermediate | intermediate | basic |
|---|---|---|---|---|
| 1. writing | ☐ | ☐ | ☐ | ☐ |
| 2. speaking | ☐ | ☐ | ☐ | ☐ |
| 3. reading | ☐ | ☐ | ☐ | ☐ |
| 4. lis. compr.* | ☐ | ☐ | ☐ | ☐ |

*Listening comprehension

**20. Have you ever been to an English-speaking country and if so, how many times?**
☐ four times and more
☐ three times
☐ twice
☐ once
☐ never

**20.1. If you have been to an English-speaking country, which countries have you been too?**
_____
_____

**20.2. For how long did you stay there?**
_____
_____

20.3. Which form of English, in your opinion, do you speak?

_____
_____

20.4. Is there an English-speaking country that you feel a special connection to? And if so, which one?

_____
_____

21. Briefly describe where and why you use English in your everyday life, both personal and academic.

_____
_____
_____
_____
_____
_____
_____
_____

**THANK YOU VERY MUCH!!!**

# Appendix C: Background Questionnaire (UM)

DATE:                           PLACE:                                          PARTICIPANT CODE (PC):
(to be filled in by the researcher)

**BIODATA**

**1. Name**                                       Family name                              (PC)

**2. Are you:** ☐ male  ☐ female?

**3. When were you born?**

**4. Where did you grow up?**

**EDUCATION**

**5. What is the highest level of formal education you have completed?**
☐ Junior High or equivalent
☐ High school or equivalent
☐ Bachelor's Degree, Diploma of Higher/Further Education, or equivalent
☐ Master's Degree, Doctorate, or equivalent
☐ PhD or equivalent
☐ none of the above, specify

**EXPOSURE TO ENGLISH**

**6. Have you ever been to an English-speaking country and if so, how many times?**
☐ four times and more
☐ three times
☐ twice
☐ once
☐ never

**6.1. If you have been to an English-speaking country, which countries have you been too?**
_____
_____

**6.2. For how long did you stay there? (How many weeks? How many months?)**
_____
_____

**6.3. Which form of English, in your opinion, do you speak?**
_____
_____

**6.4. Is there an English-speaking country that you feel a special connection to? And if so, which one?**
_____
_____

Please answer the following questions and tick off the appropriate box. Note that only **one answer** per question is possible.

**7. How often do you have a university lecture in English?**
☐ every day
☐ two or three times a week
☐ once a week
☐ less than once a week
☐ never

**8. How often do you speak English at the university in a formal context, for instance, while making a presentation or talking to a professor/lecturer?**
☐ every day
☐ two or three times a week
☐ once a week
☐ less than once a week
☐ never

**9. How often do you write academically or professionally in English?**
☐ every day
☐ two or three times a week
☐ once a week
☐ less than once a week
☐ never

**10. How often do you read English reference books?**
☐ every day
☐ two or three times a week
☐ once a week
☐ less than once a week
☐ never

**11. How often do you read newspapers or magazines in English for pleasure?**
☐ every day
☐ two or three times a week
☐ once a week
☐ less than once a week
☐ never

**12. How often do you use the Internet in English?**
☐ every day
☐ two or three times a week
☐ once a week
☐ less than once a week
☐ never

**13. How often do you listen to English song lyrics?**
☐ every day
☐ two or three times a week
☐ once a week
☐ less than once a week
☐ never

**14. How often do you watch original TV shows or movies in English?**
☐ every day
☐ two or three times a week
☐ once a week
☐ less than once a week
☐ never

**15. How often do you speak English at the university in an informal context, for instance, while chatting with your friends?**
☐ every day
☐ two or three times a week
☐ once a week
☐ less than once a week
☐ never

**16. How often do you speak English with your social contacts outside the university (close friends, relatives, etc.)?**
☐ every day
☐ two or three times a week
☐ once a week
☐ less than once a week
☐ never

**17. How often do you speak English in your family?**
☐ every day
☐ two or three times a week
☐ once a week
☐ less than once a week
☐ never

**18. How often do you use English for communication in the social networks on the Internet (Facebook, Twitter, etc.)?**
☐ every day
☐ two or three times a week
☐ once a week
☐ less than once a week
☐ never

**19. Briefly describe where and why you use English in your everyday life, both personal and academic.**
_____
_____

**THANK YOU VERY MUCH!!**

# Appendix D: Goldvarb Analyses

**Table 89:** Logistic regression analysis of the contribution of language-internal and sociolinguistic constraints to the probability of *be like* in HCNVE, 2007–2014. Goldvarb output.

| | | | |
|---|---|---|---|
| Input probability | | | .23 |
| Log likelihood | | | −936,123 |
| Total N | | | 479/2118 |
| | FW | % | N |
| **1. Grammatical subject** | | | |
| it | .904 | 68% | 52/76 |
| first | .550 | 25% | 179/712 |
| third | .439 | 20% | 225/1114 |
| second | .315 | 9% | 5/53 |
| *range* | *58* | | |
| **2. Tense** | | | |
| CHP | .730 | 41% | 84/202 |
| past | .554 | 24% | 211/874 |
| present | .450 | 19% | 70/354 |
| modal | .177 | 5% | 11/208 |
| *range* | *55* | | |
| **3. Mass media exposure** | | | |
| every day | .698 | 38% | 132/339 |
| two or three times a week | .551 | 26% | 182/681 |
| once a week | .459 | 18% | 75/409 |
| less than once a week | .333 | 12% | 65/511 |
| *range* | *36* | | |
| **4. Socio-context** | | | |
| English-dominant | .650 | 31% | 99/318 |
| mixed | .505 | 24% | 351/1435 |
| Hindi-dominant | .349 | 7% | 29/365 |
| *range* | *30* | | |
| **5. Gender** | | | |
| female | .589 | 27% | 313/1128 |
| male | .399 | 16% | 166/990 |
| *range* | *19* | | |
| **6. Mimesis** | | | |
| mimetic | .569 | 28% | 345/1201 |
| not | .410 | 14% | 134/917 |

(continued)

**Table 89** (continued)

| | | | |
|---|---|---|---|
| *range* | | 16 | |
| **7. Quote type** | | | |
| thought | [.562] | 28% | 139/489 |
| indigenous | [.520] | 22% | 22/100 |
| speech | [.479] | 20% | 318/1529 |

**Note:** Non-applicable environments in grammatical subject (n = 163) and tense (n = 480) are excluded from the respective factor group in the multivariate analysis.

**Table 90:** Logistic regression analysis of the contribution of language-internal and sociolinguistic constraints to the probability of *be like* in MaCGE, 2013–2015. Goldvarb output.

| | | | |
|---|---|---|---|
| Input probability | | | .21 |
| Log likelihood | | | −669,114 |
| Total N | | | 351/1412 |
| | FW | % | N |
| **1. Grammatical subject** | | | |
| it | .917 | 75% | 53/70 |
| first | .493 | 26% | 100/380 |
| third | .465 | 22% | 173/774 |
| second | .355 | 9% | 8/82 |
| *range* | | 56 | |
| **2. Tense** | | | |
| CHP | .677 | 35% | 42/118 |
| past | .576 | 28% | 195/677 |
| present | .408 | 20% | 51/249 |
| modal | .128 | 4% | 5/105 |
| *range* | | 55 | |
| **3. Socio-context** | | | |
| North American exposure | .595 | 32% | 159/490 |
| low-level naturalistic & high-level mass media | .532 | 28% | 66/233 |
| mixed exposure | .457 | 20% | 81/401 |
| lingua franca exposure | .396 | 16% | 38/224 |
| low-level naturalistic & mass media | .303 | 4% | 7/64 |
| *range* | | 29 | |
| **4. Mimesis** | | | |
| mimetic | .588 | 31% | 277/885 |
| not | .355 | 14% | 74/527 |

**Table 90** (continued)

| range | | 23 | | |
|---|---|---|---|---|
| **5. Quote type** | | | | |
| thought | | .586 | 31% | 105/336 |
| speech | | .479 | 23% | 237/1024 |
| indigenous | | .361 | 17% | 9/52 |
| range | | 22 | | |
| **6. Gender** | | | | |
| female | | .565 | 29% | 229/787 |
| male | | .419 | 19% | 122/625 |
| range | | 14 | | |
| **7. Mass media exposure** | | | | |
| two or three times a week | | [.519] | 26% | 151/567 |
| every day | | [.485] | 25% | 114/441 |
| once a week | | [.535] | 25% | 54/208 |
| less than once a week | | [.434] | 16% | 32/196 |

**Note:** Non-applicable environments in grammatical subject (n = 106) and tense (n = 263) are excluded from the respective factor group in the multivariate analysis.

# Appendix E: *Be like* survey

(Adopted from Buchstaller 2014: 284–294)

## Thank you very much for participating in this survey!

You are invited to take part in a research project which is being conducted by Julia Davydova at the University of Mannheim. The purpose of the research is to investigate the attitudes of English speakers towards certain characteristics of language use.

If you agree to participate, you will be asked to answer a few questions regarding your attitudes towards the use of the English language. The survey will take between 7 and 10 minutes. If you do decide to participate, you may withdraw from the project at any time without giving a reason.

The data collected in this survey will eventually be published in an international journal or a book and the results will be presented at academic conferences. Your answers will remain anonymous and your personal information will remain confidential to the researchers.

If you decide to proceed with this survey, you agree to participation.

---

Before we get started, **please do not jump ahead!** The information on future pages could bias your answers, so please view and fill out each page in order.

Appendix E: *Be like* survey — **239**

Below are two excerpts from transcribed conversations. The speakers were told to talk about food intolerances. Please read each text carefully, then fill out the following questionnaire.

Excerpt 1

A: I really like nuts but I am allergic to them. At first I was sceptical about seeing a doctor. I thought "how can a doctor help me with this?"
But finally I went to see this doctor. I said "when I eat nuts I feel as if I have a heart attack" and she was like "you will have to follow a special diet and I will do a blood test".
She said "we need to be sure that you are not reacting to anything else".
B: This is really interesting.
A: I was like "do I have to cut out nuts completely?" and she was like "yes you do. When you feel better you can reintroduce them gradually."

Excerpt 2

X: Coffee does not agree with me. When I smell it I think "oh I will just have a little one" and then I can feel my heart burning.
Y: I do love the smell.
X: So I went to the doctor and had a food allergy test. And the doctor said "do you know if there is anything you are allergic to?"
I said "I definitely think I am allergic to coffee". and she said "it might not be the coffee.
It might be what you put in it".
So she tested milk and just coffee without the milk. And she said "You are right".
She said "Please do not drink any caffeine".

## I. Personality Traits

In this section you are asked to rate speakers A and X from the excerpts above with respect to a number of personality traits with opposing features at either end. For each excerpt please indicate the value on the scale as you see fit.

### *Example:*

If you think speaker A is very attractive, you should put a cross somewhere near 'attractive'. If you find speaker X is unattractive, you should put a cross somewhere near 'unattractive'.

| **unattractive** | | | **attractive** | |
|---|---|---|---|---|
| Speaker A: ☐ | ☐ | ☐ | ☒ | ☐ |
| Speaker X: ☐ | ☐ | ☐ | ☐ | ☐ |

In what follows, you will see different personality traits. Please rate both speakers as exemplified above. The texts will be repeated on every page for your convenience – the texts will always remain the same.

**Remember: Please don't look ahead!**

## Excerpt 1

A: I really like nuts but I am allergic to them. At first I was sceptical about seeing a doctor. I thought "how can a doctor help me with this?" But finally I went to see this doctor. I said "when I eat nuts I feel as if I have a heart attack" and she was like "you will have to follow a special diet and I will do a blood test". She said "we need to be sure that you are not reacting to anything else".

B: This is really interesting.

A: I was like "do I have to cut out nuts completely?" and she was like "yes you do. When you feel better you can reintroduce them gradually."

## Excerpt 2

X: Coffee does not agree with me. When I smell it I think "oh I will just have a little one" and then I can feel my heart burning.

Y: I do love the smell.

X: So I went to the doctor and had a food allergy test. And the doctor said "do you know if there is anything you are allergic to?" I said "I definitely think I am allergic to coffee". and she said "it might not be the coffee. It might be what you put in it". So she tested milk and just coffee without the milk. And she said "You are right". She said "Please do not drink any caffeine".

|  | calm | | | | excited |
|---|---|---|---|---|---|
| Speaker A: | ☐ | ☐ | ☐ | ☐ | ☐ |
| Speaker X: | ☐ | ☐ | ☐ | ☐ | ☐ |

|  | old fashioned | | | | fashionable |
|---|---|---|---|---|---|
| Speaker A: | ☐ | ☐ | ☐ | ☐ | ☐ |
| Speaker X: | ☐ | ☐ | ☐ | ☐ | ☐ |

|  | common | | | | posh |
|---|---|---|---|---|---|
| Speaker A: | ☐ | ☐ | ☐ | ☐ | ☐ |
| Speaker X: | ☐ | ☐ | ☐ | ☐ | ☐ |

|  | educated | | | | uneducated |
|---|---|---|---|---|---|
| Speaker A: | ☐ | ☐ | ☐ | ☐ | ☐ |
| Speaker X: | ☐ | ☐ | ☐ | ☐ | ☐ |

|  | annoying | | | | pleasant |
|---|---|---|---|---|---|
| Speaker A: | ☐ | ☐ | ☐ | ☐ | ☐ |
| Speaker X: | ☐ | ☐ | ☐ | ☐ | ☐ |

|  | casual | | | | formal |
|---|---|---|---|---|---|
| Speaker A: | ☐ | ☐ | ☐ | ☐ | ☐ |
| Speaker X: | ☐ | ☐ | ☐ | ☐ | ☐ |

|  | unreliable | | | | reliable |
|---|---|---|---|---|---|
| Speaker A: | ☐ | ☐ | ☐ | ☐ | ☐ |
| Speaker X: | ☐ | ☐ | ☐ | ☐ | ☐ |

**Survey continues on next page .....Remember: don't look ahead!**

Excerpt 1

A: I really like nuts but I am allergic to them. At first I was sceptical about seeing a doctor. I thought "how can a doctor help me with this?" But finally I went to see this doctor. I said "when I eat nuts I feel as if I have a heart attack" and she was like "you will have to follow a special diet and I will do a blood test". She said "we need to be sure that you are not reacting to anything else".
B: This is really interesting.
A: I was like "do I have to cut out nuts completely?" and she was like "yes you do. When you feel better you can reintroduce them gradually."

Excerpt 2

X: Coffee does not agree with me. When I smell it I think "oh I will just have a little one" and then I can feel my heart burning.
Y: I do love the smell.
X: So I went to the doctor and had a food allergy test. And the doctor said "do you know if there is anything you are allergic to?" I said "I definitely think I am allergic to coffee". and she said "it might not be the coffee. It might be what you put in it". So she tested milk and just coffee without the milk. And she said "You are right". She said "Please do not drink any caffeine".

|  | intelligent | | | | not intelligent |
|---|---|---|---|---|---|
| Speaker A: | ☐ | ☐ | ☐ | ☐ | ☐ |
| Speaker X: | ☐ | ☐ | ☐ | ☐ | ☐ |

|  | unsuccessful | | | | successful |
|---|---|---|---|---|---|
| Speaker A: | ☐ | ☐ | ☐ | ☐ | ☐ |
| Speaker X: | ☐ | ☐ | ☐ | ☐ | ☐ |

|  | unprofessional | | | | professional |
|---|---|---|---|---|---|
| Speaker A: | ☐ | ☐ | ☐ | ☐ | ☐ |
| Speaker X: | ☐ | ☐ | ☐ | ☐ | ☐ |

|  | responsible | | | | irresponsible |
|---|---|---|---|---|---|
| Speaker A: | ☐ | ☐ | ☐ | ☐ | ☐ |
| Speaker X: | ☐ | ☐ | ☐ | ☐ | ☐ |

|  | not careful to speech | | | | careful to speech |
|---|---|---|---|---|---|
| Speaker A: | ☐ | ☐ | ☐ | ☐ | ☐ |
| Speaker X: | ☐ | ☐ | ☐ | ☐ | ☐ |

|  | articulate | | | | inarticulate |
|---|---|---|---|---|---|
| Speaker A: | ☐ | ☐ | ☐ | ☐ | ☐ |
| Speaker X: | ☐ | ☐ | ☐ | ☐ | ☐ |

|  | urban | | | | rural |
|---|---|---|---|---|---|
| Speaker A: | ☐ | ☐ | ☐ | ☐ | ☐ |
| Speaker X: | ☐ | ☐ | ☐ | ☐ | ☐ |

**Survey continues on next page …..Remember: don't look ahead!**

## Excerpt 1

A: I really like nuts but I am allergic to them. At first I was sceptical about seeing a doctor. I thought "how can a doctor help me with this?" But finally I went to see this doctor. I said "when I eat nuts I feel as if I have a heart attack" and she was like "you will have to follow a special diet and I will do a blood test". She said "we need to be sure that you are not reacting to anything else".
B: This is really interesting.
A: I was like "do I have to cut out nuts completely?" and she was like "yes you do. When you feel better you can reintroduce them gradually."

## Excerpt 2

X: Coffee does not agree with me. When I smell it I think "oh I will just have a little one" and then I can feel my heart burning.
Y: I do love the smell.
X: So I went to the doctor and had a food allergy test. And the doctor said "do you know if there is anything you are allergic to?" I said "I definitely think I am allergic to coffee". and she said "it might not be the coffee. It might be what you put in it". So she tested milk and just coffee without the milk. And she said "You are right". She said "Please do not drink any caffeine".

|  | cheerful |  |  |  | not cheerful |
|---|---|---|---|---|---|
| Speaker A: | ☐ | ☐ | ☐ | ☐ | ☐ |
| Speaker X: | ☐ | ☐ | ☐ | ☐ | ☐ |

|  | hesitating |  |  |  | fluent |
|---|---|---|---|---|---|
| Speaker A: | ☐ | ☐ | ☐ | ☐ | ☐ |
| Speaker X: | ☐ | ☐ | ☐ | ☐ | ☐ |

|  | impolite |  |  |  | polite |
|---|---|---|---|---|---|
| Speaker A: | ☐ | ☐ | ☐ | ☐ | ☐ |
| Speaker X: | ☐ | ☐ | ☐ | ☐ | ☐ |

|  | unpopular |  |  |  | popular |
|---|---|---|---|---|---|
| Speaker A: | ☐ | ☐ | ☐ | ☐ | ☐ |
| Speaker X: | ☐ | ☐ | ☐ | ☐ | ☐ |

|  | American |  |  |  | not American |
|---|---|---|---|---|---|
| Speaker A: | ☐ | ☐ | ☐ | ☐ | ☐ |
| Speaker X: | ☐ | ☐ | ☐ | ☐ | ☐ |

|  | extroverted |  |  |  | introverted |
|---|---|---|---|---|---|
| Speaker A: | ☐ | ☐ | ☐ | ☐ | ☐ |
| Speaker X: | ☐ | ☐ | ☐ | ☐ | ☐ |

|  | dishonest |  |  |  | honest |
|---|---|---|---|---|---|
| Speaker A: | ☐ | ☐ | ☐ | ☐ | ☐ |
| Speaker X: | ☐ | ☐ | ☐ | ☐ | ☐ |

**Survey continues on next page …..Remember: don't look ahead!**

Appendix E: *Be like* survey — **243**

Excerpt 1

A: I really like nuts but I am allergic to them. At first I was sceptical about seeing a doctor.
I thought "how can a doctor help me with this?"
But finally I went to see this doctor.
I said "when I eat nuts I feel as if I have a heart attack" and she was like "you will have to follow a special diet and I will do a blood test".
She said "we need to be sure that you are not reacting to anything else".
B: This is really interesting.
A: I was like "do I have to cut out nuts completely?" and she was like "yes you do. When you feel better you can reintroduce them gradually."

Excerpt 2

X: Coffee does not agree with me.
When I smell it I think "oh I will just have a little one" and then I can feel my heart burning.
Y: I do love the smell.
X: So I went to the doctor and had a food allergy test.
And the doctor said "do you know if there is anything you are allergic to?"
I said "I definitely think I am allergic to coffee". and she said "it might not be the coffee.
It might be what you put in it".
So she tested milk and just coffee without the milk.
And she said "You are right".
She said "Please do not drink any caffeine".

|  | **not ambitious** |  |  |  | **ambitious** |
|---|---|---|---|---|---|
| Speaker A: | ☐ | ☐ | ☐ | ☐ | ☐ |
| Speaker X: | ☐ | ☐ | ☐ | ☐ | ☐ |

|  | **clear** |  |  |  | **not clear** |
|---|---|---|---|---|---|
| Speaker A: | ☐ | ☐ | ☐ | ☐ | ☐ |
| Speaker X: | ☐ | ☐ | ☐ | ☐ | ☐ |

|  | **good sense of humour** |  |  |  | **not a good sense of humour** |
|---|---|---|---|---|---|
| Speaker A: | ☐ | ☐ | ☐ | ☐ | ☐ |
| Speaker X: | ☐ | ☐ | ☐ | ☐ | ☐ |

**Survey continues on next page …..Remember: don't look ahead!**

## II. Please answer the following questions about speakers A and X.

Excerpt 1

A: I really like nuts but I am allergic to them. At first I was sceptical about seeing a doctor. I thought "how can a doctor help me with this?"
But finally I went to see this doctor. I said "when I eat nuts I feel as if I have a heart attack" and she was like "you will have to follow a special diet and I will do a blood test". She said "we need to be sure that you are not reacting to anything else".
B: This is really interesting.
A: I was like "do I have to cut out nuts completely?" and she was like "yes you do. When you feel better you can reintroduce them gradually."

Excerpt 2

X: Coffee does not agree with me. When I smell it I think "oh I will just have a little one" and then I can feel my heart burning.
Y: I do love the smell.
X: So I went to the doctor and had a food allergy test.
And the doctor said "do you know if there is anything you are allergic to?"
I said "I definitely think I am allergic to coffee". and she said "it might not be the coffee. It might be what you put in it".
So she tested milk and just coffee without the milk.
And she said "You are right".
She said "Please do not drink any caffeine".

1. How old do you think each speaker is? (Please answer in years.)
Speaker A:
Speaker X:

2. What is the sex/gender of each speaker?
Speaker A:     Male ☐        Female
Speaker X:     Male ☐        Female

3. What is the social class of each speaker?
Speaker A:     Middle class ☐        Working class
Speaker X:     Middle class ☐        Working class

4. What is the ethnicity of each speaker? (For "Other", please also add the ethnicity.)
Speaker A:     White ☐     Latino ☐     Asian ☐     Black ☐     Other ☐
Speaker X:     White ☐     Latino ☐     Asian ☐     Black ☐     Other ☐

5. What is the occupation of each speaker?
Speaker A:     academic ☐     non-academic ☐
Speaker X:     academic ☐     non-academic ☐

6. Where do you think each speaker comes from?
Speaker A:     US ☐     UK ☐     Other ☐
Speaker X:     US ☐     UK ☐     Other ☐

**Survey continues on next page …..Remember: don't look ahead!**

## III. Personal Information

Please fill out the following few questions about your personal background. Rest assured that this questionnaire is completely anonymous and we require the following information for purely statistical reasons.

1. How old are you? _____

2. Are you:     Male ☐   Female ☐ ?

3. What is your ethnicity? (If Other, please write in your ethnicity.)
White ☐   Latino ☐   Asian ☐   Black ☐   Other _____

4.1. Where did live between ages 3 and 17? Please give town as well as region.

4.2. Where do you live now? Please give town as well as region.

5. What is your highest academic qualification?
☐ High School
☐ BA
☐ MA
☐ PhD
☐ Other, specify _____

6. Are you a native speaker of English?
☐ Native speaker of English
☐ L2 English speaker
☐ English learner

7. Since when were you able to speak English (fluently)?
☐ Since I was 4 years old or younger
☐ Since I was 7 years old
☐ Since I was 12 years old
☐ Since I was 16 years old
☐ Since I was 21 years old

8. How well do you feel you know English?/What is your level of proficiency in English?
☐ Basic
☐ Intermediate
☐ Upper-intermediate
☐ Advanced

9.1. Have you ever been to an English-speaking country and if so, how many times?
☐ four times and more
☐ three times
☐ twice
☐ once
☐ never

If never, please proceed to 9.4.

9.2. If you have been to an English-speaking country, which countries have you been too?

**UK:** Yes ☐   No ☐
**US:** Yes ☐   No ☐
**Other:** Yes ☐   No ☐   Please specify: _____

9.3. For how long did you stay there?

| **UK** | **US** | **Other** |
|---|---|---|
| ☐ more than a year | ☐ more than a year | ☐ more than a year |
| ☐ a year | ☐ a year | ☐ a year |
| ☐ half a year | ☐ half a year | ☐ half a year |
| ☐ several months | ☐ several months | ☐ several months |
| ☐ several weeks | ☐ several weeks | ☐ several weeks |
| ☐ several days | ☐ several days | ☐ several days |

9.4. Which form of English, in your opinion, do you speak?
☐ American English
☐ British English
☐ Indian/German English
☐ a mixture of dialects
☐ Don't know
☐ Other         Please specify _____

9.5. Is there an English-speaking country that you feel a special connection to? And if so, which one?
_____
_____

**Survey continues on next page .....Remember: don't look ahead!**

## IV. Attitudinal Survey

Please consider the uses of **like** in the example below:

B:   This is really interesting.
A:   I said "do I have to **like** cut out nuts completely?"         (Use 1)
     She was **like** "yes you do and when you feel better           (Use 2)
     you can reintroduce them gradually."

1. Do you see any difference between the two uses of *like*?     Yes ☐                              No ☐

If you see a difference, please go to 1.1. If you don't see a difference, please go to 2.

1.1. With whom do you associate these expressions? Please rate Use 1 and Use 2.

Use 1:
☐ younger people            ☐ older people                        ☐ don't know
☐ female speakers           ☐ male speakers                       ☐ don't know
☐ middle class speakers     ☐ working class speakers              ☐ don't know
☐ educated speakers         ☐ speakers with little education      ☐ don't know
☐ white speakers            ☐ speakers from an ethnic minority    ☐ don't know
☐ US English                ☐ English spoken elsewhere            ☐ don't know

Use 2:
☐ younger people            ☐ older people                        ☐ don't know
☐ female speakers           ☐ male speakers                       ☐ don't know
☐ middle class speakers     ☐ working class speakers              ☐ don't know
☐ educated speakers         ☐ speakers with little education      ☐ don't know
☐ white speakers            ☐ speakers from an ethnic minority    ☐ don't know
☐ US English                ☐ English spoken elsewhere            ☐ don't know

2. If you don't see a difference between Use 1 and Use 2, state with whom you associate expressions featuring *like* generally.

Expressions with *like*:
☐ younger people            ☐ older people                        ☐ don't know
☐ female speakers           ☐ male speakers                       ☐ don't know
☐ middle class speakers     ☐ working class speakers              ☐ don't know

| ☐ educated speakers | ☐ speakers with little education | ☐ don't know |
| ☐ white speakers | ☐ speakers from an ethnic minority | ☐ don't know |
| ☐ US English | ☐ English spoken elsewhere | ☐ don't know |

3. Do you use *like* yourself?

| | | | | |
|---|---|---|---|---|
| Use 1: | ☐ often | ☐ sometimes | ☐ never | ☐ don't know |
| Use 2: | ☐ often | ☐ sometimes | ☐ never | ☐ don't know |

If you don't differentiate between the two uses, simply state if you use expressions with *like* generally.

| | | | | |
|---|---|---|---|---|
| Expression with *like*: | ☐ often | ☐ sometimes | ☐ never | ☐ don't know |

4. Below you see a list of ten people and their occupations. Please order these people depending on how frequently you think they use *like*.

1 = the person with the most uses of *like*
10 = the person with the least uses of *like*

| | Occupations | Your score |
|---|---|---|
| A | Assistant in residence hall management office | |
| B | Marketing temp | |
| C | Waiter | |
| D | DJ, musician | |
| E | Operations manager at a large theater | |
| F | Tax lawyer | |
| G | Secondary school maths teacher | |
| H | Filmmaker | |
| I | Comedian/writer | |
| J | Assistant at a small record label | |

### Finally, please answer the following three questions:

A: I said "do I have to **like** cut out nuts completely?" (Use 1)
She was **like** "yes you do and when you feel better" (Use 2)

5. What do you think of these uses of *like* in general?

6. Where do you think they come from?




7. In what type of talk or writing do people most use *like* (jokes, news broadcasting, gossip, sermons, arguments, …)?




**Thank you very much for participating in this survey!**

# Index

*After*-perfect 189, 191
ANOVA 35, 37, 41–43
*Auffälligkeit* 187
Awareness 15, 110, 146, 188, 193–196, 198, 202–203
– dialect-mixing 52
– metalinguistic 164–170
– sociolinguistic 15

Background questionnaire 55, 63, 95, 111, 149, 228–234
*Be like* 21–22, 29–31
– across the globe 22–23
– connotations 147–148
– explicit associations 164–170
– implicit associations 153–164
– incremental spread 22–23
– origin 21
– personality judgements 147–148
– salient feature 198–205
– variable grammar 26–29
Bilinguals 10–11
– English-dominant 63, 65–70
– Hindi-dominant 64, 70–75
– mixed 75–81

Carrier material 150, 152
CHP 28, 29–30, 69, 74, 79, 85, 88, 99, 102, 106, 109, 114, 117, 118, 126, 130, 235–236
Code-switching practices 50–52
Cognitive activation 10
Common English 'core' 30
Competence 14, 15, 179
– communicative 158, 160–161
– sociolinguistic 14–16, 120, 139, 142, 175, 178
Complementiser 59
– *ki* 59–60
– *that* 59–62
Complexity 205–206, 208
– constraint 205
– interface 206
Conceptual contrast 193

Connectionist approach 179
Constraints 26–29, 120–121, 136, 175, 205, 206
– language-internal 26–29, 122, 126–127, 143
– re-organisation of 138–142
– sociolinguistic 28–29, 126–127, 130–131, 132–135
– systemic 26–29
Construction Grammar 179
Constructions 59–63, 179–180, 187
– analytical 191–192, 199
– innovative 17–18, 184
– interrogative 181–182
– quotative 18–19, 172–173, 176–177, 184–186, 199–200
– verb-argument 182
Conversational Historical Present 28

Discourse marker 59–60, 146, 184, 186
– *jaar* 60
– *jaise* (*ki*) 60
– *like* 146–147
– *matlab* 60
– *okay* (*fine*) 59–62
Discourse particle 62
Discreteness 190

Endonormative 8, 37, 39, 42, 44, 48, 50, 52, 61, 72, 80
– attitude 37, 42, 52
– mindset 39, 44, 48, 61
– orientation 44, 50, 80, 164, 169, 171, 172, 175, 177
– perceptions 53
– practice 176
– stabilisation 8
English 1, 2, 4, 7, 23, 30, 33, 42, 52, 53, 203
– American, perceptions 33
– as a foreign language 1, 11–13
– as a second language 1, 7–9
– British, perceptions 33
– Learner (EFL) 1
– in Germany 12
– ideology 44
– in India 8–10

English (continued)
- indigenised (ESL) 1
- native 1, 7, 122, 123
- non-native 1–3, 23, 30, 33, 34, 121–123, 145–146
- practices 52–53, 63–65, 175–177
Exemplar theory 179
Exonormative 12
- mindset 12, 45, 49, 52, 121, 137, 163, 169
- orientation 44–45, 50, 52, 169, 171, 175–176, 176, 177
Exposure
- lingua franca contexts 106–110
- naturalistic 91, 94–96, 118, 122–123, 131–133, 161, 236
- stay-abroad 94, 110, 143, 160
- the amount of 94, 95
- to mass media 81–89, 111–117, 128, 132–133, 134–135
- to North American English 96–100
- to UK English 100–103
- type of 95
- mixed 103–106

Face-to-face interactions 24
Factor weights 127
Feature pool 77, 137
Features 25
- superficial 24
- off-the-shelf 25
Feeling a special connection to an English-speaking country 155, 157
Frequency/Frequencies 178–187, 188–189
- high 181, 182, 185, 186, 204
- low 181, 189
- relative 15, 175
- token 181–183, 204
- type 181–183, 204

Gender 28–29, 129
Goldvarb 123, 124, 125, 127, 129, 235–237
Grammatical subject 27–28
Grammaticalisation 29–31, 75, 77, 78, 82, 100, 102, 104, 110, 117, 119, 125, 136–137, 175, 200
Great Revolt 8

*haan* 62
Hamburg Corpus of Non-Native Varieties of English (HCNVE) 3, 55, 56, 121, 125, 235
Hindi 9–10, 52
Hub/hyper-central variety 29

IDEA 39
Identity 143
Implicit learning 194–195
Inferiority complex 33
Interactionally prominent 193, 197–198, 200–201
Interface knowledge 206
Interlanguage 115, 139–142, 161, 179–180

Jawaharlal Nehru University (JNU) 2, 33, 34, 35, 39, 121, 148, 203

L1 influence 206, 208
Language 1, 7, 8, 9, 10
- acrolectal forms of 8
- additional 10
- base 10
- the evolution of 145
- first 1
- foreign 1, 7
- heritage 9
- link 7
- matrix 10
- national 8
- of instruction 9
- regional 9
- second 1, 7, 8
- shift towards English 9
Language attitudes 33–34
Language change 14
Language/dialect contact 144, 197
Language learning 161, 180, 182, 187, 196, 197
Language mode 10, 11
- bilingual 11
- monolingual 10, 12
*Langue* 179
Like
- major functions 146
- self-reported uses 170–171
- variable grammar 26–29, 118, 120, 123–135
Lingua franca 8

Mannheim Corpus of German English (MaCGE)  3, 91, 92, 121, 130, 236–237
mass media  13, 24–25
– amount of exposure  81, 94, 126, 131
– high levels of exposure  82–85, 111–114
– low levels of exposure  85–89, 114–117
Meta-discourse  196, 198, 201–203
*Mimesis*  26–27
Model
– by Grosjean (1998, 2001)  10–11
– fixed effects  124, 127, 133, 134
– grammaticalisation of *be like*  29
– language-contact  177
– mixed-effects  124, 125, 129, 132, 133, 134, 137
– random effects  124
– of 'salience'  187–198
– usage-based  179–180
– of variation  123–135
Morpheme
– bound  191, 199
– derivational  191
Multilingual inputs  23–24, 106, 137

Neuroscience  143
Neuter *it*  28, 30, 73, 78, 84, 88, 113, 117, 126, 130, 199, 235, 236
Noticing  194–195, 201
Novelty  196–197, 198, 204

*Observer's paradox*  92
Orderly heterogeneity  14
Overt commentary  196, 204

*Parole*  179
Particular semantics  192
PCA  40, 41, 43
Performance  179
Personality traits  34, 40, 41, 42, 43, 44, 151, 153, 154, 155, 156, 157, 158, 159, 160
Phonetic  190
Place of residence between three and 17′  155
Present perfect  30, 180, 191
Principle of accountability  14, 20
Proficiency in English  12, 63, 64, 148, 149, 156, 157, 159
Propagation of the variant  25

– face-to-face (interactions)  25, 132–133, 134–135
– mass media  25, 128, 133, 134, 207
Prosodically prominent  190

Quotation  3–5, 17, 18, 20, 21
– in real time  21–24
Quotative frame  18–19, 59–60
Quotative marking/markers  3, 19, 21, 26–27, 56, 59, 61–63, 64, 65, 66, 68, 70, 71, 73, 75, 76, 77, 81, 82, 86, 87, 93, 94, 97, 100, 101, 104, 108, 112, 115, 116, 128, 132, 150, 172, 183, 184, 185, 201
Quote type  27

Rbrul  123, 124, 125, 126, 129, 130, 132
Received Pronunciation  33

Salience  143, 187–205, 208
– cognitive  188, 189–193, 196
– socio-cognitive  197–198, 208
– sociolinguistic  188, 193–197
Scales
– Likert  35, 36, 37
– Semantic differentials  40, 41, 43, 151
Schools
– missionary  8, 9, 141, 170, 229
– vernacular  4, 9, 13
Second-language acquisition  5, 6, 7, 8, 17, 134, 138, 142, 145, 180, 181, 185, 187, 189, 194, 196, 197, 206
Social
– identity  14, 39, 42, 50
– prestige  34, 36, 38, 39, 47, 147
– status  34, 36, 37, 38, 39, 41, 42, 43, 44, 45, 49, 147
Social desirability bias  39
Social meaning  45, 145, 146, 155, 158, 171
Sociolinguistic competence  14, 15, 16, 110, 120, 139, 142, 161, 175, 178, 206
Sociolinguistic ecology  63, 81, 122, 128, 138
Sociolinguistic interviews  34, 45–53, 55, 63, 70, 91, 92, 106, 111, 121
Solidarity  34, 35, 36, 37, 38, 39, 43, 50, 52, 204
Speaker status  155, 156
State-of-flow  161
Stereotype  38, 44, 48, 166, 203

Suprasegmental prominence  201
Survey
– attitudinal  34–39, 148, 247–249
– be like  238–249

Television  13
Tense  28
The Big Bang Theory  38
The International Corpus of English (ICE)  2
The International Corpus of Learner English (ICLE)  2
The Official Language Act  8
Transformation under transfer  142
Transparency  192

University of Mannheim (UM)  2, 33, 34, 39, 91, 121

Variability  15, 16, 24, 59, 69, 74, 97, 105, 107, 116, 125, 126, 129, 133–135, 141, 176, 206, 207
– systemic  15
Variable(s)
– (ing)  139, 205–206
– discourse-pragmatic  18–20
– glottal replacement of (t)  139–140
– morphosyntactic  140–141
– phonological  139–140
– present perfect  30, 141
– quotative be like  29–31, 180, 191
– verbal negators  140
Variable grammar
– re-organised  141–142, 195
Variants
– be like  4, 5, 17, 56, 65, 71, 82, 86, 92, 97, 104, 108, 112, 115, 118, 125, 126, 127, 128, 129, 130, 131, 132, 133, 134, 137, 138, 145, 147, 177

– featuring like  56–57, 65, 71, 75, 82, 86, 92, 97, 100, 104, 108, 112, 115
– featuring okay (fine)  57, 65, 71, 76, 82–83, 86, 176
– featuring verb + that  57, 65–66, 71, 76, 83, 86, 176
– incoming  2, 24, 29, 137, 143–144, 147, 193, 201
– innovative  4, 5, 17, 18, 20, 39, 44, 55, 59, 66, 69, 70, 71, 72, 75, 76, 77, 80, 81, 89, 93, 94, 99, 100, 101, 103, 105, 106, 108, 110, 115, 119, 120, 121, 122, 123, 125, 129, 131, 132, 133, 137, 145, 146, 147, 148, 150, 155, 163, 172, 176, 177, 184, 187, 198, 199, 201, 204
– other  57, 66, 71, 76, 83, 86, 92, 97, 100, 104, 108, 112, 115
– traditional  56, 65, 71, 75, 82, 86, 92, 97, 100, 104, 108, 112, 115, 176
– a zero realisation  19, 20, 21, 27, 56, 65, 71, 75, 82, 86, 92, 97, 100, 104, 108, 112, 115
Variety  36
– endocentric  36
Verbum Dicendi  18, 19, 60, 61, 66, 184, 185, 186
Vernaculars  4, 13, 15, 19, 21, 24, 25, 26, 61, 67, 70, 74, 79, 80, 114, 117, 120, 123, 134, 140, 175, 176, 184, 199
VGT  34, 39, 40, 41, 43, 45, 46, 49, 149, 150, 152, 169

Well  62
Wh-question  181

www.ingramcontent.com/pod-product-compliance
Lightning Source LLC
Chambersburg PA
CBHW031351230426
43670CB00006B/500